NEW AMERICANS

NEW AMERICANS

The Westerner
and the Modern Experience
in the American Novel

Glen A. Love

LEWISBURG
BUCKNELL UNIVERSITY PRESS

London and Toronto: Associated University Presses

©1982 by Associated University Presses, Inc.

Associated University Presses, Inc.
4 Cornwall Drive
East Brunswick, New Jersey 08816

Associated University Presses
69 Fleet Street
London EC4Y 1EU, England

Associated University Presses
Toronto M5E 1A7, Canada

Library of Congress Cataloging in Publication Data
Love, Glen A   1932-
   New Americans.

   Bibliography: p.
   Includes index.
   1.   American fiction — 19th and 20th century — History and criticism.
2.   The West in literature.   3.   City and town life in literature.   I.   Title.
II. Title: Modern experience in the American novel.
PS374.W4L6   813'.009'3278   80-65717
ISBN 0-8387-5011-7

Printed in the United States of America

For Rhoda

The new Americans, of whom he was to be one, must, whether they were fit or unfit, create a world of their own, a science, a society, a philosophy, a universe, where they had not yet created a road or even learned to dig their own iron.

Henry Adams, *The Education of Henry Adams*

Contents

Acknowledgments

I am indebted to a number of persons for their assistance in the writing of this book. My principal obligation is to Professor Kermit Vanderbilt of San Diego State University, whose encouragement and perceptive criticism have accompanied the growth of the manuscript. I continue to value Kermit Vanderbilt's friendship as highly as I do his scholarship.

For a close and detailed criticism of my chapter on Sherwood Anderson, and for his suggestions on amplifying the Sinclair Lewis chapter, I cannot adequately thank Professor Walter B. Rideout of the University of Wisconsin. My further appreciation for their comments and criticism on various parts of the manuscript is gratefully extended to Professors Robert Albrecht, Terence Martin, Earl Pomeroy, and Henry Nash Smith. Other assistance and encouragement has come in a variety of forms from professors, librarians, and students, whom I wish to thank, including Jack Bennett, Edwin R. Bingham, Richard Etulain, Richard Heinzkill, Patricia Hult, Mary Land, Robert McCollough, Kip Omstead, Ruth Ellen Perlman, William L. Phillips, and Donald Taylor. Those things of darkness that remain in the book I, of course, acknowledge mine.

I am grateful to the following journals for permission to reprint from my own work as follows: *American Literature* for permission to quote several paragraphs from "*Winesburg, Ohio* and the Rhetoric of Silence" (March 1968; copyright 1968 by Duke University Press), used in chapter 4; *American Quarterly* for "New Pioneering on the Prairies: Nature, Progress and the Individual in the Novels of Sinclair Lewis" (December 1973), an earlier version of chapter 5; and *Western American Literature* for "Frank Norris's Western Metropolitans" (May 1976), an earlier version of chapter 1.

I also wish to thank Eleanor C. Anderson for permission to quote passages of Sherwood Anderson's poetry from *Mid - American Chants* (copyright 1918 by John Lane Co.) and from *Perhaps Women* (copyright 1931 by Horace Liveright, Inc.).

Finally, to my wife, Rhoda Moore Love, who during the writing of this book managed the larger share of our home and two children, Stan and Jenny, while herself teaching college biology part-time, working for environmental and educational causes, and progressing toward a doctorate in plant ecology, I can only record here my everlasting love and wonder.

Introduction

At the World's Columbian Exposition in Chicago in 1893, a White City had taken shape in Jackson Park on the shores of Lake Michigan that was to receive some twenty-two million paid admissions during the months from May through October of that year. The White City, with its architectural conception of the American future as an ordered new metropolis of the West, the creation of a triumphant technology under the direction of a group of able new American leaders, rose as an assertion of the larger forces that were rapidly reshaping American life in the nineties. Even so seasoned an observer and so habitual an ironist as Henry Adams allowed finally that the Chicago world fair was "the first expression of American thought as a unity," evidence that the American people might indeed be heading toward some "point in thought," a point that, so Adams believed, might through careful observation and study be fixed.[1] In its confident assertion of the synthesis of western, individualistic, and technological values, the White City of 1893, attractive ever since to literary and cultural historians, offers up still new and different meanings for our attention.

Another student of American culture and visitor to the Exposition was, like Adams, to find in its contemporary urban vision a portentous challenge to the American consciousness. At the same meeting of the American Historical Association on the fair grounds at which Henry Adams was elected the group's president, a young historian named Frederick Jackson Turner delivered a paper, "The Significance of the Frontier in American History," which bracketed its confident sanctioning of a frontier-determined American past within the sobering statements from the 1890 census that the frontier no longer existed. If the free lands of the great West, as Turner claimed, had provided the American

11

character with its heritage of rough individualism, then the ordered pattern of Exposition buildings, the myriad exhibits of the new science and technology, must, as he came increasingly to realize, be worked into a new cultural equation and a new moral ethic, one that would enable modern Americans to live together successfully in an urbanized and industrialized present and future.

By 1896, Turner was assessing more fully the meaning of the Exposition and the industrializing West in terms that revealed both his hopes and his apprehensions:

> The White City which recently rose on the shores of Lake Michigan fitly typified its [the old Northwest's] growing culture as well as its capacity for great achievement. Its complex and representative industrial organization and business ties, its determination to hold fast to what is original and good in its Western experience, and its readiness to learn and receive the results of the experience of other sections and nations, make it an open-minded and safe arbiter of the American destiny. In the long run the centre of the Republic may be trusted to strike a wise balance between the contending ideals. But she does not deceive herself; she knows that the problem of the West means nothing less than the problem of working out original social ideals and social adjustment for the American nation.[2]

Facing a closed frontier and the clash of conflicting forces as rapid industrial urbanization exacerbated the cultural shock caused by the disappearance of free western lands, Turner recognized here, as he would for the remainder of his life, the problem of what to make of a diminished thing. For Turner and, I would claim, for many of his western compatriots including those novelists to be studied here, new and scaled-down patterns of national unity must be sought, for which the crucial terms were to be balance, adjustment, equilibrium, and synthesis.

In a decade in desperate need of coherent new symbols of

unity the White City declared that the triumph of scientific
urban industrialism was not only inevitable but appropriate
for the American West, that the great heartland and beyond
had nothing to fear from this startling intrusion upon its
quiet cornfields and villages and raw, booming new towns.
East and West, nation and region, city and country, nature
and technology, individual and community — all of the
most deep-going and pervasive contrarieties of the national
experience — were, in the spread of gleaming halls and
exhibits, canals and bridges, which had appeared almost
overnight on the Chicago lakefront, depicted as amenable to
a progressive and harmonious synthesis. Was not this the
expression of American unity to which Adams alluded? To a
striking degree, the White City *was* the future in its most
hopeful form, that which had been projected for the year
2000 by Edward Bellamy in his immensely popular utopian
romance *Looking Backward*, published in 1888, five years
before the Chicago fair:

> Every quarter contained large open squares filled with
> trees, among which statues glistened and fountains flashed
> in the late afternoon sun. Public buildings of a colossal size
> and an architectural grandeur unparalleled in my day
> raised their stately piles on every side. Surely I had never
> seen this city nor one comparable to it before.[3]

If the White City could rival in appearance Bellamy's
distant urban paradise, could the Chicago creation not also
suggest the possibilities for a harmonious social order to
match that benign vision of the future?

There is, of course, a danger in overstating the mythic
significance of the White City. This alabaster city's gleam
was not wholly undimmed by human tears, ignoring as it
did the real and persistent failure of the actual disordered
metropolis out of which it grew. For minority Americans,
the Exposition was a "White City" indeed, as one of its black
critics indignantly noted,[4] and although the representation

of women in the Exposition was proudly noted by its supporters, it was the exotic shimmying of Little Egypt rather than the design of the Women's Building by Sophia G. Hayden, or the Congress of Women that was held there, that attracted the greater public notice. Adams himself recognized that the Chicago fair probably masked inner confusion as effectively as it promised outer harmony, and that the project bore the old marks of the booster and the trader. His former Harvard colleague, Charles Eliot Norton, was to consider on reflection that his early enthusiasm for the architecture of the White City was somewhat misplaced, as its mixtures of styles and "degrading accessories" suggested the moral uncertainties of western wealth and energy unchecked by spiritual awareness and the refinements of taste. But in their enthusiasm for the Exposition, for what Norton called "the ideal Chicago which exists not only in the brain, but in the heart of some of her citizens," both men seized upon its promise for the American future at a time of endemic uncertainty.[5] It is in this sense, especially as American writers were to address that uncertainty and that promise, that the White City is a compelling idea.

For the novelist, of course, idea is encompassed and realized through plot and character. What relationship existed between the scientific and artistic assumptions and achievements represented by the White City and those American novelists — Frank Norris, Hamlin Garland, Willa Cather, Sherwood Anderson, and Sinclair Lewis — chosen for study here? Let me admit at the start that I claim no direct line of "influence" for the Chicago experience upon these novelists, Garland being the only one who actually visited the fair. Rather I would assert that the figures who created the White City represented for thinking Americans of that period, writers as well as others, an arresting redefinition of significant lives in America. On the human level the Exposition was the creation of a rising class of new American professionals — architects, inventors, scientists, artists, engineers, technologists, governmental administrators, "visionary" businessmen, and the like. The pursuit of influence here is unnecessary because the same sorts of figures were making themselves known elsewhere in the country. The Chicago Exposition is not the source but rather the most noteworthy early example of their presence and achievements. What these figures represented, then, was the prospect of a new group of leaders, emblems of both individual and societal consequence, who were able to function successfully within the threatening context of industrial and urban America and who might thus be envisioned as assuming the place in the contemporary imagination of those essentially failed and outworn isolatoes of earlier individualistic enterprise such as the frontiersman, the yeoman farmer, and the robber baron of finance.

The emergence of these new figures of urban and industrial import was, for the most part, little acknowledged by the established major novelists of the period. Important American writers had, of course, been sensitive to the thrust of the machine into the American garden as early as the 1830s, as Leo Marx has persuasively demonstrated.[6] And the native writers who have most seized our attention have traditionally been hostile to the world of larger social significance represented by the city and the machine. In our classic literature the perpetually radical American myth of self-creation has led in the opposite direction, toward a falling out of the world and a rebirth into an individual destiny apart from and in opposition to the failures of the communal past and the muddled urban-technological present. This pattern has, indeed, informed much of the most memorable literature of Mark Twain and Henry James, the masters of the American novel at the end of the nineteenth century. But conversely these gestures of denial left them, along with Henry Adams and, to a lesser extent, William Dean Howells, facing the nineties and the emergence of the class of progressive moderns described above with, to cite

Adams once again, their historical necks broken.

Adams himself of course resonated fully to the significance of Chicago on the mythic no less than the historical and personal levels. He could herald what might have been the Exposition's representative new citizen as he looked ahead at the conclusion of his autobiography to the twentieth century and envisioned "the child of incalculable coal-power, chemical power, electrical power, and radiating energy, as well as of new forces yet undetermined" (496). But Adams was not primarily a novelist and chose not to treat the Chicago experience or the advent of industrialism in his fiction. More important, he adopted a rhetorical *hors de combat* strategy for the the narrator of his autobiography which left that figure savoring his bittersweet alienation from the new age of energy. This is not to diminish the extent of Adams's accomplishments. He defines and illuminates machine-age America as no one else does, even through this pose of isolation, insignificance, and failure. But what is called for in the new American, "a new type of man . . . .with ten times the endurance, energy, will of the old type," leaves Adams incredulous if not openly skeptical (499). He avoids treating this creature of the new age as a fully rounded actuality, preferring to leave it fleetingly and less than convincingly sketched. The only densely rendered portrait he provides is of his own "mannikin" self, who, like a parody of those Jamesian characters forever deciding, as someone has said, not to get married, perpetually discovers himself closed off from the real world.

Mark Twain, the oldest of the group of literary giants of the nineties, oscillated wildly between worship and attack in his attitude toward machine civilization, just as he often did between romantic and realistic treatments of the American garden. While Twain acknowledged the mildly heroic possibilities of the new technologist in the title figure of *Pudd'nhead Wilson*, his most memorable contemporary mechanizer, Hank Morgan, the Connecticut Yankee, is a deadly caricature of the new American, "Yankee of the Yankees," as he describes himself proudly, "— and practical; yes, and nearly barren of sentiment."[7] By the end of the novel he has become the agent of an unleashed and murderous technology, finally self-destructing, so to speak, upon the ashes of the society which he has incinerated. Twain's fictional depiction of technology here, tied, as Henry Nash Smith has shown, to his own exasperating struggles to launch the Paige typesetter upon the commercial market,[8] reflects the older conception of the machine as a means of imperializing the power of the individual rather than, as with the "cooler" conception of the nineties, as an ordered and manageable social force. And for Twain even minor artifacts of the new age of science may conceal a world whose invisible spheres were formed in fright. The nightmare events of his late, unfinished story "The Great Dark" are played out under a microscope which the narrator has innocently brought home as a birthday present for his child.

Henry James, approaching the great international novels of his maturity as the century drew to a close, revealed another kind of antipathy to lives of industrial consequence in America. Insofar as such figures remain in character and in harness, as does Caspar Goodwood of *The Portrait of a Lady*, James took little notice of them. The only major Jamesian character who might conceivably be termed a figure of the industrial age is Christopher Newman of *The American*, whose story is "intensely Western," a judgment that may be set against the information that his "sole aim in life had been to make money."[9] And of course James's interest in Newman begins at the point when the great western barbarian puts his moneymaking behind him and goes to Europe to nourish his spirit. We learn almost nothing of Newman's life before that point. Living abroad after 1866, James was to take little fictional notice of the figure of industrial and technological import who rose out of late-nineteenth-century America, and the intimation that we get of him in the ghastly specter in "The Jolly Corner" (1908), "evil, odious, blatant, vulgar," suggests some of the reasons.[10]

William Dean Howells, whose close bond of friendship with Mark Twain owed much to the fact that they were both western men who had come east and prevailed, faced the urban industrial explosion and the resultant social upheaval at the end of the century with bravery and honesty, but he was unable to conceive in his novels a full and sympathetic portrait of the consequential modern American. Silas Lapham, Howells's most sustained depiction of the American business-man, is not a new American but an old one, a rural figure essentially unsuited for the great world, who is providentially lifted out of it and returned to his healing countryside at the book's close. At first propelled toward the city and prosperity by one act of inscrutable fate, the windstorm that uproots a tree on his father's farm revealing the "paint mine" beneath it, he is as mysteriously ushered out of the urban life at the end by obscure and powerful economic forces that Howells pretends to understand no more than Silas. Equally unsuitable as a significant urbanite in the novel is Bromfield Corey, whose taste and wit can never wholly compensate for his idleness. The industrial future must be taken on faith, entrusted at the close to the union of Penelope Lapham and energetic young Tom Corey, in whom reappears that same adventuresome trading spirit of his forebears that has skipped over his father. Later Tom Corey types, Dan Mavering in *April Hopes* (1888) and James Langbrith of *The Son of Royal Langbrith* (1904), both sensitive Harvard-educated new-generation heirs of the family industry, similarly never move beyond the point of promise in their novels.

Silas Lapham's slow dissolve into pastoral humility and rectitude strikes us as far less authentic a rendering of the urban industrial dilemma than we find in *A Modern Instance* or *A Hazard of New Fortunes*. The neatly structured and controlled conclusion of Silas's story is neither as interesting nor as convincing as the troubled authorial ambiguities that attend the depiction of characters like Bartley Hubbard of *A Modern Instance* and Jacob Dryfoos of *Hazard* who are denied the escape back to nature at the same time that their moral confusion and ethical failures render them unfit for the great world as well. Howells's deeply divided conception of the urban present is most revealingly presented in authorial spokesmen like Basil March of *Hazard*, Westover of *The Landlord at Lion's Head*, and — although he is often an object of Howells's satire as well — Atherton of *A Modern Instance*, in all of whom the pattern of logical inconsistencies and of professions of despair or bewilderment toward the new age undercuts their crucial need to evaluate it properly. Basil March's characteristic retreat into irony or mild cynicism in the face of the staggering disunities of the new life reflects Howells's inability to find, despite his idealistic intentions, a foothold there for meaningful human action. Thus, forced in the opposite direction, March finally emerges, as Kermit Vanderbilt has pointed out, as a triumph of quite another sort, the first of a progression of modern urban antiheroes in our fiction.[11] However, Howells may have been a good deal less satisfied with March's achievements, or nonachievements, than the retrospective reader of today. One notes Howells's continued fascination with the type of aggressive and consequential new American depicted in Jeff Durgin of *The Landlord at Lion's Head*, published in 1897, one of Howells's last major novels. A character of boundless but anarchic energy — Norris would have loved him, indeed created several of his own versions of him — and immense appeal to the Howellsian Westover, Jeff is nevertheless bottled up in his country hotel by the author instead of being turned toward the larger world for which his energies and business talents qualify him. Clearly, for Howells this figure of primeval strength and amorality is too dangerous to be set loose. Once again Howells is caught in his dilemma, in which those with the skill and energy to cope with modern life lack the moral fiber to be entrusted with it, while those with the proper ethical credentials are deficient in the power and will required to act.

With all of this, Howells still remains, of the older generation, closest in spirit to the younger group of writers studied here. In Howells's world, where the best lack all conviction while the worst are full of passionate intensity, one could nevertheless await with hope not Yeats's rough beast but an evolutionary future for which the White City was, in the words of Howells's Altrurian traveler, who visited the fair, "'the earliest achievement of a real civic life.'" But, reflected the Altrurian fatefully, " 'I wonder what will become of all the poor fellows who are concerned in the government of the Fair City when they have to return to earth!' "[12]

If this older generation of American writers of the 1890s expressed toward machine America and its emerging figures attitudes of denial or estrangement or, in the case of Howells, of greater acceptance on the level of conscious commitment than on that of novelistic performance, it is a younger group of writers who came to maturity around the turn of the century and after the assured triumph of the machine and the city that we find searching with fresh vigor for the productive synthesis of natural and urban characteristics. Because the novelists from this group to be studied here treat the individual within the larger human setting it is perhaps appropriate to refer to them as "social novelists." In the sense that they characteristically deny the polarization of individual and society they are indeed social novelists. But the term — inescapably pejorative when set against the classic American fables of radical alienation — is inappropriate if it leads the reader to see these writers as simply presenting or adjusting to a social order rather than trying to reshape it to conform to a new vision. At their best these novelists attempt to give individual form to the gigantic formlessness of early modern American life. After a period of unparalleled expansion and mobility of population, of bewildering industrial and technological growth, of the exploitation and conversion of their native West, these writers aim, consciously or not, to order the rising urban-industrial America through new and essentially hopeful figures of individual and collective possibility. Concerned and often profoundly dismayed by the denials to creative selfhood posed by an ascendant machine civilization, they were yet unwilling to admit the social chaos that Adams and Howells portrayed. Nurtured on western and nature-inspired values of self-reliance and independence, they nevertheless acknowledge in their lives and works the necessity for new roles within a developing modern community.

While literary study has tended to look at these writers in relationship to the generic movements of romance, realism, and naturalism, the source of interest and energy in their works seems to me to lead in another direction. I believe that a fresh and revealing reading of their works is provided when they are conceived of as working in the forms of a new urban-industrial mythology. In their work may be found another sense of beginning, a machine-age version of the image R. W. B. Lewis described for an earlier day as the American Adam, "the authentic American as a figure of heroic innocence and vast potentialities, poised at the start of a new history."[13] Without ever formulating this aim so precisely these writers are engaged in organizing a confused and fragmented social order into acceptable human images and thus in satisfying a collective as well as personal need for contemporary figures of unity and hope to replace the lost leaders of the past. Their works are another version of the same impulse that led to the profusion of utopian novels in the late nineteenth century, sharing in a less visionary form the paradoxical attractions to innovation and permanence, the old life and the new, that characterize the utopian movement.

These ambivalent desires for participation in and withdrawal from the society shaped by the new industrial forces are shared also with the Progressive political movement, from about 1890 to 1920, which enclosed these five writers' critical years of development. They join in the Progressive belief that society could respond to leadership along innovative and ameliorative lines, and that strong new emblems of order were needed to overcome what historian David W. Noble calls "the expression of profound cultural crisis" that attended urban industrialism at the turn of the century.[14] Like the Progressives, these five novelists begin with the belief that Americans could subsume the city and the machine into the traditional democratic framework without sacrificing pastoral values. "Children of urban industrial America," as another recent historian, Robert Wiebe, describes the Progressives, "they looked proudly upon their cities. . . .yet pined for 'the freer, sweeter life which the country offers.' "[15] Of the historians writing upon the Progressive period, Wiebe has been most stimulating for my purposes in bringing attention to the Progressive era as a "revolution in identity." He sees the period as marked by the emergence of a new middle class of professionals, "self-conscious pioneers" of the urban industrial present, drawn together into new communities defined by similarities in talents, aspirations, and achievements.[16] Wiebe's historical analysis of a new class of men and women replacing an outmoded system of loyalties with those more appropriate to an increasingly organized and professionalized society offers a suggestive insight into the fictional lives depicted by the novelists treated here. While few of these lives match closely the characteristics of professional class identity described by the historian, many of the novelistic characters reveal an obligation to cope with contemporary life, an obsessive concern for role and career, and a need to integrate private and communal aspirations, all of which correspond to the general context of Progressivism that Wiebe describes. Similarly, of the students of American civilization contemporary with the Progressive era, Herbert Croly in *The Promise of American Life* (1909) has proved instructive for my purposes, articulating more boldly than Turner or Adams the necessity for new American figures to step forward in response to the nation's changed social conditions.

An even more essential bond between the five novelists is revealed in their self-conscious and avowed westernness, although their geographic homelands range from Ohio to the Pacific Coast. This study, then, is not strictly regional in insisting upon the influence of particular and specific western locales in their fiction. While this may indeed be the case with some of these novelists' works, I am more interested in the play of larger, shared cultural assumptions within the minds of these writers, assumptions that are as natural and vital to them as breathing — and often as unnoticed — and that reflect a West whose values were still largely frontier-inspired, with a heroic view of the past and an essentially hopeful and progressive conception of the future. That the White City was a necessarily western phenomenon, "a natural growth and product of the Northwest," wrote Adams, "offered a step in evolution to startle Darwin," but to imagine it occurring elsewhere, he concluded, was even less believable (340). As Adams saw himself isolated from the technological present of the scientist and the dynamo, so he had sardonically written himself out of the future that the West represented. Early in the *Education* (52) he had dismissed, with ironic self-approbation, the idea of going west to grow up with the country. Later, while his friends Frank Emmons and Clarence King participated in the federal government's geological survey of the Rockies and "felt the future in their hands" (309), Adams presented himself once again as the perpetual outsider, a mere tourist in the West, by which means he continued unerringly to define himself as the antihero of my book as well as his own.

The five novelists treated here, then, all Westerners born between the years 1860 and 1885, are the children of an incredibly telescoped history, growing up in a West in which the ground was literally changing under their feet. By 1900, for example, the Chicago of the Exposition was to see its population increased twentyfold over what it had been in 1860, and would become the nation's second largest city. The fiction and the personal reminiscences of the writers included here are often marked by wondering references to the rapidity and significance of this conversion from frontier and agrarian to technological and urban West. And out of this awareness arises in their books a vivifying sense of the myriad possibilities for individual lives. The swiftness of change and yet the still-unextinguished belief in progress, the newness and heterogeneity of the people and yet the growing sense of the interconnections between West and nation, the encroachment of the machine and the city upon the land and yet the continuing faith in nature as the wellspring of spiritual values — these are the shared cultural assumptions of my western figures. But the most important common attribute of all is the extent to which they are energized by the sense of themselves as Westerners. Often mordantly aware of the cultural thinness and intolerance of their region, they nevertheless saw it as the essential incubator for consequential young men and women, and the badge of their own uniqueness.

As Westerners these writers hoped to accommodate the mechanized present and future without denying the organic past. With the historian Turner their sense of a distinctive western heritage was not to be wholly sacrificed to the mechanized present. Indeed, there is a western respone to urban industrialism other than the one I present that might be written of, a response, valid in its own right, of denial, avoidance, and escape, of a sacral relationship to nature that looks beyond the temporal and the man-made.[17] In fact, my figures have characteristically been treated as spokesmen for the garden rather than the machine. Rather, what they repeatedly attempted was a proper fusion of the two.

Accepting with part of their minds the vitality and urgency of the new America, they hesitated to commit themselves fully to it. They sought to anchor their fictional moderns to earth in such a way as to permit them to embrace the possibilities of both worlds without falling victim to the destructive potentialities of either. The energy with which they pursue that elusive synthesis is the primary justification for this book.

It is, then, the response of these novelists' characters to Emerson's question of vocation as he expressed it in *The Conduct of Life*, "How shall I live?", that takes us to the center of these novels. "How shall I live?" or more precisely "What work shall I do?" — the questions reveal an insistence that lives be shaped along purposeful new lines, that consequential individualism shall also acknowledge the obligation to provide the emerging society with its new leaders. No longer will the choices for significant lives be limited to the older professions, to merchantry, or to characteristic agrarian or village pursuits. New careers emerging in response to scientifically inspired patterns of growth and change will accompany these writers' strongly felt need for original and meaningful lives in a protean nation. The figures whose lives these are, the new Americans of the title, transmute Crévecoeur's original national typology into contemporary forms, and thus project once again into our consciousness his inevitable and recurring question. "What, then," these writers seem to ask of their own contemporaries, "is *this* American, *this* new man?" The response for these novelists is a procession of moderns — the architect, the scientist, the engineer, the inventor, the scientific farmer, the forester, the ethnologist, the industrialist, the medical researcher, the artist, and so on — whose collective import suggests a new social mythology which would work to resolve the conflicts and anxieties inherent in that age of profoundly disturbing transitions. In the terms of Claude Lévi-Strauss, these figures are capable, through their union of cultural oppositions, of overcoming the deeply contradictory tendencies of their age.[18] These fictional creations, new Americans, would, as their authors sent them forth in hope and perplexity, depict means for surviving the threatening conflicts by assimilating them into promising new relationships. The characters in their individual strivings would ideally suggest not isolation or escape, although these are often alluring possibilities, but models for emulation by many men and women seeking lives of personal significance within the democratic community. And in the collective fates of these fictional characters are written the portentous actual difficulties attendant upon this social pioneering.

The elements of this new social-industrial mythology are to be found in the essential images of the novels, drawn from both natural and technological-urban contexts, in the life-shaping symbolic actions of the characters, and in the structures of the works as wholes, as various patterns of possibility emerge to attempt to encompass the fundamental disharmonies and to chart suggestive new directions for the age. Beyond this, the individual novels are, as I attempt to show, part of the larger whole of the writer's span of works in which persistent aims and overarching designs are revealed. I am concerned, then, with the novels as organized and structured repositories for the ideas which have been described above. While the books are cultural documents they are also often works of internal artistic coherence and it has seemed to me worth the risk of blurring the method-ological edges in order to interrelate the two functions where a richer sense of the work's power and significance might result. If the New Criticism erred in telling us to disregard biographical and historical context, the practitioners of mythic or historical-cultural analysis often slight the revealing density of form and texture that distinguishes literature from another type of communication.

I have, as suggested above, attempted to deal with all or nearly all of the significant body of novels by each writer in the belief that the fullest and most convincing evidence would emerge from the larger body of their works rather than in isolated novels, however brilliant or compelling. This has led me to examine a few writers in detail rather than to touch lightly upon many, but the attempted marriage of machine and garden described here could, I believe, be broadened to include the works of a number of other early modern American writers. Moreover, the treatment of these five in detail provides, at the least, the opportunity for fresh readings of a group of American writers whose body of work deserves to be known better to today's audience. I have tried to select the major writers within that frontier-inspired progress-oriented tradition defined here, ignoring contemporaries significant in their own ways, such as Theodore Dreiser, Stephen Crane, and Edith Wharton, who stood clearly apart from that tradition. In many respects, of course, the writings of Norris, Garland, Cather, Anderson, and Lewis are widely different, and a study linking them might be expected to produce more contrasts than similarities. Norris's heavy-breathing rhetoric is the antithesis of Cather's quiet understatement; Lewis's jaunty assurance grates against the searching voices of Anderson's novels and stories; Garland, according to Cather, had no more temperament than a prairie dog, and so on.[19] For all their differences, though, I find that the western-progressive synthesis traced out here in their lives and works is of sufficient importance to justify the grouping.

Finally, it has seemed apparent to me that one need not style himself a psychoanalytic critic to find evidence that writers may create out of a kind of personal hunger, that their fictional figures are often at least partly a function of their own search for place and role — particularly in an age of uprootedness such as the one considered here — and that in working out the fate of their characters they are obliquely commenting upon the validity of their own lives. For all of these writers Frank Norris's claim applies, "the novel is the great expression of modern life," and it has seemed appropriate to reciprocate this full and serious affirmation of their best art by placing it in as many relevant and illuminating contexts as possible within the scope of this study.

NOTES

1. *The Education of Henry Adams* (Boston: Houghton Mifflin Sentry Edition, 1961), p. 343. Further references will be incorporated into the text.
2. Frederick Jackson Turner, "The Problem of the West," *Atlantic Monthly* 78 (September 1896): 297.
3. (New York: Random House Modern Library Edition, 1942), p. 27.
4. F. L Barnett, "The Reason Why," in Ida B. Wells, *The Reason Why the Colored American Is Not in the World's Columbian Exposition* (Chicago: n.p., 1893), pp. 79-80, reported that only two blacks above the level of janitor, laborer, or porter were on the fair staff, both as clerks, and that there were no exhibits relating to black Americans.
5. Quoted in Kermit Vanderbilt, *Charles Eliot Norton: Apostle of Culture in a Democracy* (Cambridge, Mass.: Harvard University Press, 1959), p. 203.
6. See Marx's *The Machine in the Garden* (New York: Oxford University Press, 1964). For an alternative treatment, emphasizing the invigorating presence of the machine in the natural world, see John F. Kasson, *Civilizing the Machine: Technology and Republican Values in America, 1776-1900* (New York: Grossman, 1976).
7. *A Connecticut Yankee in King Arthur's Court* (New York: New American Library Signet Edition, 1963), p. 14.
8. *Mark Twain's Fable of Progress* (New Brunswick, N.J.: Rutgers University Press, 1964).
9. (Boston: Houghton Mifflin Riverside Edition, 1962), pp. 18, 20.
10. James, *Seven Stories and Studies*, ed. Edward Stone (New York: Appleton-Century-Crofts, 1961), p. 287.
11. See *The Achievement of William Dean Howells* (Princeton, N.J.: Princeton University Press, 1968), p. 190.
12. William Dean Howells, *Letters of an Altrurian Traveller* (1893-94) (Gainesville, Florida: Scholars' Facsimiles and Reprints, 1961), p. 34.
13. In *The American Adam* (Chicago: University of Chicago Press Phoenix Books, 1955), p. 1.
14. *The Progressive Mind, 1890-1917* (Chicago: Rand McNally, 1970), p. 1. Noble's conception of the Progressive movement requiring "the redefinition of industrialism from a force creating complexity to that of a new frontier force leading from complexity to simplicity" (p. 22) seems to parallel the attitudes of some of the figures to be studied here.

15.   Robert Wiebe, *The Search for Order, 1877-1920* (New York: Hill and Wang, 1967), p. 132.

16.   Wiebe, pp. 112, 113.

17.   On this sacral West, see, especially, chapters 1 and 2 of Max Westbrook's *Walter Van Tilburg Clark* (New York: Twayne, 1969). On the tragic aspects of western American literature, see Harold P. Simonson's *The Closed Frontier* (New York: Holt, Rinehart and Winston, 1970).

18.   *Totemism* (Boston: Beacon Press, 1963), pp. 88-91. I have profited from the discussion of Lévi-Strauss in this context found in Cecil F. Tate, *The Search for a Method in American Studies* (Minneapolis: University of Minnesota Press, 1973), pp. 140-147.

19.   Cather's remark is found in *The Kingdom of Art: Willa Cather's First Principles and Critical Statements, 1893-96,* ed. Bernice Slote (Lincoln: University of Nebraska Press, 1966), p. 331.

1

Frank Norris's Western Metropolitans

> I have great faith in the possibilities of San Francisco
> and the Pacific Coast as offering a field for fiction. Not
> the fiction of Bret Harte, however, for the country has
> long since outgrown the 'red shirt' period. The novel of
> California must be now a novel of city life.[1]

A representative action in Frank Norris's San Francisco
novels is the withdrawal of the central character or characters
from the city itself out to the Presidio and to the ruins of old
Fort Mason near the Golden Gate. There, in a setting of
solitary beach, fresh trade winds, thundering surf, swirling
foam, and great, bare hills rolling down to the sea — in
short, the sort of booming and kinetic natural landscape that
embodies the author's sense of the vital forces surging
through all life — come Norris's troubled urbanites to
straighten out their values. Here McTeague begins his
interior journey back to the Sierra Mountains of his youth as
he sits for hours, "watching the roll and plunge of the
breakers with the silent, unreasoned enjoyment of a child."[2]
Here Norris brings all three of his popular romances, *Moran
of the Lady Letty*, *Blix*, and *A Man's Woman*, to a close, and in
Blix the scene is visited repeatedly throughout the novel.
Here Norris envisioned his own recovery from his debilitating
experiences in the Cuban War in 1898. As he wrote to a
friend,

> I want to get these things out of my mind and the fever out
> of my blood, and so if my luck holds I am going back to

30

the old place for three weeks and for the biggest part of the time I hope to wallow and grovel in the longest grass I can find in the Presidio reservation on the cliffs overlooking the ocean and absorb ozone and smell smells that *don't* come from rotting and scorched vegetation, dead horses and bad water.[3]

The rejection by the fictional hero of his blighted contemporary surroundings and his rejuvenative withdrawal to a green shade is, of course, of classic ritual in American literature. But Frank Norris's version of American pastoral requires closer examination precisely because it is not the simple praise of natural setting and vilification of the city and industrial society that we have come to expect when the machine and the American garden stand in confrontation. Norris's characteristic treatment of the modern city, as exemplified for him by San Francisco, combines conventional romantic attitudes toward nature with his beliefs in a mechanistic life-force and an evolutionary process that includes the propensities for both atavism and progress.[4] If Norris can evoke the qualities of grim indifference in the San Francisco of *McTeague*, if it becomes a city of dreadful night in *Vandover and the Brute*, if it is the setting for mere society frivolity in *Moran of the Lady Letty*, the author's western metropolis is also throughout his works the emblem of an inevitable industrial future, urban and complex, in which the survivors are those who have met the city's strenuous and unique requirements.

Thus, the works of Frank Norris, whom H. L. Mencken called in 1928 "the most considerable American novelist of the modern period,"[5] offer an appropriate starting point for this study. At the threshold of the new century Norris's books boldly project a western setting that calls forth an early version of the new American, a figure of muscular modernity strikingly manifesting Teddy Roosevelt's strenuous ideal in its judicious blending of wildness and civilization. Norris, then, resists classification as a conventional defender of the natural world against the threatening city,[6] even though he occasionally seems to reveal apprehension over the emergence of technological civilization. His works may dramatize flight from the city into an exhilarating wild nature, and he could wax lyric in his critical essays over the lessons to be learned by modern, urban man in "the canyons of the higher mountains, . . . the plunge of streams and swirling rivers yet without names, . . . the wilderness, the plains, the wide-rimmed deserts."[7] Still, on the deepest and most fundamental level Norris's novels fasten upon the necessity for return to — rather than escape from — the city. For he sees the commercial and urban present as an inescapable stage in evolutionary progress and in the "Great March" of Anglo-Saxon pioneering, he emphasizes the underlying similarities between urban and natural worlds and the possibilities for beneficial interaction between the two, and he posits a hopeful future for those who master their stern lessons.[8] The pattern that emerges, then, from the total design of his novels is one of a gradual shift from characters who either are somehow unfitted for modern urban life or turn their backs upon it in favor of escapist adventuring in wild nature to those who can function successfully on both levels but who are primarily committed to an urban existence and who attempt to discover in industrialized contemporary life the opportunities for high enterprise.

Norris's three early novels, *Moran of the Lady Letty*, *McTeague*, and *Vandover and the Brute*, sketch the hopes and limitations of his western urbanites, and prepare for their more successfully realized descendants in the later works.[9] *Moran's* romantic plot follows the adventures of Ross Wilbur, an aristocratic San Francisco playboy drawn from Richard Harding Davis, who is shanghaied onto a shark-fishing boat bound for Baja California. There aboard a derelict ship he finds Moran Sternerson, an Amazonian Nordic girl with whom, after a series of adventures, he sails back to San Francisco. The muscular Moran, bested by Wilbur in a knockdown fight, has become his clinging vine, and they plan a life together adventuring on the high seas. After anchoring their ship just inside the Golden Gate, Wilbur goes ashore on business and Moran is knifed by one of the Chinese crew, who then rows ashore, leaving the ship unmanned. The wind springs up and the ship pulls free and heads out for open ocean with Moran's body lying on the deck. As the book ends, Wilbur, watching from the shore, refuses to attempt to intercept the ship and allows it to race out into the stormy ocean until it is lost on the horizon.

Summary cannot do justice to the rich absurdity of all of this, but the novel is nevertheless important in setting forth Norris's broad contrasts between primitivistic and urban values. The ending of the novel demonstrates the misgivings of both narrator and hero about the decision to follow the primitive, buccaneering life that Moran represents. As the ship lies off the lifeboat station near the Presidio, Moran grows increasingly uneasy at the distant prospect of the city:

> Wilbur could see she felt imprisoned, confined. When he had pointed out the Palace Hotel to her — a vast gray cube ,in the distance, over-topping the surrounding roofs — she had sworn under her breath.
> "And people can live there, good heavens! Why not rabbit-burrows and be done with it? Mate, how soon can we be out to sea again? I hate this place." (III, 316)

When Wilbur goes ashore to make arrangements to outfit the ship for the planned filibustering trip to Cuba, he instead paces the beach and Presidio worrying about how he is to explain Moran and his own behavior to his San Francisco socialite friends. His inordinate concern for the opinions of those whose world he has just forsworn and from whom he will soon part company forever reflects Norris's difficulty in pressing the novel's atavistic escapism any further. As Wilbur walks the beach, Norris employs the physical setting to drive home the choices open to this western renegade urbanite, with his half-tamed Valkyrie. "There, on the very threshold of the Western world, at the very outpost of civilization," Norris's new man stands poised: "In front of him ran the narrow channel of the Golden Gate; to his right was the bay and the city; at his left, the open Pacific" (318). Norris told of his difficulties with the novel at this point in a letter to Elizabeth Davenport. "I am in two minds about her [Moran's] end and do not know whether she should be killed or go to Cuba with Wilbur."[10] The choice, finally made, is a crucial one for the direction of Norris's later career. Norris allows the inevitably treacherous coolie Hoang, left aboard the ship with Moran, to dispatch her with his knife, thus conveniently solving Ross Wilbur's problem. As Wilbur hears of Moran's fate from the keeper of the lifeboat station, he rejects the idea of attempting to reclaim the ocean-bound ship or the girl's body. In a rush of Norris's clamorous rhetoric, Moran goes

> out, out, out to the great gray Pacific that knew her and loved her, and that shouted and called for her, and thundered in the joy of her as she came to meet him like a bride to meet a bridegroom.
>   "Good-bye, Moran!" shouted Wilbur as she passed. "Good-bye, good-bye, Moran! You were not for me — not for me! The ocean is calling for you, dear; don't you hear him? Don't you hear him? . . . Good-bye, good-bye, good-bye!" (325)

In this heavy-handed disposition of a troublesome problem, a "creature unfit for civilization" (310), Norris intimates the limits to his own — as well as his hero's — commitments to nature-girls and unfettered adventuring. The city on the horizon inevitably intrudes itself and brings an end to adolescent fantasies. Ross Wilbur's final farewell to Moran is a sigh of relief at his own disengagement from the freebooting life. Wilbur will once more take his place in the urban world, but it is a reasonable conjecture from the evidence of Norris's later works that he will no longer lead cotillions. The novel does not pursue Wilbur beyond the moment of Moran's disappearance, and thus closes having presented only the most extreme of contrasts. At this point, neither Norris nor his hero recognizes that modern life may offer alternatives that lie somewhere between teadancing in San Francisco and swashbuckling ocean adventure. A few months after the publication of *Moran*, Norris wrote to Isaac Marcosson, in terms that apply to Ross Wilbur as well as to his creator, "When I wrote 'Moran' I was, as one might say, flying kites, trying to see how high I could go without breaking the string. However, I have taken myself and my work much more seriously since then."[11] If *Moran* establishes the restricted possibilities for beneficent primitivism in open-air settings, Norris's later-published novels would bring his heroes back into urban and industrial life and examine the opportunities for meaningful existence there.

McTeague and *Vandover and the Brute* probe more directly the nature and requirements of modern urban life in the far West. Themes raised in *Moran* — a man's need for worthwhile work, for the companionship of a strong woman, and for bracing contact with nature — reappear in different forms in these novels. In *Moran* we are left with a hero who has added to his fine city-bred manners the strength and resourcefulness gained from an immersion into euphoric nature and his contact with an inspirational and firm-willed woman. Vandover shares Wilbur's social advantages, but not the ennobling adventure into nature, and unlike Wilbur he rejects the love of a good woman. And while Vandover has, at the beginning, a worthwhile career as a painter to pursue, he eventually allows the city's hidden sensual life to divert him from it. Vandover's father, however, and Vandover's friend, Geary, anticipate, in a fragmentary way, the emergence of heroic cosmopolitans in Norris's later works. In *McTeague*, the hero shares, even surpasses, Ross Wilbur's physical prowess, but his intellectual and social shortcomings leave him with only a tenuous hold upon his place in a bewildering urban environment. With the loss of his occupation and his wife Trina's regression, his own descent is assured, and he eventually flees back to the primitive world from which he came, with the city in deadly pursuit.

Subtitles reveal Norris's urban consciousness in both books. *McTeague* is called "A Story of San Francisco" and *Vandover* was originally subtitled "A Study of Life and Manners in an American City at the End of the Nineteenth Century." Despite its clinically naturalistic subtitle, *Vandover* is as much a western story as is *McTeague*.[12] San Francisco is named on the novel's opening page, and that city's demimonde, its notorious habits of easy and luxurious living, provide the fatal attractions for the weak-willed and self-indulgent Vandover. *McTeague* is indispensably set in San Francisco for a different reason; the city's close proximity to its magnificent natural surroundings provides the appropriate backdrop for McTeague's urban sojourn, first as observer, then as bewildered participant, and finally as fugitive. The primitive and elemental natural world that he typifies stands at the edges of the novel's action, glimpsed in the view of the open Pacific across the ugly mud flats from the B Street Station where McTeague courts Trina, intruding more fully in the scenes on the windy downs near the Golden Gate where McTeague spends his days, and reclaiming McTeague and the novel entirely in the concluding chapters set in the high Sierras and Death Valley.[13] Both books reveal the vibrant and emerging western city in search of its appropriate new man. Vandover is hopelessly weak for its stringent demands as McTeague is hopelessly stupid, a judgment that Norris is at pains to emphasize, applying the term to McTeague six times in the opening chapter alone. It is all done without malice, but should nevertheless caution us against regarding McTeague as Everyman. He is an anachronism, huge, powerful, with a kind of childlike innocence about him, but a throwback nonetheless, and thus unsuited to take part in the evolutionary march.

Indeed, none of the characters in *McTeague* is qualified to grasp the potentialities of urban life, and the first half of the work is a satire upon the Polk Street irregulars and their immigrant counterparts, Trina's family, the Sieppes. With a wink to his audience, Norris as sophisticated cosmopolitan gives us a kind of Newgate pastoral of San Francisco's bumpkin class, detailing their libido for the ugly, the sentimental, and the pretentious. In that tone of repressed amusement with which the highbrow regards the aspiring lower-middlebrow, Norris describes the interiors of their houses, their "admirable" wallpaper, Trina's wedding bouquet, "preserved by some fearful, unknown process," the pictures on their walls, cheap prints of fat English babies and incredibly alert fox terriers, and colored lithographs over the mantel of golden-haired girls in nightgowns kneeling and saying their prayers, their eyes, invariably large and blue, rolled heavenward (VIII, 191, 136-37). Trina sums it all up with the inevitable judgment: "Of course...I'm no critic, I only know what I like" (170).[14]

With similar detached amusement, Norris presents these unlikely urbanites at their leisure. A vaudeville show featuring pie-in-the-face comedy, acrobats, a "Society Contralto" in evening dress, and a performer with burnt cork on his face who renders "Nearer, My God, to Thee" on the beer bottles leaves them transported. The performance ends with little "Owgoost" Sieppe wetting the pants of his little Lord Fauntleroy suit, while his mother smacks and shakes him to his howls of "infinite sadness."[15] A picnic depicts the elder Sieppe in his characteristic comic role of inefficiency expert, marshaling the group to its destination with a series of sharp commands: "To one side!"..."Vorwarts!"..."Silence!"... "Stand back!"..."Attention!" (57-64). Another picnic with the McTeagues and their Polk Street acquaintances ends in a murderous fight, leaving a wild disorder of trampled turf, torn clothing, empty beer bottles, broken eggshells, and discarded sardine cans. The long ethnic joke that the Sieppes enact in the first part of the novel is set against their grim downward glide later. We last hear of them unsuccessfully attempting to borrow money from Trina, the father having failed in business in Los Angeles and vaguely considering emigrating with his family to New Zealand.

Trina's cousin, Marcus Schouler, is another inept urbanite who blusters through the early chapters, confusedly mouthing the catch-phrases of popular reform, choleric in his defense of ideas that he is incapable of understanding. While he professes toward McTeague (his rival for Trina's hand) the Damon-and-Pythias sentiments of popular fiction, he nevertheless rages against the unwitting dentist and throws a knife at him on one occasion. Finally, he reports McTeague for practicing dentistry without a license, the action that, in this new credentialed society, precipitates McTeague's decline. For Marcus, the bungler, the man who can do nothing well, the seething fool of words, Norris reserves an appropriate fate. Like McTeague and the Sieppes, Marcus leaves the city, but for reasons that Norris treats with some derision. Scornful of the "red shirt" school of Western fiction and the yellowback-novel shoot-em-ups, Norris depicts Marcus as a victim of their fantasies.[16] He leaves to take up a cowboy's life on the ranches of south-central California. His "entrancing vision" of himself, complete with "silver spurs and untamed broncos" (151), is deflated by Norris in the book's final chapter as, with McTeague, Marcus chases a recalcitrant mule across the blistering sands of Death Valley, shouting and cursing, finally emptying his revolver into the beast, thereby destroying the last canteen of water and any hope of survival. This entire scene — a pair of western anachronisms, the cowboy and the miner, fumbling away their wilderness chances in awkward-squad confusion — must rank with Stephen Crane's "The Bride Comes to Yellow Sky" in its puncturing of favorite frontier myths.

At the root of the failure of the Sieppes, Marcus, and the other of the novel's characters to be assimilated successfully into urban life, Norris suggests, is their confusion and insecurity over their own proper place in society: "They could never be sure of themselves," says Norris. "At an unguarded moment they might be taken for toughs, so they generally erred in the other direction and were absurdly formal. No people have a keener eye for the amenities than those whose social position is not assured" (80). In this sense, they bear another resemblance to Crane, this time in the characters of *Maggie*, who, in an uglier urban environment at the opposite end of the country, combined the behavior of "toughs" with the sentiments of Victorian gentility.

To some extent, the failure of Norris's characters to respond successfully to the demands of urban life may find its source in Norris's notorious racism. Mr. Sieppe and Marcus are excitable and confused Germanic types. Trina's penuriousness is traced to her hoarding peasant forebears. Maria Macapa is a demented Latin, a degenerate type that Norris frequently drew. Zerkow is quintessential grasping Jew, a virtual walking allegory of avarice. For good measure, he carries, and uses, a wicked-looking knife, that weapon of the depraved. (When Marcus throws his knife at McTeague, Norris describes the performance as "in the true, uncanny greaser style" [125].) Old Grannis and Miss Baker are requisite Anglo-Saxons, but too enfeebled and reticent to serve as proper models for Norris. Furthermore, their painful shyness and fastidiousness is, at one extreme, as inappropriate to the modern city as are the bungling antics of the Polk Street unwashed at the other. Of course, McTeague, too, is at least marginally Anglo-Saxon, but his stupidity renders him unfit for a complex society. Still there is something admirable in his opposition to it: indeed, Norris finds McTeague absurd not when he is behaving least like the perfect urbanite, but when he is falteringly trying to play the role.

McTeague as lowbrow, McTeague in his natural animal state, "salient"-jawed and thick-muscled, is a compelling figure: caught up in the genteel respectabilities of courting, marriage, and getting on in the world, he is usually ridiculous. One recalls his wildly comic attempt to purchase theater tickets from a supercilious cashier, his rapturous postmortem on the vaudeville performance, the pose he strikes for his wedding picture, "his chin in the air, his eyes to one side, his left foot forward in the attitude of a statue of a Secretary of State" (191).

McTeague's bewildered response to all of his urban tormenters, "You can't make small of me," foreshadows Norris's marvelously realized enlargement of the man as, after his murder of Trina, he lights out for the mountains of his youth and takes up, with an inarticulate but profound sense of appropriateness, the monstrous dentistry of placer mining: "In the Burly drill he saw a queer counterpart of his old-time dental engine: and what were the drills and chucks but enormous hoe-excavators, hard-bits and burrs? It was the same work he had so often performed in his Parlors, only magnified . . . ." Here, the great mountains take him back again and "he yielded to their influence — their immensity, their enormous power, crude and blind, reflecting themselves in his own nature, huge, strong, brutal in its simplicity" (328-29).

But if McTeague's reversion to the natural world is beneficial, it is only briefly so, for he intuitively senses that the city is his pursuer and that it is more powerful than his protective mountains. Thus he is forced further and further and further back, finally into a landscape beyond redemptive capacity, the baleful and maleficent wastes of Death Valley, where nature itself is dead. For, it must be understood, there is a larger dichotomy in Norris than that of nature and city. Overarching this conventional distinction is Norris's greater contrast between the quick and the dead, between the vast engine of life, the throbbing heartbeat of both city and country, as opposed to the interior and exterior deserts of silence, stillness, and death. The central image of this life-force, seen in *McTeague* and repeated ceaselessly throughout Norris's fiction, is that of the bourdon or the diapason, a swelling sound that emanates from both urban and wild settings and that represents the animating energy behind all life.[17] In *McTeague* it is the note "which disengages itself from all vast bodies, from oceans, from cities, from forests, from sleeping armies, and which is like the breathing of an infinitely great monster, alive, palpitating" (329). Here the description is occasioned by the colossal mountains of Placer County, but elsewhere in Norris we find the bourdon generated by a city, a crowd of people, a sea, and so on.[18] Norris's frequent interchanging of metaphors drawn from both industrial and organic sources to describe this deep murmur of the life-force demonstrates how the diapason blends the customarily and apparently opposed worlds of city and nature into one vibrant whole, a vast note whose opposite is the still void of death, the heartbeat stopped, the engine run down. Thus Trina is described as dying "with a rapid series of hiccups that sounded like a piece of clockwork running down" (320)[19] And McTeague flees the voices of life into the true wilderness of Death Valley, where

> the silence, vast, illimitable, enfolded him like an immeasurable tide. From all that gigantic landscape, that colossal reach of baking sand, there arose not a single sound. Not a twig rattled, not an insect hummed, not a bird or beast invaded that huge solitude with call or cry. Everything as far as the eye could reach, to north, to south, to east, and west, lay inert, absolutely quiet and moveless under the remorseless scourge of the noon sun (356).[20]

If McTeague were indeed "left all alone in this world's wilderness" as his one and favorite song puts it, his death might partake of the dignity of an existential isolation, but the city reaches out to wrench a final irony from this scene. For although Marcus pursues McTeague from a motive of personal vengeance, he is also, in his association with the posse, an agent of civilization, and his dying action in handcuffing himself to McTeague is a dramatic reassertion of the city's ultimate authority. McTeague is a representative modern man in his movement from the mountains of his youth to the city of his majority, although his failure there marks him as unequipped for evolutionary progress. In his regressive return to the mountains he repeats the mythic American pattern of rejection of the threatening metropolis. And in his failure to effect that escape, and to reclaim the healing and protective natural world which ought to be his western birthright, he adds another dimension to the tragic pastorals of our literature.

The young Vandover of *Vandover and the Brute* fashions his own death in the desert as he paints contentedly in his San Francisco studio pictures of broad, empty landscapes in which he places the solitary figure of an animal, "a dying war horse wandering on an empty plain" (V, 54) or a man. His planned masterwork, a huge canvas entitled "The Last Enemy," will show a soldier dying of thirst and wounds on a Sudanese desert, while in the distance a lion crouches in wait. The effects Vandover seeks are isolation and intense heat. For the young artist, this melodramatic conceptualization will turn back upon himself in the more naturalistic image of the "brute within" that brings him to his moral and physical ruin. Vandover finds his own desert of the spirit in the ironic opposite of his romantic painting. At the novel's conclusion, under the sink of a cheap rented house that he has been hired to clean, he gropes half-wittedly about, prone, in the sour water, picking up greasy refuse, a counterpart to the degenerate scrubwoman Trina McTeague. His final tormentor is a small boy who taunts him with his fallen state, " 'Hey, there! Get up, you old lazee-bones!' " (310).

Norris's fascination with San Francisco as a "story" city closely parallels Vandover's attraction to solitary figures set in immense landscapes. In describing the city for an 1897 article in the San Francisco journal, *The Wave*, Norris fastened upon its isolation: "Perhaps no great city of the world is as isolated as we are. . . .Here we are set down as a pin point in a vast circle of solitude. Isolation produces individuality, originality."[21] Isolation, Norris says, has allowed the city to develop its unique features relatively independently of outside influences. From his characteristic treatment of San Francisco in *Vandover* and elsewhere, we find the city's distinctive qualities in the sharp contrasts of its life, the mixtures of races and occupations, of corruption, languor, pleasant diversion, the tonic of nature, all existing side by side. The would-be San Francisco story writer had, in Norris's indefatigable audile imagery, but to "strike. . .the right note. . .and the clang of it shall go the round of nations."[22]

This western city, then, offers Vandover the best and worst of worlds. At the opening of the novel he lives with his father in a spacious, comfortable house on a hill on California Street with a large yard, trees, hummingbirds, sparrows nesting under the eaves, a barn, a windmill to pump water, a conservatory where orchids are raised, "altogether a charming place" although a neighboring lot full of dry weeds and heaps of ashes and ugly painted advertisements suggests the intrusion of a blighted urbanism into this nearly rural retreat (27-28). Vandover's habits of self-indulgence lead him increasingly down off his hill and into the idle and dissipated life of the city's streets. With the death of his father and the selling of the family home, Vandover's descent continues, until he reaches his nadir with the loss of his artistic talent, profligately spent "in the warm musk-laden atmosphere of disreputable houses, defiled by the breath of abandoned women,...dragged all fouled and polluted through the lowest mire of the great city's vice" (201). Accompanying his decline, images of constraint and diminution replace those of freedom and openness. Vandover moves from the spacious family home into ever-smaller and shabbier quarters until he is jammed into the tiny space under the sink of the cheap house at the novel's end. As his artistic talent ebbs away, the huge canvas on which he had planned to paint "The Last Enemy" gives way to little oval landscapes on the surface of iron safes or small horses or dogs on the sides of wagons which Vandover paints to earn a few dollars.

The sea journey which Vandover takes midway in the novel might, as in *Moran*, have served as a restorative to the citified young man, although his destination, the Hotel del Coronado in San Diego, is hardly the moral proving ground that Ross Wilbur found off Baja California. (Indeed, the homeward-bound Wilbur pays a visit to this same resort hotel and regards his society friends at their pleasures with newfound contempt.) On Vandover's return voyage to San Francisco his ship strikes a reef, and the ensuing ordeal of open boat and eventual rescue again fails to rouse the weakened and apathetic Vandover to action. Unlike the narrator of Crane's famous short story, Vandover finds the experience not important but only harrowing. At his rescue he is no more interpreter than before. Back in San Francisco, just off the rescue ship, he heads straight for the Imperial Bar, the scene of many of his previous debauches. The entire trip is a parody of the redemptive return to nature of which Norris is so fond. And once back in the city it is a further measure of Vandover's decline that he never again leaves the mean streets, never makes the healing walk out to the Golden Gate. Once Vandover moves from his father's house, the only entry of the natural world into the novel, aside from the disastrous ocean voyage, is in far glimpses of the mountains seen from the city, or in the invigorating morning air or the brisk afternoon trade winds, but these influences are too brief and ephemeral to touch Vandover significantly or to arrest his descent.

Vandover comes to a realization of his imminent destruction in a characteristic passage late in the novel. At night, and alone, in a near-hysterical state as he realizes that he can no longer draw, he stands at an open window, looking out over the city:

> All the lesser staccato noises of the day had long since died to silence; there only remained that prolonged and sullen diapason, coming from all quarters at once. It was like the breathing of some infinitely great monster, alive and palpitating, the sistole and diastole of some gigantic heart. The whole existence of the great slumbering city passed upward there before him through the still night air in one long wave of sound.
>
> It was Life, the murmur of the great, mysterious force that spun the wheels of Nature and that sent it onward like some enormous engine. . . .(202)

Here once again is the blending of the diapason, the "vast and minor note of Life," with the natural force which drives onward toward some unknown goal. Here is the harmonious merging of organic and technological metaphor — the diapason of the city, a breathing monster, a beating heart, the wheels and engine of the life-force — that denies any assumed condemnation of that mere extension of the machine, the modern city. Later, when Vandover, alone in his room at night, cries out for help,

> there was nothing, nothing but the vast silence, the unbroken blackness of the night, a night that was to last forever. There was no answer, nothing but the deaf silence, the blind darkness. But in a moment he felt that the very silence, the very lack of answer, was answer in itself; there was nothing for him. (214)

As in the ending of *McTeague*, the silence that engulfs the isolated protagonist is an intimation of his doomed state.

In the figures of the elder Vandover and Vandover's lawyer-friend, Geary, are two possible models for successful urbanites. Both are skilled in business, although at a comparatively low level compared to the captains of industry in Norris's final two books, where business becomes for Norris the acceptable and appropriate modern equivalent of such atavistic exploits as the flight into primitive nature or the urge for blood combat. Vandover, significantly, is as bewildered by business dealings as is McTeague. Thus, not only is he susceptible to sharp operators like Geary, but on a more elemental level he is represented as unarmed and helpless in the modern city's characteristic activity. Neither Geary nor Vandover's father, however, qualifies as a major urban figure. "The Old Governor" is near retirement as the book opens, and dies soon after. He is not directly pictured in the conduct of his business affairs, and from what we learn of them later his methods are narrow and unimaginative. Geary's shrewd dealings *are* closely followed, but he, too, is incapable of envisioning or carrying out a major idea. Self-centered and petty, he cheats Vandover, his friend, in a business matter, something that the more significant urbanites to come, Cedarquist and Shelgrim in *The Octopus* and Jadwin in *The Pit*, would never do. Geary, moreover, in his fondness for the pleasures of the table, shares in Norris's contempt for Vandover's sensual weaknesses. But while the elder Vandover and Geary do not qualify as major metropolitans, they do suggest a direction for Norris's future urbanites.

Blix (1899) reverses the record of Vandover's decline in the story of another artist who grasps his western city's potentialities for creative achievement while, with the aid of frequent pastoral retreats and his California girl, he resists its destructive attractions. A pivotal influence upon Condy

Rivers, the would-be writer with his weakness for all-night poker games, is his girl friend and "chum" Travis Bessemer, or "Blix," another of Norris's masculine-named, no-nonsense, yet attractive, females.[23] Although she is only nineteen years old to Condy's twenty-six, she instructs him in the lessons of purposeful living. Like Mark Twain, Norris believed that women possessed a finer moral sensibility that properly accorded them the right and the duty to improve their men. A kind of urbanized Moran, Blix rejects the debutante's role in favor of a career in medicine, although her true function in the novel is simply to help Condy fend off bad habits. San Francisco in *Blix*, although it does offer diverting temptations, is not the sink of evil to which Vandover surrendered himself. Instead, the city becomes, as Blix leads Condy to understand, a necessary, even beneficial, proving ground for manhood. To Condy's complaints that his gambling is the fault of "this city life," she counters that "a man ought to be strong enough to be himself and master of himself anywhere." When Condy pleads the difficulty of keeping up the struggle to be "clean and fine," she chides, "It's the keeping it up that makes you strong. . . . What's a good man if he's weak?" (III, 56-57). The city thus becomes in *Blix* no less a moral gymnasium than the wilds, where ninety-seven-pound weaklings, properly fortified, may be transformed into muscular and self-reliant new Americans.

Besides his association with Blix, Condy is strengthened by his recurrent relationships to the natural world. Fishing on a nearby lake, taking "their walk" out to the Golden Gate, the young couple move easily back and forth between city and countryside in a pastoral and credible version of Ross Wilbur's far-flung adventuring. Norris's customary tub-thumping in the presence of wild landscapes and "primordial" forces out at the Golden Gate is softened to complement the relationship of love and friendship between the two young people: "The huge spaces of earth and air and water carried with them a feeling of kindly but enormous force —

elemental force, fresh, untutored, new, and young" (168). The couple's pattern of interchange between urban and wild settings represents an idealized, beneficent interfusion of sophisticated and natural values that is for Norris the hallmark of his successful urbanites.

Condy is further qualified for an active role in the city by his sense that the western city's cultural diversity can provide the source of meaningful material for himself as writer. Condy's fascination with San Francisco's opportunities for fiction — which is, of course, Norris's fascination as well — leads the couple into a series of excursions and mild adventures around the town from which come the stories that eventually draw attention, and a job offer, from a New York publisher.

Thus at the end of the novel the thrice-blessed Condy — western pastoral rhythms beating in his blood, California girl by his side, his writing career fairly begun — receives with Blix on New Year's Eve the city's predictable benison; "the vague murmur of many sounds grew and spread and widened, slowly, grandly; that profound and steady bourdon, as of an invisible organ swelling, deepening, and expanding to the full male diapason of the city aroused and signalling the advent of another year" (163-64). However mawkishly, the phallic overtones here are meant to underscore the newly acknowledged love relationship between Condy and Blix; they are "chums" no longer. And the murmur of the bourdon here is of course also a clear indication of their participation in the vital and progressive life-force. The next day, in the closing scene of the novel, the two young people take their walk out to the Golden Gate where the familiar natural setting and a Technicolor sunset add to the plethora of approving signs. In unmistakable Edenic imagery the two are described on the last page as apprehensive, for the moment, "loathe to take the first step beyond the confines of the garden wherein they had lived so joyously and learned to love each other." But "work was to be done...work and the world of men," and the western city of youth and awakening life gives way "to the new life, to the East, where lay the Nation" (174). Norris's overorchestrated ending does not seriously diminish the charm of much of the novel. It retains interest and significance for the modern reader as an evocation of a lost moment of youthful optimism, as a memorialization of Norris's own courtship of his wife, the beautiful California girl Jeanette Black, and as further evidence of Norris's continuing search for the possibilities for successful and creative urban life.

Norris, as Donald Pizer and Larzer Ziff have pointed out, wanted writing to be like those more consequential activities that he regarded as the substantial business of the real world.[24] While Condy Rivers of *Blix* makes a propitious beginning in his career as writer, the "sterner note" and the compulsive exaltation of "work" that is the book's final note suggest that Norris found Condy and his San Francisco sketches lacking in worldly significance. For Norris, who wanted writers to "go a-gunning" for stories, while he portrayed in *Blix* the sedentary and tedious nature of much of the act of composition, the writer was an unpromising hero.[25] Ward Bennett, the main figure in *A Man's Woman* (1900), the third and last of Norris's popular romances, is another attempt to create a significant modern-day man of action. What the book demonstrates is that the hero as fresh-air fiend has yielded to the twentieth century and has thus virtually ceased to offer meaningful opportunities for novelistic development. In *A Man's Woman* the moronic escapades of Ross Wilbur of *Moran* have become the carefully planned polar exploring of Ward Bennett. The earlier playboy hero is now a scientist, his thrusts into the wilderness sanctioned by nationalistic motives and duly supported by "the City," a nameless metropolis which serves as a kind of base camp. (The geographic description fits San Francisco, as does the fact that it was and is "the City" to northern California and most of Nevada.)[26]

The book opens with Arctic explorer Bennett and his men losing their battle against the protean nature of the far North — cracking ice floes, groaning pressure ridges, howling winds, hissing waves — while the insistent auditory imagery once more signals the presence of elemental forces. Finally rescued, Bennett recuperates from his ordeal in a country retreat near "the City," where in the "numbing silence" of an unchallenging countryside the body of the novel takes place (VI, 97). There, to Lloyd Searight Bennett, the man's woman who frets over her husband's inactivity, it seems, in Norris's characteristic rendition of the machine of life, "as if some great engine ordained of Heaven to run its appointed course had come to a standstill, was rusting to its ruin, and that she alone of all the world had power to grasp its lever, to send it on its way" (218). Bennett's decision not to return to the Arctic and reenter the race to the Pole is paralleled by the stasis, silence, and warmth of his surroundings, imagistic equivalents of the deadening lethargy and paralysis of the will which has overcome him.

Into this lifeless world bursts the news that a rival explorer's ship is icebound, and Norris's vast machinery begins to pulse and rumble with new life. Bennett at last emerges from his inactivity and begins to mount another expedition, preparations for which occupy the last portion of the novel. As his ship sails out of the harbor of "the City" and through the narrow channel that separates it from the open ocean, it is to the inevitable bourdon of thronged crowds, bells, whistles, and guns.

> Then all at once the advancing wave of sound swept down like the rush of a great storm. A roar as of the unchained wind leaped upward from those banked and crowding masses. It swelled louder and louder, deafening, inarticulate. A vast bellow of exultation split the gray, low-hanging heavens. . . . Suddenly the indeterminate thunder was pierced and dominated by a sharp and deep-toned report, and a jet of white smoke shot out from the flanks of

the battleship. Her guns had spoken. Instantly and from another quarter of her hull came another jet of white smoke, stabbed through with its thin, yellow flash, and another abrupt clap of thunder shook the windows of the City. (241)

As an agent of civilization, a trained specialist carrying the hopes of city and nation, Ward Bennett and his polar exploring are apparently meant to command more serious attention than the mindless adventuring of Ross Wilbur. But it is difficult for the modern reader to give either work any credence. Written at least partially as a potboiler to capitalize upon contemporary interest in the race for the North Pole, blatantly nationalistic in its final pages, *A Man's Woman* demonstrates a wilderness primitivism that has played itself out for Norris. For Norris, as for the historian Turner, the geographic frontiers have disappeared. The novelist's hero is driven to the literal end of the earth to find a suitable environment for contemporary adventuring in nature. Norris's next novel was to demonstrate that the story "as big as all out-doors" was much closer to home.[27]

The expansive conception of *The Octopus* (1901) is intimated in its opening pages where Norris sets forth the poet Presley's attempt to write, in "thundering...hexameters," the epic Song of the West, "where a new race, a new people — hardy, brave, and passionate — were building an empire." Presley's efforts so far, we are told, "had only touched the keynote. He strove for the diapason, the great song that should embrace in itself a whole epoch, a complete era, the voice of an entire people" (I, 7). But while he conceives of his Song of the West as arising from valleys, plains, mountains, ranches, ranges, and mines, the sweep of events carries him not toward the back country and the frontier life which he envisions but away from it and toward the city. Presley, who dreams of the romance of the wide open spaces, is diverted from his anticipated subject by the dull but persistent commonplaces and irritating realities of freight rates and railroad-farmer bickerings. Searching for material for his epic poem in the wheat-ranching country of California's great Central Valley, Presley encounters the main characters of Norris's large and boldly drawn work. There are the two other young men central to the novel, the rancher, Annixter, and the shepherd and mystic, Vanamee. Magnus Derrick leads the ranchers, Osterman, Broderson, Harran Derrick, Annixter, and others in the fight against the monopolistic power of the Pacific and Southwestern Railroad, while Magnus's brother, Lyman, betrays the ranchers' interests by siding with the railway in order to boost his own political ambitions. Other figures of importance are the Valley working-class family the Hoovens, the railroad engineer Dyke, the dairymaid Hilma Tree, who later marries Annixter, and the San Francisco captains of industry Cedarquist and Shelgrim. Still it is the character of Presley, the Easterner who comes west with hugely romantic expectations about the frontier but who is drawn to the city and eventually to the wide world itself, who occupies most of our attention and who embodies and records Norris's purpose in the novel, as he outlined it to Howells, of illustrating the movement of contemporary civilization from an agricultural to an industrial society.[28]

Hanging in Lyman Derrick's office, in a scene midway through *The Octopus*, is a railway map of the Pacific and Southwestern Railway lines in California. The system of red lines upon a white background presents us, in Norris's relentless symbolizing, with a country sucked white by a sprawling monster, "its ruddy arteries converging to a central point" (II, 5). The central point is, of course, the city of San Francisco, and, as the actual center of the Octopus, the headquarters and meeting point of the company's rail lines. It also provides the narrative direction for the novel, as the setting shifts from the Central Valley to San Francisco to follow the lives of those who have been drawn to it. The book's action thus demonstrates the tilt of western history toward the city and the industrial future.

At the conclusion, those left behind in the Central Valley ranch country are the dead, Annixter, Harran Derrick, Broderson, Hooven, and the dying or broken, Hilma Annixter, Osterman, Magnus Derrick, and his wife. The vibrant Dyke, who fled like McTeague to the Sierras, has been hunted down and imprisoned. His mother and daughter, when we last see them, are preparing to leave for San Francisco, the old woman already anticipating her own death and the girl facing an uncertain future suggested by the fate of Mrs. Hooven and her daughters in the city. Presley's last visit to the ranch country near the end of the novel reveals an empty and desolate countryside. Annixter's abandoned ranch suggests the exhaustion of rural possibilities: "a vast stillness" hangs over it. "No living thing stirred. The rusted windmill on the skeleton-like tower of the artesian well was motionless; the great barn empty; the windows of the ranch house, cook house, and dairy boarded up" (II, 342). Of the characters who remain on the land only the mystic Vanamee remains whole. He is a potentially tragic figure, as is suggested by his characteristic presentation — like McTeague in the desert — as a speck in an immense landscape, a tiny, solitary figure in a limitless natural expanse. But he is allowed finally to join his phantom lover, and as a kind of earth father to voice the cosmic optimism with which the novel uneasily closes.

If *The Octopus,* thus described, resembles a conventional pastoral in which rural goodness is opposed by the destructive city, a closer look offers a useful corrective. The wheat ranchers, as Norris makes clear, are not Jeffersonian yeomen lovingly tilling their broad acres but cashcroppers, out for quick profit. "To get all there was out of the land, to squeeze it dry, to exhaust it, seemed their policy. When, at last, the land worn out, would refuse to yield, they would invest their money in something else; by then, they would all have made their fortunes" (II, 14). The city, on the other hand, stands identified as the emblem of the future. As the center of the Octopus, it shares the ambiguity of that central symbol: although it can be temporarily subverted for evil purposes it nevertheless participates in the general movement for good toward which, the novel's final sentence claims, all things inevitably work. Indeed, Norris's familiar metaphor of the life-force as cosmic machine is applied both to the Octopus and to nature itself. The Octopus is "a vast power, huge, terrible . . ., the leviathan, with tentacles of steel clutching into the soil, the soulless Force, the iron-hearted Power," etc. (I, 48); nature is "a vast power, huge, terrible; a leviathan with a heart of steel, knowing no compunction, no forgiveness, no tolerance; crushing out the human atom with soundless calm, the agony of destruction sending never a jar, never the faintest tremor through all that prodigious mechanism of wheels and cogs" (I, 174).[29]

As participant in the life-force, the city shares in the positive connotations of that force. Once again, as in the earlier novels, the city's potentialities for destruction or degradation are balanced by its opportunities for creative or progressive endeavor. As in *McTeague* and *Vandover*, those who are unprepared to take part, with Rooseveltian vigor, in the "hard, huge struggle" of city life must be cast aside (II, 277). What drives Mrs. Hooven to starvation and her daughter Minna to prostitution is not the city so much as their inability to adapt to its ways, or to overcome "the blind, unreasoned fear" that they feel toward the city (II, 288). Country-bred and ignorant of urban life, they are unaware "that there were institutions built and generously endowed for just such as they"; even were they aware, the "dogged sullen pride of the peasant" might cause them to turn from seeking aid (II, 278). While one urbanite, Gerard, the railroad vice-president, lives in baronial splendor atop Nob Hill and treats his dinner guests to Bluepoint oysters on pyramids of shaved ice and asparagus brought by special train, another, Shelgrim, the road's president, is a heroic manifestation of the work ethic, whose "enormous shoulders are fit to bear great responsibilities and great abuse," and who dresses almost shabbily, puts in long hours in his office, and treats an alcoholic employee with compassion and understanding (II, 281). If Mrs. Cedarquist typifies the city's bored and gullible socialites, her husband carries Norris's higher hopes as a creative and energetic knight of commerce, a visionary entrepreneur who correctly predicts that the great markets for American wheat will eventually shift from Europe to Asia, and who, at the conclusion of the novel, serves the life-force by building the line of clipper ships to carry the wheat to the Orient.

Cedarquist assumes a larger place in the novel if one considers that he is a spokesman for several of Norris's pet ideas. He espouses the theory, as Norris had done in his essay "The Frontier Gone at Last," that it was manifest destiny for the Anglo-Saxon to continue his westward pioneering until he had circled the globe and reached his original starting point.[30] Cedarquist also expresses Norris's impatience with those San Franciscans who busy themselves with trivialities — the buying and selling of corner lots, the organizing of an ineffectual trade fair, a pathetic version of Chicago's mighty Exposition, featuring a figure of California constructed out of dried apricots. All of this while Cedarquist pursues his visions of global commerce. In addition, he speaks with rare common sense against the railroad trust, and correctly identifies the source of its exploitive powers as public indifference (II, 20). Cedarquist thus forms an interesting match for Shelgrim, whose imperial rhetoric so befuddles Presley at the end of the novel. In Cedarquist's daring pioneering venture with the wheat ships he joins the Higher Business to the life-force and thereby assumes an important place in the evolution of Norris's new man. A logical outgrowth of Norris's earlier modern metropolitans, Cedarquist prepares us for the more substantial heroic urbanite, Curtis Jadwin of *The Pit*.

If Cedarquist is, as Lyman Derrick calls him, one of the city's "representative men" (II, 16), he seems to embody a distinct minority of the novel's urban characters. But if the city is frivolous, or hard, or foolish, or unconcerned, as it is depicted at various points in the narrative, these representations are subsumed under the larger impressions which the novel conveys of the inevitable movement of modern life toward urban resolutions. San Francisco as the contemporary city is indeed, as it appears on the railroad map, "that center from which all this system sprang" (II, 5), a statement that is not an indictment but a recognition of modern urbanism. The representative man of the great Central Valley, the farmer Annixter, is no bucolic tiller of the soil but a contemporary executive type who has mastered not only scientific agriculture, but finance, law, political economy, and civil engineering (I, 22-23). (Indeed all three of the novel's young heroes are college graduates and thus "new" western men.) The reception of Presley's sensationally popular poem "The Toilers" was suggested by an actual historical model, Edwin Markham's "The Man with the Hoe," which became a revolutionary call for a new laborer, the clear-eyed and intelligent workman, to replace the older ox-brained drudge, the enthralled victim of capitalistic greed and official indifference. The typical settlement of the valley is not the creeping village, but the brisk little city of Bonneville, saluted by the author as "full of the energy and strenuous young life of a new city," with its "whirring electric cars" and "zinc-sheathed telegraph poles" (I, 184, 203).

Thus, city and country merge in *The Octopus*, linked by compelling new patterns of production and distribution. What we are left with is a sense of the modern world-city, an interdependent and interconnected system like the ticker-tape machines that tie the offices of the wheat ranches not only to San Francisco, but to other great cities of the country and the world, and by which the ranches become "merely the part of an enormous whole" (I, 51).

In claiming that *The Octopus* is essentially intended as a work of progressive optimism, one can, of course, cite the novel's final page and Presley's seemingly hypnotic acceptance — in the face of evidence to the contrary — that "all things surely, inevitably, resistlessly work together for good." But the setting of this last chapter is perhaps more revealing of Norris's intention than Presley's confused reflections. We are here once again in Norris's territory of hope and possibility. As in the conclusion of *A Man's Woman*, Norris places his final action in *The Octopus* aboard a ship on a mission of larger social significance, moving out of San Francisco Bay and onto the open ocean, bearing a central character who, after a period of lethargy and dejection, is once more "up with the procession" of history's long march.

Despite Cedarquist's admirable advice to Magnus Derrick to send his wheat to the Orient, thus moving with the course of empire and helping to break up the monopolistic control over wheat prices by the Chicago speculators, Norris's determination, in his proposed trilogy of the wheat, to trace the actual historical pattern of movement from production to marketing to consumption required that he follow the flow of the wheat to Chicago in *The Pit* (1902). Although Norris was born in Chicago in 1870 and lived there until his family moved to San Francisco in 1884, the midwestern metropolis had little hold upon him. " 'Bawn 'n raise' in California,' " he wrote to interviewer Isaac Marcosson in 1898 in response to a request for personal information, and in the autobiographical *Blix* Condy Rivers says of himself, " 'Bawn 'n rais' in Chicago; but I couldn't help that, you know.' "[31] Clearly, Norris wished to be considered a Westerner and a San Franciscan. But Chicago, although Norris had in an earlier *Wave* article dismissed the place as hopeless for a fictional setting, responds to his need, in *The Pit*, for a city that takes its commerce seriously and in prodigious quantities, as San Francisco did not.[32] Chicago is the heart and center of the commercial America, the "great grey city," plundering the midlands ruthlessly, supreme examplar of the "true power and spirit of America," where "the vast machinery of Commonwealth clashed and thundered from dawn to dark and from dark till dawn" (IX, 55-58).

In the prose-poem of five or six pages that introduces the reader to Chicago, Norris repeatedly calls forth images of violent movement and strident sound to establish the city as a maelstrom of powers and forces and to prepare us for the frantic action to take place within the wheat pit. Anticipating Sandburg, Norris trumpets Chicago as "gigantic, crude with the crudity of youth, disdaining rivalry; sane and healthy and vigorous; brutal in its ambition, arrogant in the newfound knowledge of its giant strength . . ., formidable, and Titanic" (58). Chicago is the San Francisco of *The Octopus*, enlarged and galvanized for combat, a fit setting for Curtis Jadwin, the last and most ambitious of Norris's king-of-the-mountain urbanites. *The Pit* explores whether any man, even the strongest and best equipped, can withstand the pressures at the vortex of modern industrialism.

At the opening of the novel, Jadwin bears a close resemblance to Christopher Newman of Henry James's *The American*. Both are quietly aggressive and successful business-men, cut in the same hard, strong, keen-eyed physical pattern. Both are at home in country as well as city settings. Both have overcome youthful poverty, achieving wealth through powerful acts of the will. Both now seek the properly splendid woman to set atop their pile. But whereas James lifts his Newman out of industrial life, Norris takes his straight to its center. Jadwin is consistently depicted as a modern warrior and Norris drives home the business-as-battle analogy at length throughout the novel.[33] The Pit becomes, each day, the scene of warfare; at the close of trading, the littered floor of the wheat exchange is covered with "the debris of the battlefield," while at night "the wounds of the day were being bound up, the dead were being counted, while, shut in their Headquarters, the captains and commanders drew the plans for the grapple of armies that was to recommence with daylight" (98, 36). Jadwin's climactic effort to corner the wheat is done in Norris's big bowwow style, carried by the sustained metaphor of a complex and carefully planned military attack; in final defeat, Jadwin is still the Good, Grey Commander, beaten but unbowed. At the height of the great battle, Norris effectively positions his hero Jadwin at the very center of the series of concentric circles which form the novel's industrial panorama. Standing in the midst of the crowded and roaring Pit, dramatized throughout the work as a whirlpool of furious activity which his efforts to corner the wheat have agitated to an absolute frenzy, all in the midst of Chicago, the larger vortex of the nation's newfound power and energy, Jadwin is the ultimate assertion of Norris's heroic urbanite.

It is, in Norris's cosmogony, a position that no man can hold for long; Jadwin has finally gone beyond the limits of heroic personal will. In his attempt to control the entire flow of the wheat he has unwittingly thwarted the life-force itself. The inevitable "bourdon" of the massed wheat arises like "the first rasp and grind of a new avalanche..., a diapason more profound than any he had yet known" rises to a crescendo (357). Having disturbed the laws of "creation and the very earth herself," Jadwin has marked himself for destruction, and the "infinite immeasurable power," that "appalling roar of the Wheat itself coming in, coming on like a tidal wave," overwhelms and engulfs him (358, 372). Thus Norris defines in *The Pit* the limits to urban individualism. Jadwin's great "corner" was ultimately destructive not only to himself but to the poor who could not buy the bread from his cost-inflated wheat, to the farmers who were ruined by his manipulation of wheat prices, and to the institutions and individuals caught in the shock waves of his collapse. Like Poe's mariner, Jadwin has descended into the maelstrom, and, like him, although he escapes he is shaken and altered by his experience. At the conclusion, a chastened Jadwin leaves Chicago for the far West with his wife Laura, who has undergone, in her husband's defeat, the proper Norris conversion from dilettante to man's woman. Behind them remains Jadwin's young admirer and protégé, Landry Court, who, now married to Laura's younger sister, has retired to the relative sanctuary of a railroad-office position after vowing that he will speculate no more.

In Jadwin's defeat and in his retreat westward for rootholds are suggested a change in Norris's previously held attitudes toward East and West. Earlier in his career, as he dramatized in *Blix* and in his satiric thrusts at the banalities of San Francisco society in *The Octopus*, he held that one must go east to make his way, that his western metropolis lacked the high seriousness, the sterner cult of work, of its eastern counterparts. But his own later experiences living in New York, as seen in his revealing short story "Dying Fires," brought him to the opposite conclusion, that the Atlantic city was hostile to work and unstimulating and unrewarding to the serious artist.[34] Immediately after finishing *The Pit*, Norris, with his wife, left New York for San Francisco, convinced that his move east had been a mistake. The final sentence of *The Pit* suggests in its gloomy images a similar deflation of the promise of Chicago, whose frenzied industrial development, even by this time, 1902, seemed to have outrun the possibilities projected a decade earlier by the White City for a harmonious western synthesis in mid-America. Our last view, seen through Laura Jadwin's eyes as she and Jadwin ride through the city to the railway station, is of the Board of Trade building, "black, monolithic, crouching there without a sound, without a sign of life, under the night and the drifting veil of rain." The words repeat exactly those at the end of the book's opening chapter, expressing Laura's

"first aversion" to the great city (37, 71). Despite her
attraction to the city's power and force, revealed in the paean
to Chicago in the book's second chapter, Norris allows the
note of ugliness and rejection to be the final judgment — not
an exuberant Chicago but a silent, lifeless charnel house.
Thus Jadwin and Laura's move west is not a banishment but
the familiar American gesture of lighting out for the
territories, toward "the new life," as Norris indeed terms it
in a closing chapter thick with statements and images of
rebirth and renewal (401). Like James's eternal Newman,
Jadwin is still capable of growing a new man inside his old
skin.

The Pit, then, reveals that Norris was enough of a
Westerner to continue to weigh the options to modern
industrial urbanism even as he recognized its inevitability.
The novel takes its protagonist to the limits of urban
adventuring and pulls him back just short of destruction. We
may assume, for Jadwin, no more Byronic challenges to the
life-force. The glamour of the great capitalist entrepreneur
has faded. Rampant individualism is as inappropriate in the
modern city as it is anachronistic to the wilds of Norris's
earlier novels. Urban energy must be scaled down and
redirected along more progressive lines.

If, as Franklin Walker convincingly argues, Norris's own
parents are the prototypes for Jadwin and Laura, then it may
be conjectured that, like the elder Norris who left a drizzly
and dispiriting Chicago for a rejuvenative San Francisco,
Jadwin's unspecified western destination will also be that
city where the proper balance of natural and urban life can
be reestablished.[35] The denial of unchecked industrialism
with which *The Pit* concludes is echoed in some of the final
events of Norris's own life. As he and Jeanette returned to
San Francisco from New York in July of 1902, it was with a
series of new anticipations. They would take an ocean

voyage abroad to gather material for the final volume of the wheat epic. He would then do a trilogy on the Battle of Gettysburg, then a series of stories about western mountain people. He had already arranged to buy a ten-acre tract with a cabin on the ranch of Mrs. Robert Louis Stevenson in the secluded Santa Cruz Mountains south of San Francisco. It would be a retreat, and later a permanent residence. There he could fish for trout and shoot bears from the windows, as he wrote to eastern friends in a burst of redskin bravado.[36] None of these anticipations was to materialize. In October, after his return to San Francisco, Norris suffered an attack of appendicitis and within a few days was dead of peritonitis, at the age of thirty-two. For Norris, who admired the strenuous life principally from a distance, who, as one of his friends said, never knew how to rough it, and who had divided his short life between the three greatest and most dynamic cities of America, these final plans were nevertheless evidence of a continuing belief in a pattern of productive tension between progressive and primitivistic values.

The Pacific slope, the historian Earl Pomeroy reminds us, was from the beginning a region primarily urban rather than rural.[37] In the body of western American literature, which has found its primary archetype in the solitary individual set against a wilderness landscape, the novels of Frank Norris early challenged us to widen our perspective, to take into account new identities that were both western and urban. Thus these books, joined, as will be seen in the following chapter, by those of Hamlin Garland, established the figure of the new American on the western horizon and prepared the way for its fuller realization in the works to come of Willa Cather, Sherwood Anderson, and Sinclair Lewis. Norris's novels reveal an attempt to combine the sensate qualities of western life with the new rhythms of a complex urban society that he saw as the product of an inescapable evolutionary advance. From his works emerges a vital western metropolis that finds its appropriate citizens in those who respond to the compelling rhythms of both city and western setting.

NOTES

1. Letter from Norris to Isaac Marcosson, December 1898. *The Letters of Frank Norris*, ed. Franklin Walker (San Francisco: Book Club of California, 1956), p. 23, hereinafter abbreviated as *Letters*.

2. *McTeague* (Garden City, New York: Doubleday, Doran and Co., The Argonaut Manuscript Limited Edition of Frank Norris's Works, 1928), VIII, 283, hereinafter abbreviated as *Works*. All subsequent references to Norris's novels and stories are from this edition and will be limited to volume and page number and included in the text.

3. *Letters*, p. 19.

4. I am indebted to Donald Pizer's lucid and thorough explanation of Norris's conception, gained primarily from his teacher at Berkeley, Professor Joseph Le Conte, of the notion of progressive evolution. See Pizer's *The Novels of Frank Norris* (Bloomington, Ind.: Indiana University Press, 1966), pp. 3-22. An earlier study of this idea is also valuable, Arnold Louis Goldsmith's "The Development of Frank Norris's Philosophy," *Studies in Honor of John Wilcox* (Detroit: Wayne State University Press, 1958), pp. 174-94.

5. "Introduction," Frank Norris, *Vandover and the Brute*, V, x.

6. I disagree here with a principal thesis of Warren French's *Frank Norris* (New York: Twayne Publishers, 1962), pp. 60-61, et passim, and with the judgments on Norris's attitude toward the city in James R. Giles's "Beneficial Atavism in Frank Norris and Jack London," *Western American Literature* 4 (Spring 1969): 15-28.

7. "Salt and Sincerity," IV (August 1902). In *The Literary Criticism of Frank Norris*, ed. Donald Pizer (Austin: University of Texas Press, 1963), p. 220, hereinafter abbreviated as *Literary Criticism*.

8. Norris's conception of the "Great March" is found in his essay "The Frontier Gone at Last," in *Literary Criticism*, pp. 111-17.

9. *Vandover and the Brute*, although not published until 1914, was Norris's first-written novel. The writing of *McTeague*, published in 1899, also antedates *Moran's* publication in 1898.

10. *Letters*, p. 6.

11. *Letters*, p. 22. Actually, Norris had already written much of what was later to become *McTeague* and *Vandover and the Brute* during the year 1894-95, when the author was at Harvard. See Norris, *A Novelist in the Making*, ed. James D. Hart (Cambridge, Mass.: Harvard University Press, 1970), pp. 16-22.

12. For a fuller discussion of Norris's use of the San Francisco scene in *Vandover*, *McTeague*, and *Blix*, see James D. Hart's informative introduction

to *A Novelist in the Making* (n. 11) and Kevin Starr's *Americans and the California Dream* (New York: Oxford University Press, 1973), pp. 260-65.

13. A provocative essay on McTeague as frontier hero is George W. Johnson's "The Frontier Behind Frank Norris' *McTeague*," *Huntington Library Quarterly* 26 (November 1962): 91-104.

14. An excellent study by D. B. Graham explicates fully the role of art and taste in the novel. See his "Art and Humanity in *McTeague*," in his *The Fiction of Frank Norris: The Aesthetic Context* (Columbia and London: University of Missouri Press, 1978), pp. 43-65.

15. This scene is tastefully omitted from the Argonaut and other early Doubleday editions.

16. See Norris's "A Neglected Epic," in *Literary Criticism*, p. 122.

17. Despite its frequent occurrence throughout his works, Norris's "bourdon" or "diapason" has received little attention from critics. Howells was obviously playing with the concept when he praised Norris as one who "heard nothing or seemed to hear nothing but the full music of his own aspiration, the rich diapason of purposes securely shaping themselves in performance." ("Frank Norris," *North American Review* 175: 777.) In his study of Norris, Ernest Marchand calls attention to the figure and gives some examples of its use but does not analyze it. (*Frank Norris* [Stanford: Stanford University Press, 1942], pp. 178-79.) Beyond this, the diapason or bourdon receives only passing mention from Norris's critics.

Although it is doubtful that Norris was conciously alluding to it, his descriptions of "the vast and minor note of Life" bear a close resemblance to the ancient belief in the music of the spheres, a harmony arising from the order of the universe and the right relationship of human beings to this order. For a full discussion of this concept (and for evidence that the familiar reference to the diapason in Dryden's "A Song for St. Cecilia's Day" does not reflect Norris's purposes) see John Hollander's *The Untuning of the Sky* (Princeton: Princeton University Press, 1961). A more likely source for Norris's figure is the "diapason" stop on the pipe organ, which sounds a range of octaves and harmonies. There may have been an organ in the family's mansion in Chicago during Norris's youth. In any event, Jadwin's house in *The Pit* is drawn from the Norris mansion, and the great pipe organ is a focal point of the novel. (See Franklin Walker, *Frank Norris* [Garden City, New York: Doubleday, Doran and Co. Inc., 1932], pp. 13-14, hereinafter abbreviated as Walker). Furthermore, Norris occasionally mentions the word "organ" in his descriptions of the bourdon/diapason.

18. See, e.g., *Blix* (III, 160, 163-64), *A Man's Woman* (VI, 62, 64, 239), *Vandover* (V, 199, 202), *The Octopus* (II, 254), "The Guest of Honor" (IV, 155, 165), "Salt and Sincerity" (*Literary Criticism*, pp. 219-20). A particularly revealing instance of Norris's tendency to blend nature and city under the greater unity of the life-force is seen in his feature article, written for *The Wave*, on a Santa Clara carnival:

> There was another voice, that of the sea, mysterious, insistent, and there through the night, under the low, red moon, the two voices of the sea

and the city talked to each other in that unknown language of their own; and the two voices mingling together filled all the night with an immense and prolonged wave of sound, the bourdon of an unseen organ, the vast and minor note of Life. (Norris, *Frank Norris of "The Wave"* [San Francisco: Westgate Press, 1931], p. 111.)

19. Cf. the exhausted Presley, confiding to Cedarquist at the end of *The Octopus*, "There's no 'go,' no life in me at all these days. I am like a clock with a broken spring" (II, 274).

20. Similarly, in Norris's short story, "The Guest of Honor," the entrance of a character representing death is accompanied by a stilling of the background bourdon of city life (IV, 158).

21. "An Opening for Novelists: Great Opportunities for Fiction Writers in San Francisco," in *Literary Criticism*, p. 29.

22. *Literary Criticism*, p. 30.

23. Norris gave two of his story heroines the first name "Travis," and a third is *Turner Ravis* (my italics), perhaps out of admiration for Travis, the "boy commander" of the Alamo, whom Norris eulogizes in "A Neglected Epic," *Literary Criticism*, p. 121.

24. Pizer, *Literary Criticism*, p. 24; Ziff, *The American 1890's* (New York: Viking Press, 1966), p. 269.

25. In one of his journalistic essays, "The Mechanics of Fiction," Norris describes his ideal of pyrotechnic fiction: "...the complication is solved with all the violence of an explosion and the catastrophe, the climax,...fairly leaps from the pages with a rush of action that leaves you stunned, breathless..." (*Literary Criticism*, p. 60). But this all depends, as Norris admits, upon plodding brickwork by the author, and the image of Condy Rivers in *Blix* "driving his pen from line to line, hating the effort...working away, hour by hour...with the dogged, sullen, hammer-and-tongs obstinacy of the galley-slave, scourged to his daily toil" is at odds with Norris's doctrine of the strenuous life for his fictional heroes (III, 135).

26. Earl Pomeroy, *In Search of the Golden West: The Tourist in Western America* (New York: Alfred A. Knopf, 1957), p. 185.

27. *Letters*, p. 35.

28. Howells, "Frank Norris," *North American Review* 175: 772.

29. Donald Pizer correctly interprets the conflict in the novel as not between nature and technology but between those who oppose the natural life-force and those who ally themselves with it. See his *The Novels of Frank Norris* (n. 4), pp. 148-54. My reading of the novel coincides with Pizer's on this crucial point and on the importance of Cedarquist as a spokesman for Norris's ideas.

30. See *Literary Criticism*, pp. 111-17.

31. The letter to Marcosson is in *Letters*, p. 22; Condy's remarks are in *Works*, III, p. 10.

32. For Norris's dismissal of Chicago and praise of San Francisco see *Literary Criticism*, p. 28, and Norris's short story, "The House With the Blinds," *Work*, IV, p. 11.

33. For Norris's equating of the contemporary business tycoon with the warrior see his "The Frontier Gone at Last," *Literary Criticism,* pp. 111-17. An important earlier reading of Norris's treatment of business as contemporary adventuring in *The Octopus* and *The Pit* is Walter F. Taylor's *The Economic Novel in America* (Chapel Hill: University of North Carolina Press, 1942), pp. 300-304.

34. For further treatment of Norris's disenchantment with New York, see Walker, pp. 296-97, and *Literary Criticism,* pp. 22-24. Evidence of Norris's wish to return to San Francisco as early as March of 1899 is seen in *Letters,* p. 31.

35. Walker, pp. 8-9, 16.

36. Walker, pp. 304-5; *Letters,* p. 97.

37. *The Pacific Slope* (New York: Alfred A. Knopf, 1965), pp. 120-64.

2

Back-Trailing toward the Future: The Progressive Hamlin Garland

> As a matter of fact, literary power is not personal; it is at bottom sociologic. The power of the writer is derived from the society in which he lives; like the power of a general, which springs from the obedience of his army. When society changes, when his audience dies, the writer's power passes away. This is the natural law, and would take way easily and quickly were there not other tendencies to conserve and retard, just as in the animal organisms.
>
> Hamlin Garland, *Crumbling Idols*[1]

> Movement is swift on the Border. Nothing endures for more than a generation. No family really takes root. Every man is on his way. Cities come and builders go. Unfinished edifices are left behind in order that something new and grander may be started. Some other field is better than the one we are reaping. I do not condemn this, I believe in it. It is America's genius. We are all experimenters, pioneers, progressives.
>
> Garland, *A Daughter of the Middle Border*[2]

" 'Sᴇʟʟ the cook stove if necessary and come,' " wrote Hamlin Garland of the Chicago White City to his parents on the Dakota prairies. " 'You *must* see this fair.' "[3] Anxious to live closer to his ailing mother and afire with enthusiasm for the great Exposition and for the opportunities that it portended for the West to seize the cultural leadership of the nation, Garland had decided in 1893 to move to Chicago from Boston, where he had established his early reputation as a realist and disciple of the single-tax reforms of Henry George. Now the burgeoning metropolis on Lake

Michigan would become, he predicted, a literary center "more progressive than Boston and more American than Manhattan."[4] Garland's adjectives by which he heralded the emerging Chicago, progressive and American, were to be exemplified in his new novel and his best, *Rose of Dutcher's Coolly* (1895), whose publication followed his move to Chicago. And the same terms suggest a useful line of inquiry for reexamining the cultural assumptions that lie behind both his earlier fiction and the generally ignored novels that he was to write during the next twenty years, until he turned to autobiography and reminiscence for the remainder of his life with the publication of *A Son of the Middle Border* in 1917.

When he came to evaluate the achievements of Frank Norris, for example, upon Norris's untimely death, Garland found the San Francisco novelist abundantly and soundly American but not wholly progressive. For all his admiration of Norris's energetic and richly creative observations of modern western life, Garland was careful in summing up Norris's career in *The Critic* to qualify his praise in terms that are more revealing of Garland's own work than of Norris's.[5] Like Josiah Royce, the California-born Harvard philosopher, who wrote at about the same time as Garland's essay on Norris that "a general sense of social irresponsibility is . . .the average Californian's easiest failing," and that "the Californian has too often come to love mere fullness of life and to lack reverence for the relations of life,"[6] Garland thought Norris's absorption with an emerging metropolitan America somewhat disappointing in its failure to suggest any conscious design for social betterment. *McTeague*, with its "masterly" artistic originality, was nevertheless for Garland an unavailing "study of sad lives" for which no possibility of amelioration existed. *The Octopus*, "frankly sociologic," as Garland admiringly called it, with its prefacing map and its panoramic cast of characters, was an indictment of social conditions of the sort that Garland could applaud, but Norris's ceaseless attribution of these conditions to impersonal force fell short of Garland's humanitarian expectations for a western fiction that he had raised in his collection of polemical essays, *Crumbling Idols* (1894).[7] There, Garland had added his voice to Howells's earlier attacks upon romantic writing as contributing to the social evils of the day, and had correspondingly encouraged an ethically progressive but "realistic" new writing to foster social reform. For Norris, the mere presence of a Spencerian and Comptean evolutionary life-force inevitably carrying the race forward was its own justification for cosmic optimism. For Garland, going with the flow was never enough. What was required of fiction for Garland and what ties together the apparently severed halves of his career in fiction — angry realist turned benign romancer, as the conventional critical view has it — is his application of that same evolutionary and progressive force that Norris celebrated toward the resolution of social and political issues by means of skillled and capable new figures emerging upon the American scene.

To place the career of Hamlin Garland in this context, I believe, reveals it in terms other than a downhill march in which the passionate recorder of the failed dirt farmers of the Middle Border is somehow curiously transformed into the complacent fancifier of Rocky Mountain courtships and sunsets. Rather, in the best books of both periods is manifested a concern with social questions and their solutions, and Garland's changing attitudes toward these problems may be seen as reflecting new attitudes in American social thought during the 1890s and the early 1900s, the period in which Progressivism emerged as the dominant political force in the nation.

As contemporary social and intellectual historians like Richard Hofstader, David Noble, and Robert Wiebe have demonstrated, the 1890s saw the beginnings of national awareness that society could be externally managed along progressive lines. The Spencerian philosophy ascendant at the time of Garland's early writing and to which he was an early convert had assumed an inevitability to the social environment that allowed little opportunity for the exercise of productive reform. Even Henry George's single-tax proposals, which Garland wholeheartedly accepted and promoted during the late 1880s and early 1890s as a necessary means of establishing the conditions for free competition under which Herbert Spencer's "optimistic fatalism" might operate, were recognized by Garland in the mid-nineties as politically incapable of dealing with the powers of unchecked capitalism. The world was thus not likely to be made safe for the operation of Spencer's benign law of evolutionary progress. By 1899, Garland would write in his diary that the single tax system "no longer seems so vital as some other things. I do not now expect it to do more than modify thought. Once I thought it might change our way of living. So it will, but long hence, probably."[8]

Instead, then, of characterizing Garland in his middle period as a Wordsworthian lost leader who deserted the cause of social reform for the comfortable trappings of respectability, he may be seen as reflecting, under the twin influences of the political collapse of Populism and the single-tax cause, on the one hand, and the rise of Theodore Roosevelt and the Progressive movement on the other, a fairly representative and justifiable shift in public attitude. Like many of his countrymen, Garland moved away from a Spencerian, antigovernment allegiance to rugged individualism and untrammeled private enterprise toward a recognition that social justice could come about only as a result of a strong federal government enlisted on the side of progressive reform.

Thus, in the most significant Rocky Mountain novels of his middle period, Garland, in a sense, gives us a contemporary rewriting of his early fiction of the middle border.[9] The older West of these early stories is a region whose essential figure is trapped and defeated, a regional version of Markham's "Man with the Hoe" or Presley's

"Toilers" in *The Octopus*. Rural life engenders only hapless
dirt farmers and worn-out wives, or young men and women
who, even if they manage to escape the drudgery of the farm,
find their lives blocked, their opportunities for consequential
careers in a new America thwarted, by the workings of a
corrupt and greed-driven capitalism. For this early pattern
Garland fashions in his middle period another setting of
social disorder and victimization of the weak by the un-
scrupulous and powerful. But by this time, recognizing that
the individualism of his heroes, however noble and tenacious,
cannot prevail against the practices of an aggressive and
rapacious society acting out the spectacle of a debased
frontier ethic, Garland allies his leading characters with the
ameliorative forces of the new age, principally science and
progressive government, and allows them, after the obligatory
fictional conflict, a victory over these dark and essentially
anachronistic powers. In the best of his mountain fiction,
then, there is a continuation of the philosophical assumptions
of his early work that social disorder can only be counteracted
by social reform. But as participant in the revolution in
American values at the end of the nineteenth century,
Garland came to recognize that the older claims of heroic
individualism would not hold up in the face of an increasingly
collectivistic society, moreover that gross perversions of the
common good could be carried out under the soiled banner
of private freedom.

The germ of Garland's progressivism may be seen in his
early stories, such as those collected in *Main-Travelled Roads*,
and in his first novels, *Jason Edwards*, *A Member of the Third
House*, and *A Spoil of Office*. While on one level these early
works constituted an appeal for the necessity of single-tax
and Populist reform, they were also, as Garland must have
come increasingly to recognize, ironic demonstrations that
conditions had passed beyond the point at which calls for

single-tax individualism and Spencerian *laissez-faire* or personal liberty could hope to have any real effect.[10] The stories of *Main-Travelled Roads* (1891) suggest that only in neighborliness, in personal loyalty, in the voluntary social associations of a primitive farming community, can rural despair and loneliness be overcome. The neighborly assistance that the Council family provides for the Haskinses in "Under the Lion's Paw" is set against the grasping individualistic depredations of Jim Butler. Similar evidences of community neighborliness — an extension of the frontier house- or barn-raising — offered to the failing, the poor, or the defeated are presented in "The Return of a Private," "A Day's Pleasure," "God's Raven's," and "A 'Good Fellow's' Wife." A powerful benevolent figure like William McTurg of "God's Ravens" (who appears, curiously enough, again in "Up the Coulee" and as David McTurg in "A Branch Road") suggests, in his quiet strength and compassion, the appeal for Garland of a kind of transcendent agrarian leader who might set country and village aright once more. But the figure and the idea remain merely dimly sketched. The primitive social organization represented by an older pastoral neighborliness in these stories can often fashion only a temporary stay — a day's pleasure at best — against the poverty and hardship of farm life, or against the unchecked selfishness and greed of a predatory new capitalism.

Clearly, larger and more significant patterns of social organization and more effective leaders would be required to bring about the West's new day. But the possibilities for that new day are, it needs to be emphasized, an important undercurrent in these early works. Indeed, the instances of grinding and hopeless determinism in *Main-Travelled Roads* are limited to two or three stories such as "Under the Lion's Paw" and "Up the Coulee," which, perhaps because they have corresponded so neatly to the theoretical definitions of a European-derived literary naturalism, have become the favorite anthology pieces and centers of critical attention on

Garland, thus pulling his actual aims and achievements somewhat out of their own orbit.

Garland's first three novels, all published in 1892, continue the search for consequential new figures and alliances. *Jason Edwards*, a slight novel reworked, as was *A Member of the Third House*, from plays Garland had written in 1890, provides, in its subtitle, "An Average Man," an indication that the work will consider the conditions of the representative American worker. The book, dedicated to the Farmer's Alliance and its "high mission . . . to unite the farmer and the artisan . . . in a continent-wide battle against the denial of equal rights,"[11] demonstrates with perhaps unconscious irony, that the Jason Edwardses of this land are incapable of directing their own lives. First as victimized mechanic in Boston and than as failed homesteader on the western plains, Edwards is a textbook case of naturalism, helpless before a grinding profit system in the city and before the power of indifferent and violent nature in the country. But the central figure in the novel is not Edwards at all, but his daughter's fiancé, Walter Reeves, a young journalist and progressive who, although of village origins, quickly comes to "know the city like his primer" (10). He watches his opportunities, works hard, and soon rises to a position of responsibility. He falls in love with Alice Edwards, but she is determined to hold on to her freedom for a time and to do for herself and her family what Reeves had done for himself. Four years of hardship on the Dakota prairies undermine Alice's new woman convictions and leave her father near death, at which point Reeves rescues them and returns them to civilized surroundings, an act that is to repeat itself compulsively throughout Garland's fiction and that is to find its personal expression in the author's relocation of his parents, following their 1893 visit to the Chicago Exposition, in the pleasant Wisconsin village from which they had been attracted to the bleak prairies by dreams of prosperity and independence some twenty-five years earlier.

It is Reeves, then, and not Jason Edwards who carries the novelist's hopes for the future, Reeves the figure of energy and leadership who represents the possibility of improving social conditions for ordinary Americans. Reeves's final orchestration of the lives of the Edwards family suggests that the betterment of life for average Americans is less likely to be accomplished through the sort of massed action of plebeians called for in the book's preface than through the decisive leadership of skilled new urban professionals.

A Member of the Third House moves toward a similar demonstration that the general public cannot escape victimization by corrupt businessmen and legislators without the intervention of forward-looking new leaders. Garland's hero, Wilson Tuttle, a reform legislator, is an even more direct anticipation than Walter Reeves of Garland's later western moderns. Tuttle, unlike Reeves, directly confronts a social and political evil in the public arena. The book, then, looks ahead to much of the fiction of the Progressive era in which the hero or heroine's strong sense of personal morality is fitted to a satisfying public role through political reform. Even in this early work, Garland is unwilling to await the millennium promised in social Darwinism's assurance of progress. "Herbert Spencer's mighty brain might say," muses the narrative voice as it contemplates the scene of political corruption at one point in the novel, " 'What is it all? And what does it all matter?' "[12] But as the corrupters are not philosophers but activists, so they can be defeated only by activists of equal energy, armed in moral proof. While Garland could accept Norris's cosmic Spencerian judgment at the conclusion of *The Octopus* that "the larger view always and through all shams, all wickednesses, discovers the Truth that will, in the end, prevail," Garland expressed through his emerging new Americans that the process must have its catalysts.

Still, the major figures of *Jason Edwards* and *A Member of the Third House* reveal important limitations. If Edwards himself has no part to play in the new age except that of sufferer and victim, neither are his daughter and son-in-law quite fully prepared to assume their roles of leadership for the times. Alice Edwards is a new woman who has found no real work to do. She does not pursue her musical abilities sufficiently to provide herself a career, and her devotion to her father and her family acts to close her off from any significant opportunities for self-fulfillment. She finally settles for a conventional marriage. And there is no assurance that Reeves, the energetic New Englander, envisions his social role as extending beyond his charity in extricating Alice and her family from their private squalor. He, too, lacks real work. The scholarly Tuttle of *A Member of the Third House*, despite his moral crusade in a state senate, can hope for only a temporary victory against a ubiquitous system of political bribery and corruption. Moreover, he is a lifeless, cardboard figure, unable to win the reader's interest from the engaging rogue Tom Brennan, the lobbyist and corrupter of legislators for whom the novel is named, and who emerges cheerily prosperous and unrepentant at the end. Like Howells with his attractive but amoral Jeff Durgin in *The Landlord at Lion's Head*, Garland is horrified to find the combination of personal charm and diseased morality residing so comfortably within a single personality. The ending of *Member*, in which Brennan, having adroitly sidestepped Tuttle's broom of reform, enthusiastically anticipates new opportunities for intrigue, signals the resumption of dirty politics as usual. Again, more potent agents of reform than the occasional good man are needed to mend the damaged social fabric.

The roots of political corruption on the local level, as described in *A Member of the Third House*, extend to the national capital. " 'My four years in Washington showed me that,' " says one of Tuttle's friends (70). In the third and most substantial of his early novels, *A Spoil of Office: A Story of the Modern West*, Garland broadens his treatment of the theme of personal fulfillment through political reform to encompass Washington as well as the rural West. Further, he attempts to fashion out of a pair of western Populist leaders, Bradley Talcott and Ida Wilbur, the representative new man and woman to reassert the values of frontier democracy against the juggernaut of urban indifference and corruption.

A Spoil of Office has been criticized for its ax-grinding politics and its inability to bring its main characters to life, with the exception of Nettie Russell, a flirtatious girl who pursues the unresponsive hero. There is truth in both judgments, but the book retains interest for the modern reader in its depiction of the last-gasp efforts of a pastoral America to assert moral control over the powerful new forces of industrial capitalism. Bradley Talcott comes close to being an outright allegorical representation of the lost agrarian West, with his sleeping-giant strength and his stolid adherence to a code of personal integrity amid his shifty contemporaries. Western too is his association of personal fulfillment with oratorical and political prowess. He begins as a tongue-tied farmer's hired man who aspires to Chautauqua eloquence and Bryanesque rhetorical powers over his country neighbors. With Ida Wilbur, an established figure in the rural reform movement, as his inspiration and example, he eventually rises to the position of United States Representative. In setting Talcott's destination at the nation's capital Garland again underscores his hero's identity as a Westerner and obligatory optimist in the face of evidence to the contrary: "He had the Western man's intensity of feeling for Washington. To him it was the centre of American life, because he supposed the laws were made there."[13]

The satiric thrust here is carried on throughout the description of the federal legislators as Talcott first watches them conducting the nation's business. While their names suggest history to him, their appearance and manners are "amazing." One resembles a featureless oriental idol with a perpetual, babyish pout upon his face, another announces his inevitable objections in the querulous tones of a crone, another affects the style of stump oratory, still another drones on in the lugubrious monotone of the preacher. When Talcott meets his new colleagues, they pay him scarcely any attention. "Each man had his own affairs to look after, and greeted him with a flabby hand-shake and looked at him with cold and wandering eyes. It was all very depressing" (285-87). What keeps *A Spoil of Office* from approaching the sort of damning satire of Congress that Twain and Warner present in *The Gilded Age* or that Henry Adams presents in *Democracy* is Garland's continuing belief, despite the disillusioning Washington education of his hero, that the political system is still not beyond redemption and may yet respond to a just cause. Thus, although Bradley Talcott and Ida, now married, are unable to change Washington, they still hope to change the country at the grass roots, and they return to the West at the novel's conclusion where, in their separate careers, they recommit themselves to the Populist reform movement. There was, of course, as history has since revealed, more to admire in their faith than in their judgment. The tumultuous and formidable new economic and social forces which were thrust upon the national consciousness in the nineties were not to be successfully directed by Farmer's Alliance politicians working the midwestern Grange meetings and Fourth of July picnics.

In one brief but revealing scene in the novel, Talcott watches in bewildered fascination as the telegraph machine in an Iowa office clicks out the news from Chicago and New York, which is quickly translated by the office manager into telephoned financial advice to his customers. Talcott goes away, "his head full of those cabalistic sentences," conscious of the "strangeness" and "the excitment of great battles on the street which he had read of in the papers" (231). The hero's fascination and bewilderment with these Norrisian images evince both his desires and his limitations for participating in the rising urban America. He remains, even at the conclusion of his political education, an anachronistic country figure, whose simple faith in will and work, and whose vaguely realized opposition to the dark designs of "special privilege," do not quite qualify him for a role in the new times. And although Talcott properly looks toward the federal government for the correction of social injustice, he finds there, as yet, no leader and no program of the sort that will attract the more assured and capable moderns of Garland's later novels. *A Spoil of Office* marks an important shift in Garland's work away from definition of the individual through characteristics of regional determinism and local color and toward the creation of mobile new characters who are identified by their common professional achievements and goals. The novel further expresses, for the first time, Garland's sense of a large and nonsectional alliance of Westerners joined in an expression of collective reform. But without a clear conception of how this alliance might assume national significance, or a firm plan for translating an inchoate sense of injustice into new patterns of order, Bradley Talcott's experiences are a less than definitive "story of the modern West."

The major novel of Garland's career, *Rose of Dutcher's Coolly* (1895), expresses most memorably his sense of the transition of the late-nineteenth-century American Middle-Western consciousness from agrarian to urban assumptions. Rose Dutcher, an ambitious farm girl from Wisconsin, is drawn from her father and her rural home to the state university, and from there, following her graduation, to Chicago. There she is taken up by a circle that includes, besides the merely affluent and agreeable Harveys, a handful of progressive figures who bespeak the possibilities of an emerging new West — " 'We new men and women,' " as Dr. Herrick, a woman physician and member of this little group of moderns, calls them.[14] Another of this band of self-conscious urban professionals, Warren Mason, a newspaper editor, is accepted as husband by Rose at the novel's conclusion.

Rose Dutcher's sense of life's possibilities originates in a childhood memory of a physically graceful circus performer; with this brief vision of beauty before her, she resolves dumbly to lift her own life into that dreamlike world of achievement and perfection represented by her glittering acrobat. Attractive and warm-blooded as she matures, Rose nevertheless avoids early marriage through her stronger attachment to the sense of her future self as an active and full participant in the great world. She leaves home to attend the University of Wisconsin — one can imagine this fictional yearner in a class of Frederick Jackson Turner's, whose end-of-the-frontier fears and aspirations she was to live out — and she graduates with "the class of 189-." (Garland had gathered the details for graduation activities along with other material for the Madison chapters of the book during his stay in Madison during June of 1892.[15]) Rose returns home, where her widowed father has built a new house for them both, but she quickly realizes that she cannot go back to farm life, and, her sorrowing father having understood the "power of the outside world" and the pull of "progress" upon his daughter, she boards the train to Chicago. Although Garland's original conception of the novel had Rose headed toward New England at this point, his own determination to move to Chicago in 1893, convinced that the city was destined to lead the American cultural procession — witness the White City, about which Garland had excitedly written to his parents and which he celebrated in *Crumbling Idols* — caused him to shift Rose's destination to his newly adopted midwestern metropolis.

Nothing can reveal more clearly the crucial differences between the new Americans of Norris, Garland, and the other writers considered here and the textbook figures of literary naturalism such as Crane's Maggie and Dreiser's Sister Carrie than the entrance of Rose Dutcher to Chicago

when set against that of Carrie Meeber. Although both
Garland's novel and Dreiser's employ the image of the city
as attracting magnet, Carrie is the waif helplessly caught up
in these strange new forces, while Rose, inexperienced and
frightened as she is, does not doubt that the city must yield
to her assault: "She would succeed, she *must* succeed...a
fresh, young, and powerful soul rushing to a great city...."
(181) In Dreiser's novel as well as Garland's, Chicago is a
mixture of splendors and terrors, but Carrie accepts her
share of these passively and uncritically while Rose is
allowed the exercise of her will. Rose's dreams of achievement
antedate her entrance to the metropolis and help enable her
to withstand its destructive pressures and diversions. The
dreams of Carrie are entirely spun from her new urban
experiences. Carrie is seduced by Drouet, the first urbanite
to pay her serious attention, and she leaves him as casually
for Hurstwood, just as she leaves Hurstwood in turn. Rose
weighs repeated proposals of marriage against her goals of
self-fulfillment and career before finally agreeing to marry
Mason. Carrie picks up her new life in Chicago with scarcely
another thought of her rural past; Rose attempts to fashion a
balance between her strong attachment to nature and her
recognition that she belongs primarily to the new age of
cities. While she argues with a devotee of John Muir,
Joaquin Miller, and the Sierra wilderness that " 'men make
the world, bears don't,' " and she recalls approvingly
Lowell's sentiment that "the wilderness is all right for a
vacation, all wrong for a life-time," she is herself launched
upon the sea of urban possibilities by her country freshness
and strength, and she finds solace and self-perspective in
seasonal returns to the Wisconsin farm (218, 173). As Sister
Carrie adopts the protective coloration of urban anonymity,
Rose blazes into more and more distinctive individuality. In
all these senses, Rose represents that persistently anti-
naturalistic strain of the new Americans described here, as
they attempt to shape a formless urban existence into the

configuration of their heroic and yet progressive desires.
The active human will, not the inevitability of environmental
laws, leads most surely toward the improvement of individual
and social life in America.[16]

Rose's education as a new woman begins with a brief
meeting with a woman lawyer, a Mrs. Spencer, who advises
the girl tersely, " 'Don't marry until you are thirty. Choose a
profession and work for it. Marry only when you want to be
a mother' " (94-95). Dr. Isabel Herrick, who takes up Rose in
Chicago and becomes her preceptor, is a model of such
thinking. (Both of these assertive females are named for men
who Garland admired, philosopher Herbert Spencer and
Robert Herrick, the University of Chicago teacher and
novelist who, like Garland, had come to Chicago in 1893.)
Dr. Herrick is a notable feminist advancement over her
eastern Hippocratic literary predecessors, Grace Breen of
Howells's *Dr. Breen's Practice* (1881) and Dr. Mary Prance of
James's *The Bostonians* (1886). Grace Breen approaches her
medical career almost apologetically and, unable to maintain
both her femininity and her professional career, willingly
gives up the latter for the traditional role of wife, for which
she is, as are nearly all Howells's women, best suited. Tough
and technical Mary Prance has Henry James's respect for
her professional skills and her levelheadedness, but, hard,
dry, spare little creature, she must also bear her share of
James's satire for her place in the assemblage of "long-
haired men and short-haired women" who comprise his
faintly but unmistakably weird Boston reformist colony.[17]

Garland's Isabel Herrick, in contrast, is allowed both her
career and her femininity — she marries at the end of the
novel — and it is clear that her capacity to function in both
roles is an expression of a new western freedom from
stereotyped sexual roles. The emphasis in Chicago, she tells
her male friends, Sanborn and Mason, as they discuss Rose,
is on character. " 'Chicago society isn't the New York four
hundred. We're all workers here' " (246). Dr. Herrick's

accomplishments as new woman are meant to suggest to Rose that she need not choose between her ardent femininity and her dreams of achievement. Unfortunately, Garland does not carry the proposed synthesis for Rose into conclusive action. Accepting Mason's proposal of a marriage of equal partners, Rose stands at the conclusion of the novel still merely sensing the opportunities for splendor and achievement that William De Lisle, the beautiful acrobat, had roused within her as a child. Rose's achievements remain, to the end, in her potentialities. " 'She has power. I feel it,' " says Dr. Herrick (231), and Rose is repeatedly praised by Mason for her "imagination." But her early verse is so badly imitative that the magazines have steadily rejected it, and Mason advises her to burn it, which she does. Nothing comes of her literary essays either. Finally, in the book's concluding pages, she accomplishes, offstage, some admirable verse, having found her native voice in the manner that Garland had prescribed for young western American artists in *Crumbling Idols*. Mason, at last, praises her as a poet, but follows this with a declaration of her beauty and his love, and it is to these latter opinions that Rose most fully responds (401).

Rose's worldly aspirations, then, do not proceed beyond generalities, and in this sense she anticipates an important pattern for several of Cather's and Anderson's western moderns, as well as Sinclair Lewis's Carol Kennicott of *Main Street*. We are repeatedly told that Rose aspires to freedom, to achievement, to greatness. She refuses to marry — even to marry well — until she chooses to, but she does choose it at last, and in terms that may signal the subordination of her creative self. The argument between her feminine nature and her longing for achievement would seem to be best answered by her marriage to Mason, critic and lover. But the weight of evidence suggests that Dr. Herrick's earlier judgment about Rose, that " 'She's one of the women born to win her way without effort' " (299), correctly presages the ascendancy of her rich physical presence at the end.

Garland's delineation of Rose's sexuality, especially his perceptive treatment of the inner life of her girlhood, remarkable for its time, has been amply noted and praised by modern critics. If *Rose of Dutcher's Coolly* is often seen, for this innovative psychological realism, as Garland's best novel, it also may claim merit as a cultural document that, like Norris's *Octopus*, effectively records the closing of farm life as a subject of contemporary significance for its age. Garland here focuses attention upon the importance of gaining one's right to seek out and join the nascent community of professional moderns, to choose a new life in the urban-industrial world, however vaguely that life may be realized.

Garland's shifting of his fictional locale to the Rocky Mountain West in the works following *Rose of Dutcher's Coolly* provided him not so much an escape from contemporary life as it did a panoramic background against which could be projected the large public and social issues of a new West. There, the thwarted reformers and functionless progressives of Garland's earlier novels could find real new work to do, taking an active public role in the conservation of western resources and in the fair treatment of American Indians.

The novelist's interest in the mountain West, marked during the mid-1890s by increasing travel in that region and by study and observation of the conditions of its Indian inhabitants, first found important novelistic expression in *The Eagle's Heart* (1900). The book, for all of its conventional cowboy action and characterization, is actually a significant eulogy for a dying western individualism. Like Wister's *The Virginian*, whose publication as a novel it preceded by two years, *The Eagle's Heart* presents a cowboy hero who encompasses both the old West and the new, but Garland's figure goes beyond the prosaic acceptance by Wister's cowboy of private materialism and middlebrow respectability at the end. Garland's hero, a midwestern boy who goes west to become a wanderer and gunfighter, is plucked from failure and sickness at last by the acceptance of a new role, combining — Norris-style — marriage to a good woman with a significant modern western career in the field of enlightened management of Indian affairs. Here again, Garland sensed the bankruptcy of rugged individualism in the contemporary West and demonstrated that a society of atomistic individuals was changing to one of collective interdependence. The early westering urge of the young hero is thus repeated (after a disastrous return to the metropolis) at the end of the novel by another westward movement, wherein his solitary and exhilarating, but ultimately pointless, early life is transformed. Finally, he joins in helping to create an ordered and socially progressive new West which is replacing the free but lawless and disintegrative region of his youthful dreams.

The Eagle's Heart establishes the pattern which will be followed in Garland's best novels of the mountain West in the years to follow. Curtis, of the 1902 novel of the far West, *The Captain of the Gray-Horse Troop*, emerges as figure of major new proportions to embody Garland's changing conception of the representative Westerner. Modeled to some extent after Captain George W. H. Stouch, a Cheyenne Indian agent with whom Garland became friends, Captain Curtis is not only an officer in the regular army, but, significantly, a scientist, a mapmaker, an author of "articles on the forests, the watersheds, and the wild animals of the region he had traversed," and an ethnologist,[18] all of which has made him known to the scientific community represented by the Smithsonian Institution in Washington, D.C., and has resulted in his appointment, as the novel opens, as Indian agent at a western reservation. The president, it seems, is trying to put the Indian service into better order, and evidence of corruption and mismanagement under the previous agent is present as Curtis takes over his new position. Elsie Brisbane, an artist who has come west to paint

Indians, provides the novel's conventional love interest, although she and her father, a corrupt and grasping senator from the region, also represent an unregenerate viewpoint toward the Indian, she seeing them as subhuman, interesting only as artistic "material," and her father an advocate in private of genocide and in public of removing the Indian to the least desirable public lands. Lawson, a cultivated Easterner and friend of Curtis, is less the man of action, but is more knowledgeable in ethnology. In the association between Curtis and Lawson and in their discussions of problems relating to the Indians Garland suggests the Progressivist sense of a small but influential new community of professionals by which the emerging new West might be managed along principles not of greed or privilege, but of scientific skills and moral enlightenment.

The book's plot, then, focuses upon the struggle between advanced and regressive attitudes of whites toward the Indians. From Lawson, Curtis learns more fully the futility of attempting to make solitary farmers of the Indians. We should not, agrees Curtis, attempt to turn the Indians into "grotesque caricatures of American farmers. I am not of those who believe in teaching creeds that are dying out of our own life" (154), a judgment that Garland might have considered applicable to his own turning away from the dirt farmer of his earlier fiction — our own white version of the vanishing American — and toward figures of new significance. " 'I am going to tell of the red man,' " Garland wrote to a friend at this time, " 'as a man of the polished stone age trying to adapt himself to steam and electricity.' "[19] While Curtis recognizes that Indians must learn to grow their own food and meat, he accepts Lawson's teaching that the Indian is a social being, closely dependent on his tribe, and that his communal life must not be destroyed in the transition to agrarian pursuits. Reflecting Garland's antipathy toward organized religion, both Curtis and Lawson have little use for the work of the Christian missionaries represented by

Miss Colson. Lawson reprimands her for attempting to separate the Indian from his own mythology and ceremonies, and Curtis claims that he is not concerned for the future life of his wards, only for making them healthy and happy on earth. " 'If I could, I would civilize only to the extent of making life easier and happier — the religious beliefs, the songs, the native dress — all these things I would retain' " (81). But he predicts gravely that " 'when we are civilized enough to understand this redman, he will have disappeared' " (298).[20] The rabble against which Curtis, Lawson, and the Tetongs are pitted are drawn from those mythic heroes of the old West, the settlers, the cowboys, and the miners. The latter two groups, in this contemporary West, are treated, in a reversal of western stereotypes, as ignorant, foul, and cruel, while the white ranchers and farmers have no regard for any law except those that work toward their own benefit.

Curtis defends the Indians to the skeptical Miss Brisbane, arguing that Crawling Elk, the Tetong shaman whom she has painted as merely picturesque, is not widely different in his abilities and wisdom from Herbert Spencer. (Garland retained his admiration for Spencer, obviously, even though he had bypassed his philosophy). Her pictures, Curtis admonishes her, are prejudiced and condescending, failing to move beyond the elements of the Indian's external features to a sensitive delineation of the suffering man within. Curtis's criticism is just that which the early Garland aimed at conventional treatments of "picturesque" rural life, against which his harsh portraits had stood as correctives. Garland is, of course, incapable of treating Indian life with the same depth of understanding and awareness as he did that of the farm folk of the middle border, but he retains his sense of indignation for the social injustice to which the Indian has been subjected. Recognizing his limitations to treat the Indian material, he nevertheless makes the best use of enlightened contemporary views of Indian life gained from others as well as from his own experiences, and wisely focuses the action of the novel upon the conflict within the white community over the Indian.

Garland reveals the presence of progressive new forces at work in the nation when Curtis makes a trip to Washington, D.C., to argue on the Indians' behalf. He stays at the Smithsonian Society, and is introduced by Lawson to the Secretary of the Interior and the Commissioner of Indian Affairs, both friendly to the Tetong cause, in spite of strong pressure from white land speculators championed by Brisbane. The commissioner, harried but conscientious, "pestered to death with schemes for cutting down reservations and removing tribes" (110), works with Curtis in planning a defense of the Tetong lands, and, with the help of an ex-abolitionist senator who chairs the committee to which the matter has been assigned, the attempt to take over the Indian preserve is defeated. The Washington episode reveals Garland's acceptance of the federal government as the moral and pragmatic leader of the nation. Here, the capital's new cadre of professional administrators, bureau chiefs, and scientists, with equally principled workers in the field like Curtis, form a new force capable of shaping the nation's future in the West along progressive lines, in opposition to the representatives of a debased and outworn frontier individualism like Senator Brisbane.

Curtis's Washington trip also serves to inform the reader that the hero is not a native Westerner, but was born and raised near the national capital, which he loves because it is to him "the centre of national life" (89). The biographical detail seems fashioned to suggest that educated belief and identification with a new professional and managerial class have replaced western birthright as the mark of the contemporary American leader. The emerging West is not likely to find its progressives citizens from among its native sons, at least not without a massive infusion of eastern enlightenment, as Garland's own career as a back-trailer would seem to verify. Curtis's dogged devotion to wise national leadership is seen also in his conception of the army as a power whose duty is to prevent the aggression of one group against the rights of another. Senator Brisbane scoffs at this naiveté — so, too, perhaps, does the modern reader — but Garland here reveals his earnest yearning for a figure who could marry idealistic faith in national institutions with personal and professional skills, thus providing a society in transition with an appropriate new leader.

The latter half of the novel, following Curtis's return to the Tetong reservation from Washington, is less interesting, falling occasionally into melodrama — lynch mobs, gunplay, a timely cavalry rescue (of the Indians from the whites!), and the conversion of Elsie Brisbane from anti- to pro-Indian. The latter is a particularly broad stroke by which Garland first grants his hero the bride he desires, second liberates a woman from her overbearing father, and third demonstrates that reason and patience can overcome conventional prejudice against the Indian. Senator Brisbane, in the flurry of final dispensations, is cut down by a stroke in the midst of a political harangue against Curtis, as if by the hand of Divine Justice itself, and is allowed to pass off into senility like the corrupt old buccaneering West that he represents. Through it all, Curtis remains the steadfast apostle of enlightened federalism, ominously warning the crooked sheriff and his gang of rowdies that they are committing " 'a crime against Washington' " (265), and greeting the climactic arrival of the Gray-Horse Troop with a heart that "swell [s] big in his bosom" while the ruffian mob is "frozen into immobility" before this expression of "the power of the general government" (279-80). At the novel's conclusion, Curtis looks ahead to a career in Washington as the head of a department, such as Forestry or Civil Engineering. In a rush of purposeful accomplishment in the novel's last pages, he supervises planting, ditching, building, and cultivating activities on the reservation, views a ceremonial pageant depicting the swift evolutionary passage of the tribe from past to future, and, as their good white pathfinder, speaks to the assembled Indians of order and progress. Repentant Elsie murmurs to him " 'I feel your work to be the only thing in the world worth doing!' " (415). The final pageant underscores Garland's belief, which he shared with the Progressive movement, not only that society was evolving from a lower to a higher state, but also that this evolutionary process could be controlled and managed. A new sense of order, a new community, might arise, led by those who would actively direct the new age rather than merely anticipate it.

Setting aside the machinery of romantic adventure, the frequent banality of diction and sentiment, the work still repays examination as a depiction of cultural ideas in transition and as evidence that Garland had not left his social consciousness behind with his middle border stories. He had recognized, at a time of widespread ignorance of and hostility toward the American Indian, the right of the native American to a place in the country's future. Garland had also indicated his continuing determination to treat the Indian honestly and compassionately in fiction, an intention that was to be successfully culminated in his collection of stories *The Book of the American Indian*.[21] Moreover, he had found in Curtis a new pioneer, a scientific administrator and conservationist who identifies himself with the emerging power of an advancing government and who offers for the modern West a hopeful alternative to the earlier failures of frontier individualism on the middle border.

The Captain of the Gray-Horse Troop, in which policies for Indians, formerly determined by local western whites for their own advantage, are shifted to a forward-looking national administration, owes much to the influence of Theodore Roosevelt, indeed Garland's "progressive" period is roughly concurrent with Roosevelt's years in the White

House. Garland had first met Roosevelt in 1895 when the latter was Police Commissioner of New York City, and they had found common ground in their knowledge of and interest in the West.[22] Never one to let an influential acquaintance slide, Garland continued to see Roosevelt, and they exchanged autographed books. The serial publication of *Captain* in 1901 occurred as Roosevelt was succeeding to the presidency, and Roosevelt listened to Garland's advice on Indian matters during his years as president, while providing the novelist with access — along with another western novelist with conservationist ideas, Stewart Edward White — to the decision-makers in the Department of the Interior. Garland shared Roosevelt's desire to preserve the strenuous ethic of an agrarian past and came, under the influence of Roosevelt and the Progressive movement, to recognize that this could not be accomplished, given the power of great, emerging social forces, without the leadership of a strong central government entrusted to a new professional class of scientist-managers and administrators.[23] Under Roosevelt, the national government was to be made the most important force in the country. Garland could discover in Roosevelt's own volumes on *The Winning of the West* a compelling new assertion of national unity. And Garland would find written large in progressive reform the spirit of local mutual aid and cooperation that had characterized the farming communities of his youth, that had ennobled the actions of downtrodden country people of early stories like "Under the Lion's Paw," but that had proved no match for an increasingly rapacious economic system.

Roosevelt's ability to elicit loyalty and admiration from others is frequently noted by historians; Garland's devotion to him is shared by other civic-minded Americans of the time like Gifford Pinchot, Felix Frankfurter, and Henry L. Stimson.[24] For Garland, Roosevelt was our one president "who could talk art with artists, literature with writers, and politics with politicians . . . the biggest, most interesting and versatile man I ever knew."[25] Further, the novelist's admiration arose in response to Roosevelt's contemporary reassertion of the figure of the frontier hero, now effectively blending the elements of nature and civilization into a vigorous first citizen. Garland's support of the President reached its literary apogee in his 1910 novel, *Cavanagh, Forest Ranger.* Here Garland treats most directly the issue that Roosevelt had cited in his first message to Congress in December 1901, when he claimed that "the forest and water problems are perhaps the most vital internal problems of the United States."[26] *Cavanagh* contains frequent approving references to Roosevelt and his reforms in the field of natural resources conservation and the book becomes a defense of Roosevelt's policies in the then-current controversy between Gifford Pinchot, appointed director of the U. S. Forest Service in 1898, and Richard A. Ballinger, named Taft's secretary of the interior when Roosevelt lost the presidency to Taft in 1908. Pinchot had long been a leader in the movement for scientific conservation and land use in the West and was a member of the inner circle of Roosevelt's most valued and trusted division heads. The new marriage between science and the federal government that began with figures like John Wesley Powell, whom Garland greatly admired,[27] and Alexander Dallas Bache, had found its home in the Department of Agriculture in which Pinchot's Division of Forestry was located, and its mission in the cause of conservation of public resources in the West, a movement with which Pinchot's name soon became widely identified. The Pinchot-Ballinger dispute grew into what was seen by the country as a whole as a clear struggle between conservationist and exploitive policies toward the public lands. Pinchot pressed the attack, citing evidence of corruption on Ballinger's part and publicly denouncing him as an enemy of conservation. Taft accepted Ballinger's rebuttal of the charges, and Pinchot, who continued the attack, was removed as the head of the Forest Service in January 1910.[28]

Garland had first been invited to meet Pinchot by President Roosevelt at the capital in April 1902, after the author had presented Roosevelt with a copy of his newly published *Captain of the Gray-Horse Troop*. Garland quickly became a supporter of Pinchot's, regarding him as a talented patrician who had enlisted in the conservation movement out of a sense of personal commitment to the western future as it emerged from its tin-can-and-barbed-wire stage. "This meeting," recalled Garland, "turned out to be a most important event in my literary career, for it led to a ten year's study of the forest ranger and the mountain West."[29] The simmering controversy between Pinchot and Ballinger after Taft's election brought Garland's interest in forest conservation to the surface, and his *Cavanagh* was published just months after Pinchot's removal from office in 1910. Although historians now no longer view the Ballinger-Pinchot affair as a sharply defined dispute between conservationists and exploiters, Garland accepts that contemporary view of it in *Cavanagh*. Pinchot and Roosevelt had shared a public view of the world as morally divided into warring camps of good and evil, and the dispute with Ballinger and Taft was easily pressed into that mold. " 'The Conservation question is a question of right and wrong,' " declared Pinchot in the same terms in which Roosevelt had seen good and evil as the causes of social virtue and vice.[30] Garland, whose moral system was also fashioned along these rough-hewn lines, joined the battle on Pinchot's side, sent him the proofs of *Cavanagh*, and included Pinchot's reply as the introduction to the novel. Pinchot's letter, dated March 14, 1910, just two months after his removal from office by Taft, praises Garland's "sympathetic understanding of the problems which confronted the Forest Service before the Western people understood it." Pinchot's letter further cites the "new order" of support for conservation policies in the West and offers the politic judgment that the Forest Service has "won the contest — an episode of which you have so well described —" because Westerners have come to believe in the cause of conservation of the public lands.[31] For Pinchot, Garland's new book was another salvo in his battle with Ballinger, still far from over. For Garland, the blessings of the country's chief spokesman for the new conservation ethic validated his claim to deal authoritatively with social concerns in his novels of the mountain West. At the same time, one can imagine Garland basking in Pinchot's reference to the writer as one of the "old hunters," (vii) a phrase by which Garland's historic connections with the western border country — none of your upstart newcomers or effete eastern environmentalists — was asserted to the mutual benefit of both politician and novelist.

The militant social rhetoric of *Cavanagh* was further emphasized by its dedication, "To the Forest Ranger, whose lonely vigil on the heights safeguards the public heritage," and by an accompanying black-and-white photograph of an anonymous forest ranger, fully uniformed and mounted on horseback, looking out from an alpine meadow over a sweep of forested hills and valleys. The forest ranger, with his frontiersman's skills and his loyalty to a public ideal was, to Garland, "a hero made to my hand."[32] The contemporary social and political freight of these introductory pages, then, tempers the book's subtitle: "A Romance of the Mountain West," and encourages the reader to view the work as something more than an unabashed rural love tale in the genre of contemporary bestsellers like *The Trail of the Lonesome Pine.*

Cavanagh opens with a contrast between the old and new Wests as the heroine, Lee Virginia Wetherford, returns from the East to her home town of Roaring Fork, from which she has been away since childhood. (Garland's actual locale was the Big Horn Range country of Wyoming and the towns of Buffalo and Dayton.[33]) The transformations include not only the evidences of apparent progress — automobiles instead of stagecoaches, alfalfa and wheat fields, irrigation ditches and painted farmhouses — but the signs that her pleasantly remembered western town has turned ugly and dirty, its picturesque cowboys, the knights of her youth, having given way to an assortment of drunks, loafers, and hell-raisers. Lee's mother, unkempt and ill, keeps a dingy boarding house, featuring greasy food and flies, for this motley patronage. Disgusted by all of this, Lee nevertheless feels an obligation to help her mother. The girl meets Cavanagh, a federal ranger of the new Forest Service, and his superior, Redfield, a rancher turned forester who functions, as did Lawson in *Captain of the Gray-Horse Troop*, as a knowledgeable and influential senior ally of the hero. Redfield characterizes himself and Cavanagh to Lee as "believers in the New West" (46) and explains that the term suggests a kind of house-cleaning.

> The Old West was picturesque and, in a way, manly and fine — certain phases of it were heroic — and I hate to see it all pass, but some of us began to realize that it was not all poetry. The plain truth is my companions for over twenty years were lawless ruffians. . . .We didn't want settlement, we didn't want law, we didn't want a State. We wanted free range. We were a line of pirates from beginning to end, and we're not wholly reformed yet. (46-47)

In the regenerate Redfield's younger associate, Cavanagh, Lee perceives the emerging "man of the new order" (28). Again, as in *Captain*, Garland is careful to establish his hero as a nonnative, a Westerner by choice, in this case an Englishman who has served under Roosevelt in the Cuban War, who has tried the cattle business, and who has joined the Forest Service out of a love for the wilderness and a wish to help sustain it. As with the earlier Captain Curtis, Garland perceives that the mountain West's creative leadership must come from enlightened outsiders who adopt the country out of a sense of its natural heritage and acknowledgment of one's mission to preserve its resources, both attitudes which are characteristically scorned by the local inhabitants. These unreconstructed locals are represented in *Cavanagh* by Sam Gregg, a stockman openly contemptuous of the new laws for grazing on National Forest lands.

In the struggle for the future of the Western lands that the novel records, Lee functions in an allegorical role. She instinctively gravitates toward the progressive New West of Redfield and Cavanagh, but her father, an old-time cowboy and gunfighter, and her slovenly mother tie her to the past and to that sordidness into which emerging western life seems to slide. At one point, Garland baldly terms the girl "a symbol" of the contemporary West, "and the law of inheritance holds in her as it holds in the State. She is a mixture of good and evil, of liberty and license. She must still draw forward, for a time, the dead weight of her past, just as the West must bear with and gradually slough off its violent moods" (153). Cavanagh, for his own part, must overcome the class distinctions of his English upbringing by accepting the West and Lee, for, while he dislikes the social rigidity of his native England, he is unable to rid himself entirely of its habits of classification. While he finds himself falling in love with the girl, he shares with Mrs. Redfield doubts as to her character, given that of her mother. Cavanagh praises Lee's cleanup of her mother's hotel early in the novel as "something heroic" (84), associating it in his mind with the work necessary to bring about the New West which Redfield had called for. But as in *Captain* the heroine must be separated from the Old West parent before she can join the hero in helping to fashion the country to the future's new design. (Garland had also used this pattern in his 1905 novel of psychic phenomena, *The Tyranny of the Dark*, wherein the hero, Serviss, an eastern scientist and progressive, acts to free a young western girl from her repressive and debilitating associations.)

In the meantime, Cavanagh's hands are full in dealing

with the lawless Greggs and their followers. In the tradition of the typical western, which Garland is also helping to create here, the "decent citizens" are nowhere to be found when trouble arises, and Cavanagh, with the help of Lee and her mother, must fend off a mob. Later, the ranger discovers the massacre of several Basque sheepherders, their bodies chopped and burned, victims of cattlemen's vengeance. Sickened by this act, Cavanagh promises that he will wash his hands of America and return to England if the murderers go unpunished. While attempting to find the guilty ranchers he hears from an associate that the new president has " 'fired the chief — the man that built up the Forestry Service. The whole works is goin' to hell. . . . We'll have all the coal thieves, water-power thieves, poachers, and free-grass pirates piling in on us in mobs. They'll eat up the forest. . . . They'll put some Western man in, somebody they can work. Then where will we be?' " (212) This is the final outrage for Cavanagh and he resigns from the Service amid the jeers of Gregg and the townspeople, telling Redfield that he is "done with America" (214).

It is at this point that Roosevelt's influence upon the work is most strikingly presented. The new president had for some time enunciated a doctrine of strenuous morality in alliance with practical politics. The honorable man must not, he vigorously maintained, recoil from public life because of its dirt and unpleasantness. A private moral honor is not sufficient for the survival of democracy. One must accept the obligation to participate fully in public life, for all its degradations. "The real service is rendered," he claimed, "not by the critic who stands aloof from the contest, but by the man who enters into it and bears his part as a man should, undeterred by the blood and sweat."[34] In Roosevelt's martial conception, it is only by showing that one can give and take heavy punishment on the field of public battle that one can establish himself as an effective and worthy leader in the fight for reform. As if in response to Roosevelt's injunction that "it is sheer unmanliness and cowardice to shrink from the contest because at first there is failure, or because the work is difficult or repulsive,"[35] Cavanagh has second thoughts and eventually rejoins the effort to find the Basques' murderers, who are caught and brought to trial at last. A decent successor is named to replace the chief forester, and Cavanagh tears up his resignation. He is offered the supervision of a national forest in another state and swallows his abhorrence of Lee's mother long enough to propose to the girl. That Cavanagh's distaste for the older woman is shared by the author and his audience, however, is revealed in the gratuitous disclosure — of which Cavanagh, to his credit, is unaware when he proposes — that Lize is not Lee's real mother, who had been an eastern gentlewoman who died in Lee's infancy.

These sprightly dispensations of rewards to the worthy and retribution to the wicked do little credit to Garland, and skew the book's conclusion too far in the direction of romance, and away from the social and political commentary of the main story. Garland sensed the work's inadequacies, as he wrote in his diary, while putting the book through the press, that he feared that "it may not be as good as it ought to be," and that it veered off toward shallowness or foolishness.[36] To his own apprehensions must be added the modern reader's bemusement at Garland's growing intolerance of moral slackness from any quarter. We are put off by his jowl-shaking imprecations against what he sees as a nearly ubiquitous contemporary sordidness and vulgarity. The town is a "pest-hole," a gathering of "criminals and ungovernable youths"; the cowboys and town loafers are all "coarse," "unspeakably vile," "depraved," "libertine," "drunken beasts," etc. Most of the town's women are "slatterns," "unsexed," and the like. Lee, the heroine, is "the lovely flower of corrupt stock," until, with a sigh of relief by all, she is granted a real mother who had been "nice." Here is that later Garland who will become something of a literary curiosity for his fierce denunciations of contemporary social and sexual behavior as depicted in fiction, film, and the stage. Here, too, is the obverse of that disgust at moral decadence, a passion for good health, for physical strength and "cleanness," that he shared with Norris and Roosevelt.

But as with *Captain of the Gray-Horse Troop*, Garland's strongest contribution in *Cavanagh* is his depiction of an emerging national land ethic based upon scientific principles and embodied in a new professional and managerial elite who assume the stewardship of public resources in the West. The heroic old West is once again harshly examined in *Cavanagh* and found wanting: "in truth," Garland writes, "it had never existed at all!" (14) The new West as represented by Cavanagh, Redfield, and the Forest Service, is assured of no untroubled existence either. A memorable minor character, a newspaper reporter who helps Cavanagh at one point, describes his paper as representing the " 'New West, but to us the New West means opportunity to loot water-sites and pile up enearned increment. Oh yes, we're on the side of the fruit and alfalfa grower, because it pays. If the boss of my paper happened to be in the sheep business, as Senator Blank White is, we would sing a different tune.' " But even this sardonic judgment is followed by his claim that a few good men like Cavanagh " 'could civilize this cursed country' " (275), and it is this skein of evolutionary hopefulness, of appeals to right-thinking, progressive Americans to join in shaping the future, that characterizes these western novels. Thus, Ross Cavanagh comes finally to accept the necessity for taking up the strenuous life in pursuit of a visionary future for the American West, and by implication for the American nation. He becomes, among other things, an exemplum of Roosevelt's maxim that "every man who wishes well to his country is in honor bound to take an active part in political life."[37] The theme of an old West, passing inexorably and not without struggle into oblivion as the country marches toward a more hopeful future, is held before us constantly. Men like Lee's father " 'had to go like the Indian and the buffalo, and these hobos like Ballard and Gregg will go next,' " Cavanagh tells a companion (157). Later he thinks, " 'This generation, these fierce and bloody hearts, must die; only in that way can the tradition of violence be overcome and a new state reared' " (188), and again, " 'a new and splendid State can rise even out of the ashes of these murdered men' " (191). A supervisor in the Service tells him that " 'Public sentiment is coming our way. The old order is already so eaten away that only its shell remains' " (260). At the conclusion of the novel, Cavanagh tells Lee that the Forest Service " 'taught me to regard the future' " (286), reinforcing his earlier conception — doubtless born out of Garland's Washington associations — of the West as an inspiring testing ground for tomorrow: "Here the problems of popular government and industry were to be worked out on the grandest scale. . . . 'Some day each of these great ranges will be a national forest, and each of these canyons will contain its lake, its reservoir. . . . Surely in this development there is a place for me' " (152).

In the book's romantic conclusion, Cavanagh and Lee "entered upon the building of a home in the New West" (301), and the final emphasis upon a home, a fixed and humane habitation — something between the train-station disorder of Lee's mother's fly-specked hotel and Cavanagh's ivory tower, his isolated bachelor's cabin at 9,000 feet — signals the couple's accession into a productive, rooted new existence. Cavanagh's solitary cabin, in whose remoteness he has formerly found refuge, burns to the ground at last, and in its ashes may be read the hero's renunciation of the appeals of escapist individualism or of mollycoddle avoidance of the crowded arena of battle, and his descent from the plane of social superiority that had characterized his earlier attitude toward Lee. Cavanagh's acceptance of her marks his assent to the New West and his recognition that one must enter its corridors of consequence and responsibility with a willing heart.

Without formal education in the new profession of forestry, Cavanagh, we are told, is destined to occupy only a transitional position, a middle place "between the cowboy . . . and the trained expert who is being educated to follow him" (173). But like the highly qualified and knowledgeable figures whom he precedes, Cavanagh verifies the presence of a new force in the American West, an ordered new leadership characterized by active and purposeful professionals whose aims are both hopeful and pragmatic. Faith that the new power of science and enlightened management can be joined successfully with a visionary conception of the future is a basic tenet of Garland's novel and of the emerging West that it sought to portray. "Indians, soldiers, woods, waters, he teaches me that they may all be considered to the national advantage," wrote Howells as he praised these later novels of Garland's for their record of social history.[38] Like the elder Frederick Jackson Turner, Garland had accepted the necessity for an "adjusted liberty" in the new West, and had recognized that scientific and governmental leadership might provide the opportunities for heroic individualism which had seemed to fade with the closing of the frontier.[39]

The Forester's Daughter (1914) was Garland's last novel of the mountain West, indeed his last novel, before he turned primarily to autobiography and reminiscence during the latter part of his life. The book's title suggests what its introduction makes clear: the waning of Garland's energies for the significant new Westerner — concurrent with the decline of Roosevelt's own career and the dimming of the Progressive dream in the decade of the first World War. Here Garland slips again into the scenic romance beyond which such earlier mountain novels as Her Mountain Lover, Hesper, and Money Magic did not reach. "It was my intention," wrote Garland in his introduction to this last novel, "originally, to write a much longer and more important book concerning Supervisor McFarland, but Berrie [his daughter] took the story into her own strong hands and made of it something so intimate and so idyllic that I could not bring the more prosaic elements into it."[40] This coda to the "sociologic" works of his middle period is Garland's own admission of their fault, his continuing tendency toward soft pastoral, until he submits to it with a gesture of tolerant self-apology at last. The book's relinquishment of consequentiality parallels Garland's own decision at about this same time that he would move to New York City and leave to others the same Chicago and West that he had approached so enthusiastically two decades earlier. "It is a place for young, vigorous, enthusiasic business men, builders, not men of meditation," he wrote in his diary after he had settled himself and his family in New York.[41] Reflecting upon his progress in his later autobiographical work, *Back-Trailers from the Middle Border*, he sees that his life's direction has been the result of two divergent pulls, one toward western wildness and the other toward eastern civilization, of which the move to New York had been simply another manifestation of these alternating responses.[42]

But it is perhaps more appropriate, in the light of the works studied here, to consider his career as less of a dialectic than a continuing thrust toward synthesis, his middle-period novels asserting the possibility of a marriage of East and West within a landscape rational and yet heroic, peopled by new Americans who subsume within themselves urban as well as natural values. Garland's striving toward such a synthesis is indisputably present in the sequence of his autobiographical works — *Trail-Makers of the Middle Border, A Son of the Middle Border, A Daughter of the Middle Border,* and *Back-Trailers from the Middle Border* — with which he closes his career. In these works he records the social history of the nation in the saga of his own family, from its westering pioneer stages, through the sodbusting homestead and farm era, passing at last into the urban industrial present, in which the competing strains of frontier and civilization seem to pause in contemplative balance.

As a follower of Taine, a believer that the memorable writer must reflect his own period and place, the inner life of his nation, and as a defender, in *Crumbling Idols*, of the right of the modern artist to be freed of the requirements of a dead past, Garland seems to have provided his own best defense of a significant portion of the fiction of his middle period. After 1900, relative prosperity having returned to the farming country of the middle border, the conditions that had stirred Garland's social conscience in his early fiction had all changed. The West's "mighty rush toward civilization" had passed on to a new stage of development, and Garland was determined to accompany it: "I must be part of things in the city and the nation," he wrote of himself.[43]

Garland's early work is rightfully praised by Henry Nash Smith as "the end of a long evolution in attitudes. It had at last become possible to deal with the Western farmer in literature as a human being instead of seeing him through a veil of literary convention, class prejudice, or social theory."[44] But if Garland's early work represents the end of one tradition in which the Westerner is seen, in Smith's words, as "a representative of suffering humanity," Garland goes on to record, in his best mountain fiction, such as *Captain, Cavanagh*, and his Indian stories, the beginning of still another tradition. There, acting in concert with other professionals representing an enlightened science and government and led by a national president whose personal presence seemed to confirm to the country the productive union of eastern intelligence and western vigor, new Westerners might, like new emblems of possibility, move beyond the frustration and dissent of the 1880s and early 1890s to the actual amelioration of the social conditions of American life.

NOTES

1. Ed. Jane Johnson (Cambridge, Mass.: Harvard University Press, 1960), p. 140.

2. *A Daughter of the Middle Border* (New York: Grosset and Dunlap, 1921), p. 347.

3. Hamlin Garland, *A Son of the Middle Border* (New York: Macmillan, 1922), p. 458.

4. *A Son of the Middle Border*, pp. 428-29, 457.

5. "The Work of Frank Norris," *The Critic* 42 (March 1903): 216-18.

6. Royce, *California* (Santa Barbara and Salt Lake City: Peregrine, 1970), pp. 393-94.

7. "The Work of Frank Norris," pp. 216-17.

8. *Hamlin Garland's Diaries*, ed. Donald Pizer (San Marino, Calif.: The Huntington Library, 1968), p. 9. Hereinafter abbreviated as *Diaries*.

9. Garland's middle period is the subject of several recent studies and alternative interpretations. Robert Gish's pamphlet, *Hamlin Garland: The Far West* (Boise, Idaho: Boise State University Western Writers Series no. 24, 1976), provides an admirable survey and review of criticism of this middle period. Gish argues persuasively, also, for the importance of the theme of travel and the trail metaphor throughout Garland's work. Joseph L. Carter, in his unpublished doctoral dissertation, "Hamlin Garland and the Western Myth" (Kent State, 1973), finds Garland's middle period part of a lifelong preoccupation with a psychological and literary myth of the West. George Howard Savage, in another unpublished doctoral thesis, " 'Synthetic Evolution' and the American West: The Influence of Herbert Spencer on the Later Novels of Hamlin Garland" (University of Tulsa, 1974), finds Spencerian evolutionary ideas informing the structure and characterization of Garland's far-western novels. (I argue here that Garland's admiration of Spencer did not extend to the philosopher's deep-seated antipathy toward government. See also n.10.)

10. I am indebted to Donald Pizer, *Hamlin Garland's Early Work and Career*, University of California English Studies no. 22 (Berkeley: University of California Press, 1960), for his elucidation of the influence of Spencer and Henry George upon the early Garland. I disagree here, however, with Pizer's estimate of the extent to which Garland remained committed to their doctrines during his middle period. See, especially, Spencer's *Man versus the State* (New York: D. Appleton, 1908), for evidence of that philosopher's strong antigovernment bias. I also contradict here Pizer's conclusion that Garland was unable to adjust to the new social and political needs of a society in transition (*Hamlin Garland's Early Work and Career*, pp. 168-69).

11. *Jason Edwards: An Average Man* (Boston: Arena Publishing Company, 1892), n.p. Further references will be incorporated into the text.

12. *A Member of the Third House: A Dramatic Story* (Chicago: F. J.

Schulte and Company, 1892), p. 200. Further references will be incorporated into the text.
13. *A Spoil of Office: A Story of the Modern West* (Boston: Arena Publishing Company, 1892), p. 268. Further references will be incorporated into the text.
14. *Rose of Dutcher's Coolly* (Chicago: Stone and Kimball, 1895; repr. introduced and edited by Donald Pizer, Bison Books, Lincoln, University of Nebraska Press, 1969), p. 213. Further references will be incorporated into the text.
15. I am indebted to Donald Pizer's introduction to the novel for the biographical details in this paragraph.
16. Stanley R. Harrison correctly notes the failure of traditional theories of literary naturalism to account for that mode's conception of freedom and escape which, with the genre's traditionally noted despair, forms a productive and characteristic tension. ("Hamlin Garland and the Double Vision of Naturalism," *Studies in Short Fiction* 6 (Fall 1969): 548. Harrison's essay deals only with Garland's early stories, and finds three avenues of liberation in these works: the physical beauty of nature, inner vindication, and the hope for possible escape. My own view is that all of these channels of hope may be seen as coalescing in the search for contemporary roles by Garland's new Americans in the novels which followed the early stories.
Further corrective general theoretical treatments of American literary naturalism may be found in Donald Pizer's *Realism and Naturalism in American Literature* (Carbondale: Southern Illinois University Press, 1966) and Edwin Cady's *The Light of Common Day* (Bloomington: Indiana University Press, 1971).
17. James, *The Bostonians* (New York: Modern Library, 1956), p. 72.
18. Garland, *The Captain of the Gray-Horse Troop* (New York: Harper and Brothers, 1902; Border Edition, 1930), pp. 88, 54, 9, 72. Further references will be incorporated into the text.
19. Quoted in Albert Keiser, *The Indian in American Literature* (New York: Oxford University Press, 1933), p. 285. The book is devoted to Garland as "Friend of the American Indian," as is the recently published *Hamlin Garland's Observations on the American Indian 1895-1905*, compiled and edited by Lonnie E. Underhill and Daniel F. Littlefield, Jr. (Tucson: University of Arizona Press, 1976). The latter is a full and useful collection and analysis of Garland's Indian writings.
Jack L. Davis, it should be noted, argues that Garland was unaware of Indian botanical skills and knowledge when he assumed, in *Captain*, that the red men were ignorant of agriculture. See Davis's "Hamlin Garland's Indians and the Quality of Civilized Life," in *Where the West Begins*, ed. Arthur R. Huseboe and William Geyer (Augustana College, Sioux Falls, S. D.: Center for Western Studies Press, 1978), pp. 58-59. Further discussion of Garland's weaknesses (and strengths) in treating Indian life in *Captain* is found in John C. McGreivey's thorough study of the novel,

"Art and Ideas in Garland's *The Captain of the Gray-Horse* Troop" *Markham Review* 5 (Spring 1976): 52-58.

20.   In his reminiscent volume *Companions on the Trail,* (New York: Macmillan, 1931), pp. 23-24, Garland had recorded his similar impressions from a reservation visit in 1902: "How arbitrary . . .to make them conform — to cause them to act like white people — to cut them off from all that is deep-seated in them, is the purpose of their teachers. They sing our monotonous, worn-out hymns and they wear shoddy agency clothing. In the end they will be merely imitations of poor whites."

21.   *The Book of the American Indian* (New York: Harper and Brothers, 1923).

22.   Jean Holloway, *Hamlin Garland: A Biography* (Austin: University of Texas Press, 1960), pp. 130, 178-79. Hereinafter abbreviated as Holloway.

23.   The extent of Roosevelt's actual dedication to the principles of the Progressive movement has frequently been questioned by recent historians, but, insofar as his attitudes toward conservation of western lands and waters and his image in the eyes of Garland and a large segment of the public, the connection remains generally valid.

24.   William H. Harbaugh, ed., "Introduction," *The Writings of Theodore Roosevelt* (New York: Bobbs-Merrill, 1967), p. xxi.

25.   *Diaries,* p. 212, Holloway, p. 245.

26.   Harbaugh, ed., *The Writings of Theodore Roosevelt,* p. 141.

27.   Garland, *A Daughter of the Middle Border,* pp. 55, 253.

28.   James Penick, Jr., *Progressive Politics and Conservation: The Ballinger-Pinchot Affair* (Chicago: University of Chicago Press, 1968), provides a useful summary of the controversy together with a modern scholar's survey of its historical interpretations. I am indebted to Penick for many of the historical details here.

29.   Garland, *Companions on the Trail,* pp. 135-36.

30.   Robert Wiebe, *The Search for Order* (New York: Hill & Wang, 1967), p. 153; Penick, *Progressive Politics and Conservation,* p. 14.

31.   "Introduction," Garland, *Cavanagh, Forest Ranger: A Romance of the Mountain West* (New York: Harper and Brothers, 1910), pp. vii-viii. Further references will be incorporated into the text.

32.   *A Daughter of the Middle Border,* p. 343.

33.   *Diaries,* pp. 99-100.

34.   Theodore Roosevelt, "The Manly Virtues and Practical Politics," *The Forum* 17 (July 1894): 552. Hereinafter abbreviated "Manly Virtues."

35.   "Manly Virtues," 556.

36.   *Diaries,* p. 100.

37.   "Manly Virtues," 552.

38.   Howells, "Mr. Garland's Books," *North American Review* 196 (October 1912): 527-28.

39.   On this stage of Turner's thinking, see Ray Allen Billington's "Frederick Jackson Turner and the Closing of the Frontier," in *Essays in Western History in Honor of T. A. Larson,* ed. Roger Daniels, University of

106 NEW AMERICANS

Wyoming Publications 37, no. 1-4 (October 1971): 54-56.

40. Garland, *The Forester's Daughter* (New York: Harper and Brothers, 1914), pp. vii-viii.

41. *Diaries*, p. 20.

42. Garland, *Back-Trailers from the Middle Border* (New York: Macmillan Company, 1928), p. 360. John R. Dove comments insightfully upon this split in Garland's sensibility in "The Significance of Hamlin Garland's First Visit to England," *Studies in English*, University of Texas 32 (1953): 96-109.

43. The West's "mighty rush toward civilization" is quoted from Garland's *Crumbling Idols*, ed. Jane Johnson, p. 13. "I must be part of things..." is quoted from Garland's diary by his daughter, Isabel Garland Lord, in Hamlin Garland: *Centennial Tributes and a Checklist of the Hamlin Garland Papers in the University of Southern California Library*, ed. Lloyd A. Arvidson, University of Southern California Library Bulletin no. 9, 1962, p. 6. See also *A Daughter of the Middle Border* p. 257.

44. *Virgin Land: The American West as Symbol and Myth* (Cambridge: Harvard University Press, 1950), p. 249.

3

The Cowboy in the Laboratory:
Willa Cather's Hesitant Moderns

> In Nebraska, as in so many other States, we must face
> the fact that the splendid story of the pioneers is
> finished and that no new story worthy to take its place
> has yet begun....The generation now in the driver's
> seat hates to make anything, wants to live and die in an
> automobile, scudding past those acres where the old
> men used to follow the long corn-rows up and down.
> They want to buy everything ready-made, clothes, food,
> education, music, pleasure. Will the third generation —
> the full-blooded, joyous one just coming over the hill
> — will it be fooled?...Surely the materialism and
> showy extravagance of this hour are a passing phase!
> They will mean no more in half a century from now
> than will the "hard times" of twenty-five years ago —
> which are already forgotten.
>
> Willa Cather, "Nebraska: The End of
> the First Cycle"

IN these sentences from *The Nation* for September 5, 1923,
at a period in which she later claimed the world broke in
two for her, Willa Cather nevertheless sounds a characteristic
western note — a forced hope, an almost obligatory statement
of new possibility — that often goes unnoticed in the
commonly accepted opinion of her as the elegist of a lost
frontier, one who saw the heroic past cut off from any
meaningful contact with the present, and who found little
or nothing in modern life worthy of her consideration.[1] In
The Art of Willa Cather, the distinguished collection of essays
presented at her centenary celebration in 1973, reassessments
of Cather and her work underscored her international and
historical heritage. One is again struck by her pervasive

sense of the continuity of history, of moderns reaching back
to touch the ancient American civilizations or experiencing
in the classical or folk past of the Old World their own shock
of recognition.[2] As Cather's conception of the past and its
influences upon her and her work are restudied, as we find
our understanding enlarged of that part of her mind that
goes back beyond the frontier period, even beyond the early
cultures of the cliff dwellers and the civilizations of Greece
and Rome to their archaic and primitive roots, as we
recognize the length of her historical perspective and the
antiquity of her values, so her attitudes toward the present
and the future are placed in bolder relief and may yield
further meanings. Her conception of the record of cultures
as cyclic and her insistence upon hope for the next phase
seem to summon moderns — including, of course, that less
sanguine side of herself — to acknowledge intimations of
hope and promise even during a period of decline and
defeat.

Recognizing the complex and contradictory nature of her
attitudes toward modern life, and without denying the force
of Cather's lament for a lost past, it may nevertheless be
claimed that in the books of her early and middle period,
from *Alexander's Bridge* (1912) to *The Professor's House* (1925),
the span which includes nearly all of her most famous
novels, Cather accompanies her elegies with a procession of
contemporary Westerners whose pursuit, successful or not,
of new opportunities for consequential living in an increasingly industrialized and urbanized America demonstrates
how passionately and insistently Cather sought those
connections between present and past, present and future,
which are supposedly wanting in her work. Although her
sympathies do indeed lie with the pioneering age and the
heroic figures who peopled it — like Alexandra Bergson of
O Pioneers!, Ántonia Shimerda of *My Ántonia*, and Captain
Forrester of *A Lost Lady* — Cather is too consciously
historical and too deeply an American and a Westerner not to

attempt repeatedly, like Norris and Garland, to define an appropriate and essential role for her present-day Americans and in doing so to project the qualities of a mythic past upon a recalcitrant contemporary nation. As if she realized the extent to which her admiration for the early pioneer committed her to a philosophical acceptance of the later stages of pioneering and the emergence of an urban and technological present and future, she gives us a rather remarkable group of new Americans — variously, a bridge designer and engineer, an opera star, a railroad lawyer and writer, a soldier, an architect, a scholar, and a cowboy turned physicist and inventor.

These contemporary Westerners share with their predecessors a current of primal creative energy, a birthright emanating from the land itself and manifested in the motion of the rough, red prairie grass blowing in the wind, in the larks of the fields and the eagles of the mountains, in the dazzling white summer sandbars of the western rivers, freshened and renewed each year by the floods of winter, with their tiny, dried skeletons of small creatures, where her youth come to camp and dream of the future amidst suggestions of an evolutionary past.

This primal West is enhanced for Cather's young Americans by evidences of heroic human achievement: the astonishing stone cities and the graceful pottery of the cliff dwellers of the Southwest, the relics of Spanish explorers, the rutted tracks of covered-wagon wheels in the prairie sod, the ordered and fertile farms. Possessed of a unique claim to these sources of power and accomplishment and often reacting in opposition to the graceless and narrow patterns of life that have, since the time of the old pioneers, imposed themselves upon this numinous land, Cather's young moderns leave their birthplace and "go east." To go east for Cather is to acknowledge one's place in the larger world, to find and accept a role in the social order and to attempt to achieve one's fullest human potentiality. This new role characteristically must allow the hero or heroine to combine obligations to society with those to the essential, or western, self. It is an uneasy union in which the great world may fail to justify and fulfill the expectations of the western seekers. Nevertheless, the attempt must be made. Despite Cather's fundamental misgivings about the possibilities for integration of western values and eastern opportunities and obligations, an examination of her contemporary moderns reveals that she allows none of them to avoid the challenge of new pioneering.

Cather published her first novel, *Alexander's Bridge*, in 1912 and her second, *O Pioneers!*, in 1913. The first, it has often been concluded, was a failure, a misfire resulting from an attempt to deal with materials and modes external to her native abilities which she was, as a novelist, to first tap in the world of the Nebraska divide of *O Pioneers!* Although a growing body of critical opinion, beginning with Maxwell Geismar's praise of *Alexander's Bridge* in his 1949 *The Last of the Provincials* and continuing through to the most recent studies of Cather, has tended to place this first novel back within Cather's main tradition, *Alexander's Bridge* as an expression of her deepest and most characteristic attitude toward her country and the appropriate role for its postfrontier hero deserves thorough examination.[3]

Willa Cather herself dismissed *Alexander's Bridge* almost as soon as it was written and in a 1922 introduction to a second edition of the novel. Again, in a 1931 article, she passed it off as an irrelevancy, a typical young writer's attraction to extrinsic materials, to new and diverting subject matter, "the thrill of novelty" and "the glitter of the passing show."[4] The beginning writer, she claims in her 1922 introduction,

must have his affair with the external material he covets; must imitate and strive to follow the masters he most admires, until he finds he is starving for reality and cannot make this go on any longer. Then he learns that it is not the adventure he sought, but the adventure that sought him, which has made the enduring mark upon him. (viii)

As these and other statements in this introduction reveal, Cather claims for the writer a deterministic inner "life line," a homing device that eventually brings the writer back to that material which is truly his own, that has been his from youth, and that, whether he is aware of it or not, has shaped itself into the wisdom of his intuitions. "When a writer once begins to work with his own materials, he realizes that, no matter what his literary excursions may have been, he has been working with it from the beginning," she concludes. "He had less and less power of choice about the moulding of it. It seems to be there of itself, already moulded" (viii).

Students of Cather will recognize the similarity of these necessitarian judgments to those elsewhere in Cather: Thea Kronborg of *The Song of the Lark* says about her own youth, "the point to which I could go was scratched in me then"; Jim Burden, at the conclusion of *My Ántonia*, comes home to himself "having found out what a little circle man's experience is"; and in *My Mortal Enemy* Myra Henshaw realizes that "as we grow old we become more and more the stuff our forbears put into us. . . . We think we are so individual and misunderstood when we are young; but the nature of our strain of blood is inside there, waiting, like our skeleton." But the image of the mold suggests most pointedly those lines which Professor St. Peter recalls of a translation of an Anglo-Saxon poem, near the end of *The Professor's House:*

> For thee a house was built
> Ere thou wast born;
> For thee a mould was made
> Ere thou of woman camest.[5]

Although the passage refers most immediately to the grave and to Professor St. Peter's anticipation of his own death, it applies as well to the buried life, the essential, primitive self that has surfaced within the Professor, and it shares with Cather's 1922 statements on the inerrable creative process a strongly naturalistic conception, a sense of human inevitability that cannot be separated from her mind and her work.

If this sense of inevitability is turned back upon her own first novel, *Alexander's Bridge* emerges as a great deal more than the false start which Cather claimed it to be. Despite her disparagement of it, the work dramatizes the presence of those deeper awarenesses which she claims eventually seek out the artist in whom they reside. Cather's characterization of the creative process compels us to recognize that *Alexander's Bridge*, with its repudiated Jamesian or "eastern" surface, may also convey significant if masked attitudes toward West and East that have already taken intuitive shape in the novelist's mind, that will clearly emerge within a year during the writing of her first overtly western book, *O Pioneers!*, and that will be present in her great novels of the next two decades. Furthermore, these attitudes extend beyond theme and into the pattern of unconscious authorial self-revelation that will become characteristic of many of Cather's main figures. Finally, it may be seen that *Alexander's Bridge* anticipates, in a number of striking parallels, that most fascinating and difficult of all her novelistic treatments of the contemporary Westerner, *The Professor's House* (1925).[6] In short, *Alexander's Bridge* unintentionally reflects Cather's own regional and psychic absolute: you can take the writer out of the West, but you can't take the West out of the writer. This rejected first novel is Cather's best evidence that her deterministic conclusions are profoundly just.

Alexander's Bridge is the story of Bartley Alexander, an engineer and bridge designer of great energy and ability, who is, at the book's opening, in middle life and at the peak of his career. Married to a woman of elegant beauty and distinction, renowned for his achievements as a builder, Bartley personifies the pragmatic and yet creative American hero. But within Bartley is a primitive self, a seeker who yearns to recapture the sense of freedom of his youth, and who is increasingly restless under the constraints and expectations which have accompanied his fame. In an attempt to regain his early, unfettered self he renews an old love affair with an Irish actress, Hilda Burgoyne, and finds himself drawn deeper into the narcissistic and destructive pursuit of his own youth. At the same time, he ignores his work on the latest and most significant project of his career, the Moorlock Bridge over the St. Lawrence in Canada, the longest cantilever in existence. Cramped by a shortage of money for the project and driven to emulate current engineering practices that he regards as unsound, he finds that he has created, in his half-finished bridge, a flawed structure. On inspecting it, he discovers signs of strain threatening collapse and realizes that no choice remains but to pull it down and start over, but before he can get the workmen off the bridge, it begins to buckle and fall.[7] Thrown into the water, Bartley, a strong swimmer, could have saved himself, but he is seized by others who are drowning and carried down to his death.

The setting of *Alexander's Bridge* is indeed eastern, alternating between Boston, New York, London, and Bartley's bridge on the St. Lawrence, but the physical scene is negligible in the novel; Cather gives us simply a series of one-dimensional backdrops — Bartley's elegant Boston house overlooking the Charles River, the theater or Hilda's apartment in London, an ocean liner in mid-Atlantic, and the like. There is little intimation here of the reflective and descriptive treatments of landscape — the silent and beautiful places — that deepen the aesthetic texture of the great novels to come. One scene, however, suggests the direction of her most characteristic work: Bartley, aboard a train from New York to Canada, looks out at sunset to see a group of country boys sitting solemnly around a campfire and recalls his own experiences as a boy camping along a western river.[8] Here, as with the other references to Bartley's western boyhood, the West represents to Bartley that time when he was possessed of "the full consciousness of himself," filled with the sense of his "continuous identity," a seamless vision of potentiality that is now soiled and faded (32-33). The scene outside the train window is a glimpse into the meaningful past, but more than that, it suggests one of those familiar Catherian opening windows, the window to which Cather compared Tom Outland's story, set in the cluttered and petty world of *The Professor's House.*

> Just before I began the book I had seen, in Paris, an exhibition of old and modern Dutch paintings. In many of them the scene presented was a living-room warmly furnished, or a kitchen full of food and coppers. But in most of the interiors, whether drawing-room or kitchen, there was a square window, open, through which one saw the masts of ships, or a stretch of grey sea. The feeling of the sea that one got through those square windows was remarkable. . . .
>
> In my book I tried to make Professor St. Peter's house rather overcrowded and stuffy with new things; American proprieties, clothes, furs, petty ambitions, quivering jealousies — until one got rather stifled. Then I wanted to open the square window and let in the fresh air that blew off the Blue Mesa, and the fine disregard of trivialities which was in Tom Outland's face and in his behaviour.[9]

It is in this respect, in the extent to which heroic individualistic values — nurtured by, and reflected in, the primitive West — are critically measured against those of the man-swarm of the great world, that *Alexander's Bridge* asserts its unity with those novels which are to follow.

Cather's selection of an engineer as the hero of her first novel may seem odd to today's reader, familiar with her frequent attacks upon machine civilization, but a Cather dramatic review roughly contemporaneous with *Alexander's Bridge* suggests that at that time she saw material accomplishment as no less necessary than artisitc: "a kind of power can be extracted from youth that can be obtained nowhere else in the world — or in the stars; and this is the only power that will drive the world ahead. It makes the new machine, the new commerce, the new drama, the new generation."[10] All achievement is progressive and admirable, all is dependent upon the potency of youth. There is further evidence, however, in her creation of heroic engineers like Bartley Alexander and Captain Forrester, in the physicist-inventor Tom Outland, the white knight of all her fiction, as well as in *My Ántonia*'s Jim Burden, the patron saint of railroading, Niel Herbert of *A Lost Lady*, who becomes an architect at last, and a host of lesser figures, that for Cather the essential American genius was scientific and progressive. In this view, Cather mirrors a cultural attitude emergent during the late nineteenth century that American technology had triumphantly asserted its place in world civilization as both an expression of national development and a leading force in international understanding. By 1900 in America, as Hugo A. Meier points out, "the record of a century of technological achievements in the interests of mankind possessed an authority which defied pessimism."[11] At the same time, however, Cather characteristically will muffle the implications of surrender to a technological present by presenting her significant moderns in the role of artists and romantics as well. In the tenaciously autobiographical cast of her writing, the outlines of her own youth are here suggested: she was herself close enough to the pioneering period she so admires to recognize its dependence not only upon visionary dreams but upon objective and pragmatic skills. Her early desire to become a scientist or a doctor[12] was transmuted into a career as a writer, but, as her own necessitarian assumption would have it, the original impulse remained, "waiting, like our skeleton," and was later to find itself embodied in many of her most admirable fictional figures.

Among the characters of *Alexander's Bridge*, Lucius Wilson, a professor of philosophy at a western university and Bartley's former teacher, is a less fully developed Professor St. Peter in *The Professor's House*, just as St. Peter's star pupil, Tom Outland, bears important resemblances to the early Bartley Alexander. Both young men are figures of heroic action in contrast to their reflective mentors. Both make so strong an impression upon the older men that the professors spend the most significant portions of their later lives surveying their young pupils' achievements. Professor Wilson says of Bartley, "I was always confident he'd do something extraordinary. . . . He was simply the most tremendous response to stimuli I have ever known" (8-9). By the end of the novel, the aged Professor Wilson has become a close friend of Hilda Burgoyne, Bartley's lover, and Wilson and Hilda's deepest attachment is to Bartley's memory. With them, as with Bartley's wife, "nothing can happen to one after Bartley" (175). Professor St. Peter of *The Professor's House* similarly lives his later life in the shadow of Tom Outland's accomplishments and meanings. "In a lifetime of teaching," he says, "I've encountered just one remarkable mind" (62). Although, unlike Professor Wilson, St. Peter has a wife and two daughters, they are part of the world of social obligation from which he increasingly withdraws in favor of those evocations of heroic value and achievement which Tom Outland represents to him. Since Professor Wilson of *Alexander's Bridge* remains relatively undeveloped in comparison to Godfrey St. Peter of *The Professor's House*, the treatment of Bartley Alexander is enlarged to encompass what will become the principal roles of both Tom Outland (Bartley's idealistic and productive youth) and Godfrey St. Peter (Bartley's doubt-ridden and regressive later years).

The similar structures of the two novels also reflect this contrast in proportions: Professor Wilson is the focus for the opening and closing pages of *Alexander's Bridge*; the rest is given over to Bartley. In the later work, Professor St. Peter occupies books I and III of the novel, and Tom Outland's story of the discovery of the Blue Mesa is the middle book, "a turquoise set in dull silver," as the epigraph images it.[13] In both cases, Cather frames the story of an active and consequential young Westerner within that of a reflective, contemplative older man whose life has assumed vicarious meanings from the visionary accomplishments of his young pupil.

Resemblances of characterization and structure in the two novels are accompanied by similarities in central theme: both works center upon Cather's characteristic conflict between the obligations to the self and to society. Bartley Alexander is an essentially American genius in this object-ification and mastery of the pragmatic arts that carry civilization forward. He fulfills the conception of the American, as Bartley's English friend, Mainhall, would have it, that "they should be engineers or mechanics. He hated them when they pretended to be anything else" (28). Bartley objectifies what Cather had earlier admired as "the monumental pluck and nerve of the Americans."[14] Bartley's characterization as "a natural force" (19, 21), who "looked as a tamer of rivers ought to look" (11), with his powerful shoulders and purposeful manner, underscores his appropriateness as an agent of social progress. Bartley's identification with bridges, of course, raises associations from Whitman and, for the modern reader, Hart Crane, of science and technology as reservoirs of hope and achievement, and of a past, present, and future unified by a creative vision. The force that Bartley signifies, as Wilson and Bartley's wife agree, "builds the bridges into the future over which the feet of every one of us will go" (22). In the light of the rest of the novel, indeed, of the rest of Cather's work, this responsibility is ominous both in its threat to the selfhood of the heroic creator, inescapably bound to the society he leads, and in its unqualified acceptance of a doctrine of technological progress, an acceptance that the novelist was finally unable to sustain. Bartley's task begins in hope and promise, like his first bridge, "over the wildest river, with mists and clouds always battling about it, and it is as delicate as a cobweb hanging in the sky. . . . You had only to look at it to feel that it meant the beginning of a great career" (22-23). In this early period in his career, Bartley's idealistic self-aspirations are successfully integrated with public expectations; the bridge is both a graceful work of personal expression and a contribution to society's needs. At this point, he resembles the young Tom Outland of *The Professor's House* who has discovered the hidden cliff city and its artifacts and wishes to convey their significance to his fellow countrymen, or who later invents the Outland vacuum that revolutionizes the design of aircraft engines. Or, Bartley is another young Godfrey St. Peter at the moment when he first conceives of his design for what will be his great lifework, the multivolume history of the Spanish explorations in North America.

The transcendent idealism of all of the young men's principal accomplishments is represented in their Catherian leap from earth: Bartley's first bridge is dramatically hung in the sky; for St. Peter riding in a boat along the Spanish south coast, "the design of his book unfolded in the air above him, just as definitely as the mountain ranges" (106); Tom Outland lifts his head from studying the treacherous ground below the Blue Mesa to discover high in the air above him the miraculous city of stone (201). Even Outland's later scientific invention is peculiarly airborne.[15]

But unlike Tom Outland, who is killed in the World War still possessed of his unviolated selfhood, Bartley Alexander slips into a middle age in which the demands of society upon its standard-bearers have become increasingly oppressive. Like the older Professor St. Peter, Bartley finds that public success has brought him only unwanted duties and vexations, a sensation of being buried alive in the obligatory trivia that has accompanied worldly fame. St. Peter's reflections on the dead Tom Outland are as appropriate to Bartley Alexander as to the Professor's own lost youth:

St. Peter sometimes wondered what would have happened to him [Tom], once the trap of worldly success had been sprung on him.... What change would have come in his blue eye, in his fine long hand with the backspringing thumb, which had never handled things that were not the symbols of ideas? A hand like that, had he lived, must have been put to other uses. His fellow scientists, his wife, the town and State, would have required many duties of it. It would have had to write thousands of useless letters, frame thousand of false excuses. It would have had to "manage" a great deal of money, to be the instrument of a woman who would grow always more exacting. He had escaped all that. He had made something new in the world — and the rewards, the meaningless conventional gestures, he had left to others. (260-61).

As Bartley chafes under the obligations that his fame has pressed upon him, he recalls the feeling of the strength of his previous life, "the boy he had been in the rough days of the old West" (50) and the full consciousness of self that is the "only one thing that had an absolute value for each individual" (51). Bartley, in love with his own youth and its conviction of full self-awareness, finds that he has, in imagistic terms, been transformed from a creature of feeling into a merely mechanical man. The sensations of his young life, "that original impulse, that internal heat, that feeling of one's self in one's own breast" have given way to a later man who is "only a powerful machine" (50-51). The city to which he has given himself is itself a huge machine, rhythmically vibrating, as Cather depicts it, "like the muffled pulsations of millions of human hearts" (119), and Bartley, its representative man, must march to this compelling beat. Society tolerates only those mechanistic functions of the creative individual useful to itself, and relentlessly works to expunge the other, private self. With both Bartley and Professor St. Peter, the old, primitive, self, however thwarted, struggles for release. With the Professor it is not the scholar, but the "original, unmodified Godfrey St. Peter" (263), "a primitive . . ., solitary . . .;he had never married, never been a father. He was earth and would return to earth" (265). So Bartley imagines an old self growing stronger within him. This sense of an inner self is variously depicted in terms of a window opening onto a fresh-smelling spring garden, a range horse who has tasted loco weed, a pleasure-loving simpleton, and finally a strong sullen man fighting for his life (128-30). Driven by society's expectations and its blindnesses (the insistence that ever-longer bridges be constructed and the failure to allow the builder full control over his methods and materials), Bartley fashions in the Moorlock Bridge the objectification of his own inner ruin. Had he not been drowned in the collapse of his bridge, Cather intimates, he would have found some other escape from a suffocating public world. "The mind that society had come to regard as a powerful and reliable machine, dedicated to its service, may for a long time have been sick within itself and bent upon its own destruction" (166).

In these terms, then, *Alexander's Bridge* is central to Cather's best and most characteristic Western novels. It is her first full-length portrayal of the conflict between individual self-expression, rooted in a lost Western youth to which the hero cannot return, and the obligation to participate in the great world, a world that may ensnare and victimize the creative individual even as it exalts him. While this first novel fashions a typical role for the young American as visionary builder and society's bridge into the future it reveals a deep ambivalence about the nature of that role and that future. Thirteen years and six novels later, Tom Outland of *The Professor's House*, whose invention makes possible new machines for man's service, dies before his career thrusts him into the disintegrative obligations of fame or before the professor's sardonic attacks upon science can be laid at the young man's door. By that time, Cather leaves no doubt that he is well out of it. If the world indeed broke in two for Willa Cather, as she claimed, "in 1922 or thereabouts,"[16] we may detect the cracks in the facade of *Alexander's Bridge*.

The ambiguous treatment of Bartley's primitivistic inner self that struggles against the social man imprisoning it will continue to characterize Cather's work. By allowing Bartley's essential self to be manifested in the illicit affair with Hilda Burgoyne, Cather clouds the larger issue of the demand for individual self-expression in conflict with social expectation, for, as John H. Randall and Blanche Gelfant have pointed out, sexual indiscretion is always punished in Cather.[17] Is Bartley's sexuality behind the author's judgment of him as "sick within himself" at the conclusion of the novel? Can we see in Bartley's death the punishment for sexual license — even in the service of freedom and self-expression — that signals the deaths of Emil Bergson and Marie Shabata in *O Pioneers* and the fall from grace of Marian Forrester in *A Lost Lady*? Is it the taint of sexuality that leads Bartley to come to regard his inner self as shameful, a Londonesque beast within, "strong and sullen, . . .fighting for his life at the cost of mine? . . .Eventually, I suppose, he will absorb me altogether. Believe me," Bartley writes Hilda, "you will hate me then" (130).[18] Dissociated from the disturbing reverberations of sexuality, Cather's portrayal of Bartley and of those creative seekers of her later work will demonstrate a persistent unwillingness to accept the implications of a surrender of the virbrant self to the world of public expectation. Bartley, who can bridge neither to his private past nor to a public future, Bartley, the strong swimmer, dragged down to his death by the drowning workmen, is a disturbing portent for the questing individual in society.[19] A part of the primitive, sacramental West of Bartley's childhood, the inner, singing self is the source of creative power for the young searcher. To attempt to deny this self is to deny what Cather describes for Bartley as the "only one thing that had an absolute value for each individual," (50) and what she describes for herself as artist, in her introduction to the book, as the writer's "deepest experience," the "inner feeling" that lies "at the bottom of his consciousness," that which is "truly his own," and is the ultimate integrity of his work (vi-vii).

Thus, the distance between Cather's first novel and her second is, despite her attempts to contrast the two, primarily a matter of mere surface differences. She is, from the first, writing about her own country of the spirit, and the Alexander of *Alexander's Bridge* is as much a part of this home region as the Alexandra of *O Pioneers!* Like the great novels to follow, *Alexander's Bridge* meets the test of serious writing that Cather quoted approvingly from Sarah Orne Jewett: " 'It is things like that, which haunt the mind for years and at last write themselves down, that belong, whether little or great, to literature.' "[20] Her disavowal of *Alexander's Bridge* is really an eloquent defense of it, and infallibly links her own artistic self to the first of her novelistic heroes. As she said of the young writer, with a wisdom which surpassed her intentions, "he learns that it is not the adventure he sought, but the adventure which sought him, which has made the enduring mark upon him."

While *O Pioneers!* (1913) is Cather's first novel actually set in the West, it, too, finds its essential meaning less in a celebration of agrarian experiences and characters than in a movement of alternation between primitive and progressive values. The "pioneers" are often themselves drawn from the stock of European urbanites, skilled craftsmen and tradesmen, often unsuited for the hard conditions of the frontier, but pulled into the cycle of a new civilization in its founding stages. What these newcomers discover is a land with a kind of terrifying and powerful life of its own, depicted here, as it will be in *My Ántonia*, as untamed and fierce and beautiful in its strength, struggling against encroachment. As a wild thing, an unbroken horse that "kicks things to pieces," this protean landscape bewilders the sociable *handwerkers* now turned farmers.[21]

Three kinds of human responses to this primitive new land are recorded in the novel. The first, that of Alexandra's father, John Bergson, is a recognition of the failure of pioneering, a final willingness, after hard struggle, to surrender to the land's greater strength and to die and be buried deep under it. Other new settlers share this belief that the country is unfit for living, and talk of going back to the settled lands of Iowa or Illinois or to cities like Chicago, where a job and a few pleasures would make them happy enough to forget the struggle for life on the prairies. This response is treated with understanding by Cather, but is finally rejected as lacking the heroic vision and imagination that interest her.

The second response to the land is to live in active harmony with it, to melt into its wildness without any attempt to alter its biological patterns. To some extent, all of the early settlers merge with their surroundings. Their sod houses are unobtrusive, their roads only faint paths through the shaggy grass. But this is only envisioned as a temporary phase in the rise of a new order, an admission of the land's greater strength, for the moment. By their efforts, the pioneers will eventually alter the landscape to reflect man's presence. The character "Crazy Ivar," however, is a human extension of the land itself, living "without defiling the face of nature any more than the coyote that had lived there before him had done" (36). Except for its rusty stovepipe, his dugout is indistinguishable from the surrounding prairie. There is no shed, no corral, no well, not even a path; his acres are unplowed. He protects the wild birds and animals that share his land. To his visitors he shouts, " 'No guns, no guns!' " (39). But his version of ecological noninterference is also unsuitable as a model for Cather's pioneer. His nickname reveals how much regard his neighbors have for all of this. By not working his land he is unable to "prove up" on it, and eventually, despite Alexandra's prodding, his "mismanagement" loses him his claim (45, 87). He accepts Alexandra's guardianship, without which he would be institutionalized as a madman. Ivar's biblical vision of a peaceable kingdom is impotent in a land of struggle and conquest. The plow and the gun, anathema to this powerless old man, are the tools of the pioneer and the portentous determiners of the book's action.

The third response to the wild land is, of course, to "pioneer" it, to alter it in accordance with some preconceived notion of the future. While Cather respects those like Ivar and the Indians of the southwestern deserts in *Death Comes for the Archbishop* who will not try to master nature and who leave the country as though they had not passed through it, she reserves her brightest admiration for those whose years upon the land are validated in their tangible achievements, the sheaths of their desire: Father Latour's cathedral, Captain Forrester's miles of rails, Ántonia's garden, Alexandra's farm. In *O Pioneers!*, where talk of the future is on nearly everyone's lips, the "last struggle of a wild soil against the encroaching plowshare" must be overcome, so that finally the land yields itself to the plow "with a soft, deep sigh of happiness" (47, 76). But the historical process, as might be divined from the always-problematic Catherian sexual imagery here, carries its own risks.

Although Alexandra is first of all a pioneer, she mediates successfully between these three responses. As a girl, she shares her father's awe of the land's power, at one point wishing that she and all of the family could join their father in death "and let the grass grow back over everything" (16). But she accepts the leadership of the family after his death and becomes one of the tamers of the wild country. She recognizes Ivar's gifts, his gentleness, his skill at doctoring animals; she takes his part against her skeptical and callous brothers, Lou and Oscar, and against those in the community who would place him in an institution. But she cannot understand his unwillingness to shape his land to human purposes. The aspects of nature with which Alexandra is most strongly identified are not those of wildness and unbridled power, but those of order and purpose: the straight, clean, mile-long furrows of her farm, the "ordered march" of the stars, the regularity of the crops and seasons, the dependable cycles of death and rebirth (70, 309). The one aberrant exception is her recurring daydream of being lifted up and carried away by someone very strong, a kind of earth-god ("he was yellow like the sunlight, and there was the smell of ripe cornfields about him"), an emblem of the still-primordial power of the land (206). This sexual fantasy, followed by self-anger and cold showers, suggests Alaxandra's continuing fascination with a surrender, like her father's, to primitive force, and also her own need to place more rigid bonds upon these impulses in herself. Late in the novel, when she sees the same figure as death ("the mightiest of all lovers"), she seems satisfied to replace the troubling sexual dream of her youth with this shadowy figure of final release (282-83). Carl Linstrum, whom Alexandra is to marry as the book closes (she is now past forty), is a spokesman for the displaced wild prairie, to which he had always instinctively responded, and he questions the process which has tamed it into a land of milk and honey. But Carl, thin and frail, five years younger than Alexandra, more friend than lover, represents a diminished and thus merely comfortable version of the primitive presence.

When Alexandra tells Carl that his wandering life in the cities is preferable to the heaviness of unrelieved farm life, and that she would see no reason to go on working " 'if the world were no wider than my cornfields,' " she touches an important chord in the novel: the dangers of provincialism and the need for an interfusion of farm life with that of the wider world (124). The sight of the great bridges over the Platte and the Missouri rivers is enough to convince a discouraged neighbor farm girl that her life is worth living when such things are happening, and Alexandra agrees that " 'it's what goes on in the world that reconciles me' " (124). At the same time, there are warnings against this sort of easy optimism. The Bergsons' growing prosperity frees Alexandra's brothers from the brutalizing toil of the early days, but what has come of it? Lou's leisure has allowed him to aspire to politics and has turned his childish ignorance and excitability into ugly blustering. Emil, the favored younger brother, has received a college education and is fit for the new age, but he retains the violent emotions of his father, and his love for Marie Shabata, a married woman, leads to their disastrous affair and to their murder by Marie's husband, Frank. When Alexandra visits Lincoln, the emerging metropolis on the western horizon, she finds not only a university, a monument to frontier aspirations which she views with pride and satisfaction, but also the penitentiary, in which she sees the broken Frank Shabata and is left appalled. As with the prison at the opening of *The Scarlet Letter*, we are reminded of how ugly realities undercut the hopes of frontier dreamers, "whatever Utopia," in Hawthorne's words, "of human virtue and happiness they might originally project." Lou Bergson, repeating a catch-phrase of contemporary Populism, assures us that " 'the West is going to make itself heard,' " but its message is at best equivocal (112).

Alexandra herself is a troublesome figure for Cather. Not clever or talented beyond a native good sense and a blind faith in the future of the Divide as farming country, deficient, as Cather tells us, in the imagination which the pioneer should have, she is a heroine of extremely limited possibilities for her creator. (48, 203). Alexandra's general endorsement of the great world and her agrarian achievements do not measure up to the requirements of the major figures to follow. Furthermore, there is no other character who can, like Jim Burden in *My Ántonia*, provide a consciously sophisticated frame for her pastoral life. Even as a figure of the soil, she is less vital than Antonia Shimerda. Alexandra, childless and past forty at the end of the novel, stands as a kind of barren earth mother. And her judgmental role is as unsatisfactory as her biological one. As Alexandra must admit that she has completely misinterpreted the relationship between Emil and Marie ("Emil was a good boy, and only bad boys ran after married women"), so we perceive how Alexandra's optimistic earlier assumptions about the results of the pioneering experience are called into question: "It had been worth while; both Emil and the country had become what she had hoped" (284, 213). In the light of what we have seen, then, Cather's final tribute to her heroine is not wholly satisfying: "Fortunate country, that is one day to receive hearts like Alexandra's into its bosom, to give them out again in the yellow wheat, in the rustling corn, in the shining eyes of youth!" (309). There is an abstractness to this, a diversion of attention from Alexandra back to the land into whose "bosom" her heart will be received. The figure is genteel and evasive, and its upbeat sentiment obscures the troubled nature of the future toward which this pioneering has been moving. The land will remain, although people come and go, these last pages of the novel tell us, but Cather's greater concern will be not with an abiding land but with whether pioneer conquest will lead to an advance or a decline in the lives of those who follow.

The only character in *O Pioneers!* who might have emerged as one of Cather's new Americans is Alexandra's younger brother, Emil. A "splendid figure" of a young man, intelligent, sensitive, an athlete and a musician at the University of Nebraska, from which he has just graduated, he is clearly destined, in Alexandra's mind, to live out her mute faith in the future and her wish to reach beyond her own fields to touch the contemporary world. He has not been worn by the struggle against the land in which "so many men broke their hearts and died," and which has marked his older brothers and Alexandra. Part of "the brighter pattern" of the new western life, he seems ready to step into the role of professional or technological figure which Cather elsewhere posits for her striving moderns (78, 213). He talks of studying law, or of opening up new land further west; he eventually goes to Mexico City to work for one of his university acquaintances who heads an electrical plant. But his wandering is really an unsuccessful attempt to shake himself free from his love for the beautiful and impulsive Marie Shabata, and he cannot make a successful start at anything. Returning from Mexico, he tries once again to break with Marie, planning to enter the law school at Ann Arbor that fall, but he draws her into the adultery that results in their murder, two more victims of that swift and deadly retribution which, as Gelfant says, strikes Cather's illicit lovers. Still, Emil Bergson, spotted as he is for Cather by the sacrifice of his potentialities to sexual passion, may be seen as an uncompleted version of those young Westerners who will in later Cather novels attempt to project the heritage of a pioneering past onto a contemporary world.

Thea Kronborg of *The Song of the Lark* (1915) adds to the strong-willed Alexandra Bergson the intellectual and cultural achievements of the artist in the great world. Thus she becomes the first of Cather's major figures in whom western and eastern values combine in a sustained and productive relationship. She belongs not with the pioneers like Alexandra but with the following generation, and like her contemporaries she must fight her way through the narrow and repressive atmosphere of her western town in order to find the meaning of her own life and ambitions revealed in the land itself. Setting in Cather's western novels functions so as to provide an integrated and powerful outward configuration of the central character's strivings, a design that both invites and affirms his or her dreams. In *O Pioneers!* Alexandra Bergson both seeks and is sought by the promise of fecundity and increase in the rich farmland of the Divide. Pastoral richness, ripeness, bland assurance of time's fruition — how can one say where the land ends and Alexandra begins? In

The Song of the Lark the essential West for Thea Kronborg is not vegetative but mineral. The configuration that attracts and impels Thea is that of the landscape as a precious stone, or jewel. Her home town is Moonstone, Colorado, its name suggesting not only a precious stone, but also a kind of lunar landscape unsuited to the growing of crops.[22] The characteristics of this western setting, repeated in the life and mind of its young seeker, are brilliance of color and light, hardness, permanence, and value.

The opening chapter reveals the town of Moonstone on a night in winter, stars flashing in the sky, the nearby white sandhills gleaming in the clear air. Within this jewellike setting, Doctor Archie, the town physician, attending the birth of the immigrant Kronborgs's seventh child, finds his attention taken by one of their other children, Thea, ill with pneumonia. Angry at the parents for ignoring Thea in the fuss over the new baby, he thinks to himself that Thea is " 'worth the whole litter,' " wonders " 'where she ever got it from,' " and reflects upon how he would "cherish" such a creature if she were his.[23] With her strong constitution, Thea recovers rapidly from her illness, and we observe her and her relationships to the townspeople and to her country in the following chapters. To Professor Wunsch, her piano teacher, a dreamer and an occasional drunkard, but a spokesman nevertheless for the great tradition, she suggests "a yellow flower, full of sunlight, perhaps. No; a thin glass full of sweet-smelling, sparkling Moselle wine. He seemed to see such a glass before him in the arbour, to watch the bubbles rising and breaking, like the silent discharge of energy in the nerves and brain, the rapid florescence in young blood" (38). Besides Doctor Archie and Professor Wunsch, Thea's other kindred spirits in the town are the railroad worker, Ray Kennedy, and Spanish Johnny, the musician, handsome, wild, "gold-coloured, with wavy black hair, a round, smooth throat, white teeth, and burning black eyes" (53). Against most of the drab and cloddish townspeople, an artist like Spanish Johnny stands out brightly to the young girl. Ray Kennedy she likes for his adventurous past and because he takes her to her favorite place, the sand hills, "a constant tantalization; she loved them better than anything near Moonstone,...the Turquoise Hills, the Mexicans called them,....many-colored hills; rich, sun-baked yellow, glowing turquoise, lavender, purple; all the open, pastel colours of the desert" (58, 60). Here, in a kind of natural amphitheater, the desert converts its own life into jewellike objects, "bits of brilliant stone, crystals and agates and onyx, and petrified wood as red as blood. Dried toads and lizards were to be found there, too. Birds, decomposing more rapidly, left only feathered skeletons" (60). This country of brilliant air, of color and light, of silver mirages in which cattle are magnified to look like prehistoric mammoths, seems to call up in the young girl both the desire to achieve a beautiful permanence and the recognition that all achievement must be measured against the ages.

The reciprocity between this Moonstone country and the heart of young Thea is underlined in Doctor Archie's later observation, when Thea as an opera star is at the peak of her career, that "the only things we cherish are those which in some way met our original want; the desire which formed in us in early youth, undirected, and of its own accord" (488). At the end of the novel, looking back upon the girl who left Moonstone for Chicago and the beginnings of her struggle toward success, Thea, now the supreme opera star, concludes, " 'The point to which I could go was scratched in me then' " (552), where even the characteristically necessitarian Catherian judgment is imaged in terms of Thea's mineral West, suggesting the etching of diamond upon material of nearly equal hardness.

This setting of not a farming but a mining West is suffused with the idea of *making it,* of the big strike, the hope of sudden riches — "a fortune kicked up somewhere in the hills...an oil well, a gold mine, a ledge of copper" — as Ray

Kennedy dreams it (67). The luckless Kennedy's dreams are actually achieved by others. Doctor Archie strikes it rich in his silver mine and moves to a sumptuous hotel in Denver, that western metropolis that for Cather has accepted the standards of the mining West, easy money and a good time, just as Lincoln, Nebraska, is elsewhere identified with the less flamboyant West of the farm and the family and the traditional aspirations toward education. Doctor Archie, his hand in new industries and state politics, settles into that comfortable life of the courtly western exploiter upon which Cather occasionally beams so approvingly. Thea's more powerful aspirations take her to Chicago and the East. Along with her romantic yearnings, we are told, Thea has "a hard kind of cockiness, a determination to get ahead," that leads her to view the weaknessess — and even the strengths — of others with a kind of contempt. Whereas all her young contemporaries meant to have things, "the difference was that she was going to get them!" (274) The "hard glint in her eye" that drives Thea onward leaves her at the top at last, in a state of jewellike brilliance and self-sufficiency. The ideal of achieving a beautiful and unassailable permanence pervades and shapes her aspirations. For her, to be alone in a high place is an expression of deepest desire — her childhood room up under the eaves, or the cliff dwellings of Panther Canyon, "a nest in a high cliff, full of sun," or the opulent New York towers where as prima donna of the opera she lives in godlike isolation (371). Through her art she finally becomes one of "the things that last," a moonstone of the self, beautiful, cold, prized, unearthly, called now, as one of the greats, simply "Kronborg," literally crown-fortress.[24]

There is an opposite side to Thea's westernness that complements the impermeable, gemlike state to which she responds and aspires, and that is found in the intimations of passionate life to which she responds. Within the young girl, an almost uncontrollable sense of creative power exists, as is seen in the passage in which she lies on the floor of her room

in the moonlight, her body "pulsing with ardor and anticipation" (177). As with the Nebraska Divide on which Alexandra
Bergson is perhaps the first to turn a face filled with love,
Thea's West is also a vital land rich with the evidence of
human achievement. Thea's conception of this heritage is
first awakened in her as a child when she visits Wyoming
with her father. There, on a windy, high plain backed by
snowy peaks, she sees the furrows cut by the wheels of
pioneer wagons, while eagles fly overhead. The old rancher
who has shown her the place tells her of hearing the first
message that came over the new telegraph across the
Missouri River, "Westward the course of Empire takes its
way," and Thea resolves never to forget the message or the
spirit of courage whose evidence she has seen on the high
plain with the eagles. Thea finds an even more forceful
inspiration among the buildings and earthen vessels of the
cliff dwellers of Panther Canyon in Arizona where she
spends a summer as a young woman. Again, an eagle in
flight compels her imagination and links her to an older
human heritage:

> O eagle of eagles! Endeavour, achievement, desire, glorious
> striving of human art! From a cleft in the heart of the
> world she saluted it. . . . It had come all the way; when men
> lived in caves, it was there. A vanished race; but along the
> trails, in the stream, under the spreading cactus, there still
> glittered in the sun the bits of their frail clay vessels,
> fragments of their desire. (399)

From the remains of the Ancient People of the cliff dwellings,
Thea learns what she comes to believe is the lesson for every
artist, " 'the inevitable hardness of human life. . . . You have
to realize it in your body; deep. It's an animal sort of feeling.
I sometimes think it's the strongest of all' " (554). Thea is
influenced so deeply by her experiences in Panther Canyon,
then, because she finds there her homeland's most profound
expression of passionate human desire and rocklike permanence and perfection.

Thea's conscious use of her western past marks her recognition that while she cannot match the Easterners' elegance and confidence, her western standards will prevail because they are so deeply a part of her, a manifestation of the strength of her will. The six hundred dollars from Ray Kennedy's life insurance that financed her first year as a music student becomes, as she tells Doctor Archie, the figure by which she measures monetary value, just as she still judges high buildings by the height of the Moonstone standpipe. In this sense Thea, although a striving Westerner and thus bound toward the East and the city, will remake the city on her own terms. Although Thea's preacher father believes that big cities were "places where people went to lose their identity and to be wicked" (196), it is the cities that lose their identity to Thea's force of will. As a child, she finds Doctor Archie reading Balzac's *A Distinguished Provincial in Paris* and discusses the book with him. The title prefigures her own presence in New York at the conclusion of the book, at which time Doctor Archie reflects that Thea " 'was born a cosmopolitan' " (457).

Chicago, in which she spends her first winter away from home studying music, does not, for many months, break in upon Thea's reserve. The city is a "wilderness" as her West never was (244). She feels no quickening of pace from the accelerated life of Chicago, and takes little notice of its new sights and sounds, with the exception of the jeweler's windows, whose tokens of earthly power attract her strongly: "she had always liked bright stones. . . .These seemed very well worth while to her, things worth coveting" (244-45). Later a visit to the Art Institute begins to awaken in her some awareness of the larger world of art, although the picture that pleases her most, "The Song of the Lark," which depicts a peasant girl in the morning stopping to look up and listen to a lark, and which Cather calls "second-rate" in her preface, is primarily a reminder and evocation of Thea's western plains. Her introduction to symphony music is also

significant not for the unfamiliar experience that is presents
but for the power that the music, Dvorak's "New World
Symphony," has to raise up and vivify her earlier memories
of the West. Chicago itself, with all its activity and bustle, is
"a spent thing, its chief concern its digestion and its little
game of hide-and-seek with the undertaker. Money and
office and success are the consolations of impotence." What
is important, we are told, are the hungry, proud youth who
walk its streets, "who are the Future, and who possess the
treasure of creative power" (332-33). It is the same creative
power that has built the cliff city of Panther Canyon which
Thea visits after her second winter in Chicago and which
coalesces in her mind her previously undirected yearnings.
That fall she sails for Europe and study in Germany.

New York, the city of "Kronborg's" successful maturity,
has no evocative power and becomes merely another urban
backdrop for the career of the heroic artist and achiever. Her
life, by this time, is in her work and on the stage, and her
personal life and its relationships to the real world become,
as Cather admits in her preface, increasingly pale and dull.
Her marriage to wealthy Fred Ottenburg does not touch her
essential self. New York recedes into insignificance —
expensive hotel suites and performances at the Met, with
taxi rides between — before the triumphant desire of this
western artist.

The book closes not in New York, but back in Moonstone
in an epilogue wherein Thea Kronborg's rise to brilliance is
placed in the context of fable. It is twenty years since Thea
left the town for Chicago. Moonstone is "smarter" now, the
women look younger, and "the children look like city
children" (575). Thea's adoring Aunt Tillie is the last
Kronborg left in the town. In her copy of a New York
newspaper she reads of Madame Kronborg's triumphs in
London, and that the king of England has presented her
with a jewel. Thea is, by this time, enshrined (along with a
local boy turned rich Omaha businessman) in the town

consciousness as an example of Moonstone enterprise, although, Cather adds, "a voice has even a wider appeal than a fortune," an assertion of the communal importance of art. News of what their native sons and daughters are doing in the great world, Cather's final sentence intones, "bring to the old, memories, and to the young, dreams" (581).

Thea Kronborg is, to this point in Cather's career, the most successful of her new Westerners because she preserves the integrity of her inner will at the same time that she performs, as a great artist, an important social and cultural function. Although she lives in a kind of personal isolation, through her art she speaks from her inner self "to all those second selves" which lie within each of us, and music is the most powerful and universal of all the artistic communicators (273). Still, art in its timelessness speaks to the ages, leaving Thea not so clearly a representative figure of the post-pioneer America as Bartley Alexander, Emil Shimerda, and those other figures to come. For that America, *The Song of the Lark* suggests some directions, but no clear path. The railroad conductor Ray Kennedy, self-taught, resourceful, chivalric, admirer of the cliff dwellers, talented in mathematics and physics, but not blessed by luck, is an early draft of Tom Outland, the wandering cowboy who turns to the science of the new age, at the same time that he recognizes the eternal values of art. Doctor Archie as mine director and industrial entrepreneur retains Cather's respect, although one senses that his success is more a reward for his faith in Thea than evidence of the author's interest in his fate. Among the minor figures, Thor Kronborg, Thea's little brother, is a born mechanic and becomes Doctor Archie's chauffeur, after failing at a business college and an engineering school. Madison Bowers, Thea's voice teacher in Chicago, is a cold and bitter man who works with a voice "as if he were in a laboratory, conducting a series of experiments" (271), an imagistic rejection of the new science when divorced of human passion. But none of these figures is more than a side-melody in the imperial performance of Thea Kronborg.

Without the presence of Jim Burden as first-person narrator, *My Ántonia* would have been simply another *O Pioneers!*, a tribute to the vital immigrant girl of the Nebraska frontier. But Jim represents, in part, Cather's persistent attempt to graft upon the heroic past a figure of contemporary significance, and as such he marks an advance over all of his predecessors. Bartley Alexander embodies the uprooted Westerner, the modern builder who has lost contact with his primitive source of power and feeling and has been sucked dry by the great world to the east. Alexandra Bergson is merely a remembrance of the past, a prairie stalwart whose avowed concern for the wider world beyond her cornfields is never novelistically realized. Thea Kronborg successfully converts her western heritage into a triumphant artistic career that inevitably lifts her out of the real world and into the realm of fable. In Jim Burden, a Westerner, an artist, and a functioning representative of the world of modern consequence and action, Cather has imaged a figure of major importance in the development of her heroic design. He looks ahead to Tom Outland as the supreme creation of that design; if Tom is a richer composite of princely attributes, Jim Burden is more fully realized as a major character. His importance is signaled in the introduction to *My Ántonia*, in which Cather sketches Jim's role as narrator and as attendant spirit to Antonia and her western world. Cather, or the "I" of the introduction, begins by describing a day spent on a train crossing the hot fields of Iowa with Jim Burden. She tells us that she and Jim are old friends who have grown up together in a Nebraska town, that they agree that no one who has not grown up in that kind of place can know anything about it ("it was a kind of freemasonry, we said"), that they both now live in New York, where Jim is legal counsel for a "great" western railroad.[25] Their memories center upon a Bohemian girl who seems to represent the country most meaningfully to them. Further, we learn that Jim is not happily married, that he has had disappointments, but that he remains unchanged from his youth:

> The romantic disposition which often made him seem very funny as a boy, has been one of the strongest elements in his success. He loves with a personal passion the great country through which his railway runs and branches. His faith in it and his knowledge of it have played an important part in its development. (2)

The introduction concludes with Jim, some months later back in New York, bringing a manuscript to the narrator, an account of the Bohemian girl whom they had discussed and of whom Jim's mind had been full on that day on the train. He has not titled the manuscript, and so writes "Ántonia" across the front of its portfolio. Frowning at this he adds the word "My," making it "My Antonia." "That seemed to satisfy him" (2).

One of Cather's purposes in providing this introductory material on Jim Burden, rather than allowing it to filter in during the course of Jim's narration, is to delineate clearly and unmistakably the essential elements of his life and character. First, he is a Westerner, an insider whose participation in prairie life has marked him forever, like some member of a secret society. Next he has gone east, as has the narrator of the introduction, and despite marital unhappiness has become a success in his work, a consequential modern whose faith in and knowledge of the home country through which his railroad runs have helped that land to grow and prosper. Furthermore, Jim's career with the railroad provides him with the opportunity and the obligation to return to his home country, allowing him, in a familiar Catherian pattern, to revivify his eastern, contemporary self from the primitive wellsprings of his youth. Finally, we know that Jim has also become a writer. He has fashioned the potent but chaotic memories and impressions of this primitivistic world of his youth into a work which may — his reader shall soon see — break the closed circle of "free-masonry" that has isolated this western country and its representative figures like Ántonia and even Jim Burden himself from the wider world.

All of this amounts to an extraordinary series of accomplishments for the Catherian hero. A number of potentially destructive or at least limiting stresses are, in Jim Burden, placed in productive balance to form the outlines of a larger and more complex figure than has yet emerged from among Cather's heroes and heroines. The book, then, may be seen as primarily Jim Burden's story, as his insistence upon the word "My" in his manuscript title indicates. Ántonia Shimerda, as vital a character as she is in her own right, is more important for what she does to, and for, Jim Burden.[26]

Jim is ten years old at the opening of the novel when he comes to Nebraska to live and first meets the Shimerdas. Orphaned in Virginia, Jim is brought by train to Black Hawk, Nebraska, to live with his grandparents, traveling with Jake Marpole, one of his father's hired hands who is now going to work for his grandfather in Nebraska, and who is as naive and unacquainted with the world as is young Jim. This pair of innocents who "set out together to try [their] fortunes in a new world" arrive after a journey of several days, having heard of an immigrant family in the next coach whose destination is also Black Hawk and who have a young girl (Ántonia) who can speak a little English. Jim is too shy to meet Ántonia, and Jake remarks that one might catch diseases from foreigners (5-6). Arriving in Black Hawk at night, and jolting across the prairie toward his grandparents' house in a wagon with Jake, Jim feels "erased, blotted out" by the huge, unfamiliar land (9).

These opening pages are richly sown with the implications of Jim's future growth. Jake's superstitions about foreigners disqualify him in this respect as Jim's mentor, but Jake, along with the other hired man at the Burden farm, Otto Fuchs, an Austrian turned rough laborer and wanderer, provides Jim with comradeship and a sense of the lure of the old, cowboy West, like the "Life of Jesse James" that Jake buys for young Jim on his train journey to Nebraska and that Jim recalls later as "one of the most satisfactory books I have ever read" (5). Still, in the fate of Jake and Otto, who head off to the Colarado mountains to take up prospecting in what Otto calls "the 'wild West,' " and who after one postcard are never seen or heard from again, is a portent for Jim of the "defenceless" Westerner in a world that has gone past him and a warning of the insubstantiality of human relationships (97, 56).

The one communicant from among the foreigners on the train, the immigrant girl Ántonia, whom Jim comes later to find interesting because like the transplanted narrator himself she had "been early awakened and made observant by coming at a tender age from an old country to a new," helps to transcend in Jim's education the narrow and spiritless town life of Black Hawk (131). Ántonia and her sensitive and artistic father will kindle in Jim's mind the desire for wider knowledge and understanding that accompanies his wish to shape the raw, wild Nebraska landscape ("not a country at all, but the material out of which countries are made") into meaningful form (8). The intimation of Jim's later hope to " 'be the first, if I live, to bring the Muse into my country' " is present in these opening pages in Jim's choice of the writer-to-be's images ("erased, blotted out") as he arrives in Nebraska (171, 9). (Later he will describe the famous image of the plow magnified in the sunset as "a picture writing on the sun" [159].)

While Jim and Antonia grow up sharing the richness of the western land and the sense of greater worlds beyond their Nebraska horizon, Ántonia's greatest gift to Jim is that she arouses in him, as a young artist, the powerful and deeply felt pictures of his own youth. Ántonia "leave[s] images in the mind that did not fade — that grew stronger with time," at the same time that she suggests elements of the most memorable human importance: "she lent herself to immemorial human attitudes which we recognize by instinct as universal and true" (228). Thus she calls up in Jim the most significant reverberations of private and common experience which he must possess and unite if he is to become an artist.

More than serving as a rich source of human images and attitudes, Ántonia also encourages Jim directly in his early efforts at expression, realizing that he possesses an ability that she cannot command but that she instinctively recognizes as precious. When Jim gives the high school commencement speech, Ántonia is deeply stirred, saying, " 'It must make you very happy, Jim, to have fine thoughts like that in your mind all the time, and to have words to put them in. I always wanted to go to school, you know.' " (150). When Jim tells her what she had already sensed, that he had been thinking of her father when he wrote the speech, Ántonia is so moved that Jim admits to having had "no other success that pulled at my heartstrings like that one" (150-51). On this occasion and again when Jim is implored by Ántonia to tell the girls the story of the early Spanish explorers (" 'I've tried to tell them,' " says Antonia, " 'but I leave out so much' " [158]) the reader senses that the effect upon Ántonia of Jim's early achievements with words helps to nurture his desire to write and to shape his conception of the writer's responsibilities. Like George Willard of Sherwood Anderson's *Winesburg, Ohio*, Jim assumes the "burden" of the artist: to communicate the truths of the inarticulate to the great world, revealing the heretofore unacknowledged significance of the voiceless ones to a wider audience, which is itself enriched by this sympathetic enlargement of its experience.

Jim's education is furthered by his association, while a student at the newly emerging state university at Lincoln, with a

brilliant young scholar, Gaston Cleric, who introduces him
to intellectual life through the Greek and Latin classics.
Reading Virgil's *Georgics* Jim discovers the universality and
timelessness of man's search for his own past and his desire
to memorialize the land-hunger within him for his native
soil. At the same time, Jim recognizes that he can never be a
scholar because he cannot lose himself among "impersonal
things" and that while Cleric brings him to new ideas the
familiar figures from his own past, "strengthened and
simplified," keep arising in his mind to grasp his attention
(170).

Cleric and Ántonia both contribute to Jim's education in
urging him that he not allow himself to be diverted from
the high road of idealism. Both warn him away from the soft
and alluring Lena Lingard. Ántonia is determined that he
will not turn out to be a fool for the girls or an idler, like
some of the town boys, but will go away to school and make
his mark in the world. Cleric takes Jim with him when he
leaves Lincoln to take in instructorship at Harvard. Yet both
Cleric and Ántonia are victims of the entrapping personal
relationship against which they warn Jim. Cleric, Jim
believes, has missed being a great poet because he has spilled
out his inner potency in his brilliant conversation, wasting his
talent "in the heat of personal communication" (169). Ántonia
is seduced by the railroad conductor Larry Donovan, and
then, pregnant, is deserted by him. She eventually recovers
herself through her marriage to a young Bohemian, Cuzak,
and raises a large family, but the lesson of her experience
has not been lost upon Jim, who follows the familiar
Catherian path of avoidance of the potentially destructive
passionate sexual realtionship. The marriage that he
eventually makes is loveless and childless, but leaves him
free to pursue his own interests. Despite Jim's admiration for
the exuberant farm girls like Ántonia and Lena and his
professing as a teenager that he "knew where the real women
were...and...would not be afraid of them, either!" it is the

nonthreatening, asexual relationship with Ántonia that most clearly fulfills the requirements of the Catherian hero. Jim joins Cather's heroines in the two previous novels in finding a marriage that does not touch him so deeply as his career. When Jim sees Antonia after the birth of her first child he voices her proper role in his personal life precisely: " 'I'd have liked to have you for a sweetheart, or a wife, or my mother or my sister — anything that a woman can be to a man' " (208). Once more Antonia's function is to *lend herself* to Jim's requirements. At the end of the novel, when Jim meets Antonia after a number of years, she is a "battered" woman, a mother of many, a "rich mine of life," selflessly serving her husband and children, her farm, its animals, its encircling orchard, the activities of planting and cultivating and harvesting, just as she has served the narrator's artist's hunger for representative human attitudes (228-29).

Jim's distancing of himself from the batterings of close human relationships is both the price and the reward of his artistic creation. His failure on Antonia's familial and personal level frees him from the self-effacement that accompanies submersion into the social world. Antonia achieves immortality through her nurturing of life and Jim through his creation of a work of art. She has her children and he his book. To see Jim as a failure because he is landless, childless, unhappily married, is to ignore Cather's more compelling loyalties to the higher achievements of art.

The true marriage in Jim's life is the chaste and vicarious one that has, in the end, linked him to his idealized Antonia, to his treasured past, and thus to his own deepest sense of self. The book closes with an underscoring of these connections as Jim recalls his first night in Nebraska as a boy:

> I had only to close my eyes to hear the rumbling of the
> wagons in the dark, and to be again overcome by that
> obliterating strangeness. . . . I had the sense of coming

home to myself, and of having found out what a little circle man's experience is. For Ántonia and for me, this had been the road of Destiny; had taken us to those early accidents of fortune which predetermined for us all that we can ever be. Now I understood that the same road was to bring us together again. Whatever we had missed, we possessed together the precious, the incommunicable past. (240)

If the past is indeed incommunicable then it is paradoxically so, since the force of Jim's narrative has gone toward communicating it, and, in doing so, toward fashioning an answer to the "obliterating" cancellation of individuality which had overcome him as a youth on his first journey across these prairies.

Jim's final tribute to the past should not obscure the fact that for him there is also both a present and a future. He has both his meaningful career with the railroad and his newfound relationship with the Cuzaks to look forward to. He happily anticipates hunting trips with the boys and getting to know Cuzak himself better, and his mind is filled with "pleasant things" as the novel closes (239).

As a railroad man Jim basks in Cather's benevolent approval of that industry, despite her antipathy toward machine civilization. Of her most admirable characters, many work for the railroad in some capacity — Ray Kennedy of *The Song of the Lark*, Jim Burden, Captain Forrester of *A Lost Lady*, Tom Outland of *The Professor's House* — and relationships between these men and their work are often mutually beneficial. (Cather's own beloved brother, Douglass, was a brakeman for the Sante Fe Railroad when she visited him in Arizona in 1912). A thoroughgoing rotter like Ántonia's seducer, Larry Donovan, is a conductor for the line running through Black Hawk, but he is guilty of knocking down fares and is fired and blacklisted by the company, a punishment that even Ántonia (who "cannot believe ill of anyone she loved") views as justified (202). Ray

Kennedy is killed in a railway crash, but the accident, Cather is at pains to make clear, was the fault of a careless co-worker, a cynical fellow who collected pictures of undraped females. For Cather, as for Jim Burden, the railroad seems to have been accepted as simply a part of the geographical and cultural given of the prairie.[27] The railroad was there when they arrived, and thus it belongs. While critics have placed Cather in the camp of the Populists, she is clearly in opposition to them in her benign acceptance of the railroad, whose evils were principal targets of Populist reform.[28] Her treatment of the railroad, then, suggests that it was not machine civilization as such that called forth the bitterness and scorn of *One of Ours* and her following novels, but those aspects of it, like the automobile, that postdated her own formative years and which were therefore not subsumable into her closed and carefully ordered western world.

Among the threatening possibilities, Jim Burden carefully picks his way. He adds to his achievement in art and to the resuscitation of his lost past the accomplishments of an honorable contemporary man. Jim finds the means to carry on the process of pioneering, which he has recorded in the life of Ántonia, through his position with the railroad, which enables him to help nurture and guide the growth of his home country. Not "merely" a minor artist, that is one who, like Ántonia's father, is unable to find a suitable role in a new age and a new environment, Jim is also a significant and functioning modern American. As one who finds a satisfactory balance-point between the conflicting pulls of West and East, individualism and society, old ways and new, he joins Thea Kronborg as a successful survivor from among Cather's new Americans.

With her novel on World War I, *One of Ours* (1922), Cather shifts her confrontation of West and East from an American to a global stage. Claude Wheeler, her Nebraska farm-boy hero, is another of Cather's western seekers, one whose sense of yearning for "something splendid" in life grows stronger within him as his opportunities progressively diminish. His love for learning is cut short as he is forced to give up his studies in Lincoln in order to take over the management of the family farm. Later, he wanders into marriage with a frigid and Puritanical girl. Finally, he is caught up in the war, and finds his spiritual fulfillment as a soldier in France. Awkward and unfinished in speech and dress, untalented artistically, and deprived of the opportunities for further education, this social "clod" (whom Cather admitted privately to be a representation of her earlier self[29]) would seem to offer his creator few opportunities for novelistic development into a figure of cultural consequence. But Claude's sensitivity and intelligence, combined with his footballer's physique and his physical courage, are sufficient virtues to allow Cather to add the Warrior to her gallery of New Americans. Claude's football-playing may be validated as Catherian heroic action by reference to an essay from her student days, "The Poetry of Football," which might as well have been written by Norris, another avid devotee of the game. The essay extols the Anglo-Saxon stength and the crude, savage instinct to which football appeals. When the last spark of barbarism is dead in us, she concludes, in terms prophetic of Claude and *One of Ours*, "then providence will be done with us and will have some new barbarian people ready to come and conquer."[30]

But Claude's mid-American, mooncalf yearning itself is, of course, the indispensable quality. Perpetually on the brink of what might be an apotheosis, an experience, as Fitzgerald would say, commensurate with his capacity for wonder, he is forever sensing an imminence just outside his reach, yearning for meanings just beyond the range of his perception, but suggested, as by the snowflakes of a winter storm that exhale to the young man "a faint purity like a fragrance almost too fine for human sense."[31] Claude, then, is "one of ours" because his heart is set upon the highest goals, another Catherian figure whose reach exceeds his grasp.

And this hunger, as we have seen, is for Cather's Westerners a kind of power. Claude realizes that his father, too, must have once possessed the same longing when he ran away into the new Nebraska country, which a generation of cash-crop farming has converted into Claude's open-air prison. Now, the example of the father, sunk into trivial political and business dealings and that thoughtless, cruel brand of indigenous midwestern "kidding" that Sinclair Lewis and Ring Lardner were to flay, gives urgency to Claude's struggle for release. Claude's brothers are opposites, but equally unsympathetic to his dreams. Bayliss, the elder, is a greedy and dour little Philistine; the younger, Ralph, is a mindless and profligate buyer and tinkerer of the family's too-many machines. The boy's mother is evangelical and submissive. Claude's Bohemian friend, Ernest Havel, is simple and forthright, open to new experiences, free from the alternate grasping and sanctimoniousness of his Anglo-Saxon neighbors, but his Old World capacity for acceptance of the limitations of individual human life marks a crucial difference with Claude. Ernest's easygoing passivity is unacceptable to Claude, as it would be to Cather's other questing moderns, a petering out of the heroic will and a denial that life can — or ought to — be possessed of splendor. The Ehrlichs, the German-American family in Lincoln that befriends Claude, introduce him to a more graceful world of human relations than he has yet known. Their home is a place of many visitors, of animated conversation, of music and books. His experiences there combine with his brief stay at the university, where he studies history enthusiastically, to form the beginnings of his rebirth, but he is called back to the farm and resigns himself to accepting that "he belonged out in the big, lonely country, where people worked with their backs and got tired like the horses, and were too sleepy at night to think of anything to say" (73). In the extended treatment of the contemporary agricultural West (more than the first half of the novel) Cather records the failure of the modern farm to offer a satisfying life for her young seekers. There is simply nothing left in the rural West out of which their longings can shape constructive patterns for living. Looking at a statue of Kit Carson, on horseback and facing westward, Claude realizes that "there was no West, in that sense, any more" (104).

The reader's first impression is that Cather attributes the decline of the American West to the material prosperity brought on by machine civilization. In a famous passage, Cather presents her indictment of the contemporary West:

> The farmer raised and took to market things with an intrinsic value; wheat and corn as good as could be grown anywhere in the world, hogs and cattle that were the best of their kind. In return he got manufactured articles of poor quality; showy furniture that went to pieces, carpets and draperies that faded, clothes that made a handsome man look like a clown. Most of his money was paid out for machinery, — and that, too, went to pieces. . . .
> [In former times] the farmers took time to plant fine cottonwood groves on their places, and to set osage orange hedges. . . . Now these trees were all being cut down and grubbed up. Just why, nobody knew; they impoverished the land. . .they made the snow drift. . .nobody had them any more. With prosperity came a kind of callousness; everybody wanted to destroy the old things they used to take pride in. (88-89)

Cather's apparently unqualified attack upon the new ascendancy of the machine is carried on through the plot and imagery of the novel as well. Claude's brother, Ralph, loads the family down with more machinery than it wants or needs; a noisy truck is partly responsible for causing Claude's mules to bolt, resulting in a serious injury to him. Natural and mechanistic images are continually set against each other: a water-powered mill gives way to an engine, and the change, regretted by Claude as a young boy, parallels the mill owner's own spiritual decline; the woodlot on Claude's farm is a haven for birds and the boy's refuge from the technological muddle which surrounds him; when Claude goes off to do battle with the German juggernaut, the metallic nightmare of the front is alternated with pastoral interludes in the brilliant summer landscape of France. Indeed, Cather seems determined to humanize the allied effort by demechanizing it. It is Claude and Our Boys against "the Hun bombers." At the height of the battle, Claude stands atop a parapet, commanding the fire of his men, "directing them with his voice and his hands. . . . Their eyes never left him. With these men he could do anything" (385). If Cather's fervor has produced an improbable triumph of midwestern flesh and will over the Hun machine, her novelistic intentions are nevertheless carried to their ends. By elevating her soldier hero into the role of artist, a kind of guest conductor at a symphony of carnage, Cather provides unmistakable corroboration that Claude has at last achieved the sort of significance which will grant him his rightful place among her western achievers.

Claude's high position is further underscored by the same sort of Catherian elegy in the book's final pages that is given to the memory of Bartley Alexander at the conclusion of *Alexander's Bridge* or to Thea Kronborg's shining career at the end of *The Song of the Lark*. Like his more illustrious predecessors, Claude Wheeler has become his admirers. And like Tom Outland, still to come in *The Professor's House*, Claude has not only achieved a hero's death, he has cheated life of its inevitable revenge of disillusionment.

Despite her apparent wish to exclude allied technology from its place in the war effort, Cather is enough of a modern to recognize that such a position would be ludicrous, and enough of a partisan not to apologize for Yankee mechanizing in what she fervently believed was a just cause.

German submarines are sinking our transports, but it is only a question of time before American knowhow turns the tide. " 'In another year,' " Claude confidently tells his mother, "the Yankees will be flying over. They can't stop us' " (220). And it is, after all, American firepower and not a cavalry charge or a luminous ideal that gives Claude his final victory. Modern warfare has clearly gone beyond the personal and the passionate, even for Cather; so that if the Hun will be the technological aggressor, Our Boys will give him back his iron blitzkrieg in spades.

Cather is actually able to resolve this ambivalence toward the machine in *One of Ours* by dramatizing that it is not the machine, but its worship or misuse, that is behind her indictment of modern life. Claude dies for a homeland that is not Nebraska, nor even America, but France, because France, "flowery France," for Cather and her young hero represents an exaltation of spiritual over mundane concerns. With respect to the machine, this means that the French have successfully subsumed their technology into a larger conception of the worthwhile life. As Claude's troop train rolls through the blooming French countryside, the soldiers see not the creeping rusticity they had expected, but a landscape that is both modern and at the same time human:

> The thatched roofs they had so counted upon seeing were few and far between. But American binders, of well-known makes, stood where the fields were beginning to ripen, — and they were being oiled and put in order, not by "peasants," but by wise-looking old farmers who seemed to know their business. Pear trees, trained like vines against the wall, did not astonish them half so much as the sight of the familiar cottonwood, growing everywhere. Claude thought he had never before realized how beautiful this tree could be. . . . At home, all about Frankfort, the farmers were cutting down their cottonwoods because they were "common," planting maples, and ash trees to struggle along in their stead. Never mind; the cottonwoods were good enough for France, and they were good enough for

him! He felt they were a real bond between him and this people. (289)

France, which knows how to treat both its cottonwoods and its machines, must be, for this disinherited Westerner, both the right place and the right people. That he dies for them is a measure of his faith, however idealistic, in the possibilities for a productive union of spiritual values with the industrial present.

A Lost Lady (1923) occupies a special place in the Cather canon because it dramatizes most pointedly both the attractions and the dangers of secession from one's own times. Niel Herbert, the hero of the novel, is more than just another of what Edmund Wilson called Cather's "limpid and sensitive young men."[32] Niel is a contemporary Westerner whose relentless mythicizing of his home country and its people threatens to isolate him forever from the modern world to which he belongs. Although the novel is characteristically seen as a lament for the pioneering past, with Niel dramatizing Cather's own disillusionment with the decline of the modern West, the work reveals that Niel is, almost from his first appearance, an unreliable consciousness, not merely a dreamy and romantic youth, but a persistently self-deluding one. While he shares many of his creator's attitudes, and while one hesitates, given the pattern of close involvement between Cather and her leading fictional characters (Jim Burden, Thea Kronborg, Claude Wheeler, and others) to grant her the degree of objectivity and distance required for irony here, still there is considerable evidence that she consciously uses Niel to demonstrate an excessive devotion to a romanticized past, and to reveal the folly of attempting to order the present and the future in the terms of that past.[33]

The "Lost Lady," Niel's most treasured fiction, is Marian Forrester, the captivating young wife of Captain Forrester, twenty-five years her senior, a pioneer railroad builder now retired in Sweet Water, Nebraska, where the boy, Niel, is growing up. Idolizing Mrs. Forrester, Niel has elevated her into an impossible combination of provocative charm and stolid pioneering loyalty. She, however, like some figure out of comedy, refuses to hold still for the marble toga in which her young admirer would encase her. During the period of the old captain's invalidism, she is discovered by Niel in an affair with a youger man, Frank Ellinger. When the captain dies, she will not grieve her life away, as Neil's rigid code would require. To his chagrin, she rejects the cold comfort of respectability and widow's weeds, and in the embrace of the disreputable Ivy Peters leaves Niel, now a young man, to ponder the meaning of her character: that life on any terms is preferable to self-sacrifice to the past. Ironically, Niel's contempt for her failure to take up the role of Pioneer Widow provides the impetus for him to break free from his devotion to a dead past. Liberated by her survivalist evasions from the obligation to continue worshiping at her shrine, Niel goes east to take up his study of architecture at M.I.T. and eventually to fill the place that awaits him in the real world. Thus, though Marian Forrester is finally and unremittingly "lost" for Niel in several senses of the world — a fallen woman, an aimless wanderer, a creation of the remembrances of his youth — she frees him from his bondage to mythland and vicarious experience, and thus gives him the gift of his own life.

Cather's difficulty during the composition of the novel in deciding between first- and third-person point of view, and her final choice of the more flexible third-person narration, a limited omniscience that reveals most, but not all, of the events as seen through Niel's eyes, alerts the reader to the possibility that Niel's is an unreliable consciousness: his inveterate memorializing of western pioneering leads him to disregard reality so flagrantly that we cannot accept his judgments about either the past or its last survivor, Marian

Forrester.[34] Unlike *My Antonia, A Lost Lady* was to dramatize ironies that could not be wholly trusted to an insider. The strategy of the novel's opening pages substantiates this reading. Niel Herbert is not introduced until the second chapter; in the first, Cather establishes a balancing of realistic and romantic materials and foreshadows the ascendancy of the romantic in what is to come. The opening chapter, then, gives us both the propensity for glorification of the pioneering past and the underlying reality that resists this sort of illusion-making. The first sentences of the novel are as follows:

> Thirty or forty years ago, in one of those grey towns along the Burlington railroad, which are so much greyer to-day than they were then, there was a house well known from Omaha to Denver for its hospitality and for a certain charm of atmosphere. Well known, that is to say, to the railroad aristocracy of that time. . . .[35]

The chapter goes on to pick up the elements introduced here — the town of Sweet Water, the house and its inhabitants, and the railroad executives who visit there — and gives us something of a double view of them all. The town's past is less dreary than its present, but it was "grey" enough even then. The house, we are told, "was not at all remarkable." Yet "the people who lived there made it seem much larger and finer than it was" (4). Here the materials for both realistic and idealistic conceptions of subject are set side by side. Similarly, the "railroad aristocracy" and their fellow executive types who have come "to 'develop our great West,' as they used to tell us," are not spared, in these terms, a sardonic thrust, nor are the Burlington men who liked to stop off for a night at the Forrester house "where their importance was delicately recognized" (4). Cather's benevolent attitude toward the western railroads in her other works heightens the significance of even such muted satire as this. (She might, had she truly belonged in the Populist tradition to which she has occasionally been assigned, have included a variety of sharp practices — rate fixing, stock-watering, influence peddling, appropriation of public lands, and the like — which the Burlington Line practiced openly at this time, during which the Burlington and the Union Pacific companies divided much of the political and economic control of Nebraska between them.[36]) Captain Forrester, "himself a railroad man," that is, a brother to these self-congratulatory gentry, is introduced in terms of only mild approbation. To his credit, he appreciates the beauty of his land, but the disclosure that he basks in the approval of his gentlemen friends, that he was "well off for these hard times, and he had no children. He could afford to humour his fancies," is hardly the stuff out of which legends are made (5). His unqualified deification must await the appearance of Niel in the following chapters.

Marian Forrester is to prove less malleable material; she is a triumph of opposites from the beginning: "she was attractive in dishabille, and she knew it . . . . whatever Mrs. Forrester chose to do was 'ladylike' because she did it" (6-7). The "magic of contradictions" (79) that characterizes Marian Forrester will become for Niel not only the source of her charm, but for an incorrigible and resolute simplifier like himself, a mocking, almost maddening quality.

Niel's unreliablility as a judge of Mrs. Forrester is most clearly indicated by the fact that, although he dares not admit it to himself, he is in love with her from the beginning. The early incident in which Niel, as a boy, is carried into Marian's bedroom after an accident, is perhaps the most erotic scene in all of Cather's novels: "What soft fingers Mrs. Forrester had, and what a lovely lady she was! Inside the lace ruffle of her dress he saw her white throat rising and falling so quickly" (23). The room is darkened by shutters on the windows; she sheds her rings to comfort him, runs her fingers through his hair, and kisses him. Further in the novel, when Niel is older and home from college, he seizes Marian Forrester in her hammock and lifts her in his arms, thinking,

> How light and alive she was! like a bird caught in a net. If only he could rescue her and carry her off like this....
> She showed no impatience to be released, but lay laughing up at him with that gleam of something elegantly wild, something fantastic and tantalizing, — seemingly so artless, really the most finished artifice! She put her hand under his chin as if he were still a boy.
> "And how handsome he's grown!" (105)

Her sexuality, provocative and enticing as it is to the young man, is also deeply troublesome to him. Later, when Marian grips Niel's wrist and tells him " 'I feel such a power to live in me....It's grown by being held back,' " her admission is strangely unsettling to Niel, in retrospect, and causes him to shiver (120-21). Niel's instinctive sense of "evil" in Frank Ellinger has strong overtones of sexual jealousy. Mrs. Forrester intimates to Niel that she prefers Ellinger to him, and when Niel later overhears Frank and Marian in bed together it is more than "admiration and loyalty" that are destroyed for him (74, 81). His rage and shock are better explained by the fact that he has been drawn back to her house and her bedroom, ostensibly to bring her flowers, early on a morning when he knows that the captain is out of town (indeed, he wants to get there "before Frank Ellinger could intrude his unwelcome presence" [79]), and that Niel has then overheard the lovers through the same shutters with which he was first closed off from the world to receive the lady's caresses. Thus he writhes to discover that his place has been usurped by a more potent sexual rival. Unable to acknowledge to himself the unspeakable, his erotic and incestuous fascination with the captain's wife, he fashions for her a prim and sexless character, The Pioneer Wife, to which she — and this is what Niel finally cannot forgive her for —

refuses to conform.

Niel "burns" to ask her how she can be so exquisite and yet take a lover like Ellinger, to know "how she could recover herself, and give one — give even him — the sense of tempered steel, a blade that could fence with anyone and never break?" (95). "Even him" — he who feels so agonizingly the disparity between her actual behavior and the figure of perfection that he wishes her to be. Small wonder that he leaves Sweet Water at the end of the novel with such "weary contempt for her in his heart," this little warrior who fights his rigid idealizing to a standstill.

With the captain and his friends, Niel has easier going. The boy fashions for himself from the beginning a closed aristocratic hierarchy that includes the captain and Marian (a version of Arthur and Guinevere, perhaps), the railroad knights of commerce, Niel himself (a Lancelot in Galahad's clothing), and, as chancellor, Judge Pommeroy, the boy's matenal uncle, whose probity may be assessed by his claim that he knows " 'the difference between a white man and a nigger.' " (87). Niel admires his uncle not only as the captain's financial and legal advisor, but as an intimate of "all the great men" who visited the Forresters (25). Niel is curiously cold toward his own father, a widower, and virtually deserts him because of the air of failure and defeat that dogs him. When his father moves to Denver to try a fresh start, Niel coolly remains behind with the judge, the representative of that maternal side of the family to which Niel cleaves. The boy, we are told, resembles his proud mother, who had died when he was five, who had, significantly, "hated the West" and had come there only to attempt to cash in on the new land along with the rest of the exploiters (25). Instead, the years bring hard times and the family fortunes decline, as do those of the Forresters and other Sweet Water aristocrats and gentlemen farmers who return disillusioned to the East, and as do those of the railroad elect, now anxious to hurry by a town into which they had "sunk money that would never come back" (28). Niel stubbornly refuses to acknowledge what every modern reader must sense, to some degree: that this sort of carpetbagging cannot be made unreservedly heroic, even when pushed back a generation to the Captain's building of the railroad on which these dreams of success were predicated.[37]

Indeed, the early conquests, which Niel insists upon converting into heroic myth, do not differ in substance and effect from the actions of a latter-day sharper like Ivy Peters. " 'He gets splendid land from the Indians some way, for next to nothing'....'I don't admire people who cheat Indians. Indeed I don't!' " exclaims Mrs. Forrester in referring to Peters's Wyoming land boondoggles (118-19), tenderly ignorant of the expropriations of Indian lands by the government and her husband's railroad. Even the Forrester house stands on the site of a former Indian encampment. The captain had seen the land during those early days when Indians where living on it and, without so much as twinge of conscience, had marked out the place for his own.

The captain has transformed this era of plunder into the comfortable blandness of illusion. " 'We dreamed the railroads across the mountains, just as I dreamed my place on the Sweet Water,' " the old man tells his hushed after-dinner audience. None of them is more uncritically receptive than Niel, for whom this bowdlerized history seves as model for his own reveries, his musings on the "dreamers" who had tamed the West (51, 102). Niel's adoration of Captain Forrester elevates the old man's laconic remarks to his guest into "inscriptions cut in stone," verbal equivalents for the majestic natural images which he calls up in the boy's mind — trees, mountains, old Indians (44, 50, 51, 110). There is, of course, much that is admirable in Captain Forrester, his kindness and consideration for his friends, his assumption of full responsibility for a ruinous business debt when his partners refuse to come forward,[38] his quiet and mature acquiescence in Marian's affair with Frank Ellinger. Niel unfortunately practices a selective emulation of the captain's qualities, which does not include the old man's tolerant understanding that a young woman with an elderly invalid husband might seek something more for the remainder of her life than to be, as one of my students once put it, the caretaker of a national monument. Thus while Niel is a dreamer like the captain, he does not know, or rather *refuses* to know, as the old man does, when to stop dreaming. The captain concludes his remarks to his listeners with the assertion that what you dream is what you get in this world, unless you are destined to get nothing. Niel is unable to sense the double edge to these words, to understand that one may end up with what one wants even though that may *be* only illusions. In his unremitting habits of self-delusion Niel very nearly narrows his own future to nothing but an exquisite sense of loss.

Against Niel's persistent romanticizing of the captain and his lady, Ivy Peters stands as a ruthless debunker. " 'I'm just as good as she is,' " he boasts to the other boys at the opening of the novel; later he says to Niel of the Captain, " 'Good deal of bluff about all those old-timers....he had the delusion of grandeur' " (15, 100-101). It is immediately clear why, as we are told, Niel and Ivy had always disliked each other, "blindly, instinctively, recognizing each other through antipathy, as hostile insects do' " (101-2). Unfortunately, Ivy's aggressive egalitarianism and pragmatism are not allowed full play in the novel because the reader's view of Ivy is almost wholly dominated by the disgusting personal characteristics associated with him: repulsive in appearance, a sadistic torturer of animals, a grasping money-grubber, devoid of personal charm or honor. One sides with Niel merely in reaction to all of this, but a less odious characterization of Ivy by the author might have prompted Niel and the reader to ponder more fully the implications, both heroic and actual, of the western past, and to confront the curious similarities between the old "developers" and the new.

On the other hand, perhaps only the shock of seeing Marian Forrester embraced by such a monster as Ivy Peters would have been sufficient to rupture Niel's attachment to his illusions. Approaching the conclusion of the novel, Niel decides to interrupt his college education at M.I.T. to serve the Forresters in their days of declinging fortunes. Niel's act of charity may, however, also be seen as his thinly disguised attempt to prolong his own boyhood and to hold together as long as possible the little dream world that he has created. While the fast-fading Captain Forrester sits unmoving for hours in his garden, gazing at the sundial that counts off the hours toward his death, Niel unwittingly wishes to hold back the currents of time and change. Cather, however, skillfully intimates, through her control of action and imagery in this final section, the folly of Niel's hopes. As the captain (who becomes physically incapacitated and has throughout the novel been linked to images of immobility) passes into the absolute stasis of death, Marian Forrester, typically depicted as a figure in motion (rushing out to greet her guests, being chased by a bull, dancing, running, birdlike, etc.), seems to quicken her pace to near-frantic activity near the end. While this excited movement incorporates in it something of Marian's loss of stability after her husband's death ("without him, she was like a ship without ballast, driven hither and thither by every wind"), it also suggests a warning to Niel to bestir himself ("He could still feel her hand upon his arm, as she urged him faster and faster up the lane") or he may fall out of his own place in time (150, 121). Although he is, after a year back in Sweet Water, anxious to return to his study of architecture in Boston, he also surrenders himself to the sweet sorrow of his leave-taking. He realizes that he is making an irreparable break with the past and that henceforth "there would be nothing to come back to" (167). Niel's fond recollections of "the sunset of the pioneer" with which the book's final chapter opens are in the familiar Catherian vein of elegy, but there are further indications of excess here — Niel's rather incredible little salute to the buffalo hunter, for example — that keep the question of the young man's reliability before us. Most pointedly there is his cold dismissal of Marian Forrester for her failure to arrest her downward glide: "she was not willing to immolate herself, like the widow of all those great men, and die with the pioneer period to which she belonged; . . .she preferred life on any terms" (168). Yet life on, at best, other than one's own terms is what Niel must accept finally for himself. It is less Marian's admonition to him to "hurry and become a successful man" than the blow of seeing her in Ivy's arms that convinces Niel, at last, of this (108). Niel's "weary contempt" for Marian is the price of his own loss of illusion.

The fall is fortunate, then, because it frees Niel to take up his role in his own age, exchanging the paralysis of immolation to the past and the might-have-been to a place in the real world. He becomes, by the skin of his teeth, a contemporary man, a functioning modern who, if he rejects his first career choice of law because of its attraction to modern shysters like Ivy Peters, accepts the possibilities for new pioneering and a progressive union between hope and actuality that are reflected in his decision to become an architect. The faded western town of Sweet Water and the lost house of Captain Forrester with which the book opens are balanced at the end by the world of New York and Chicago and Europe, and by the intimations of building for the present and the future suggested in Niel's professional success. He has become the figure of modern import that Cather recognizes and, not without apprehension, accepts.

When Niel last hears of Marian she has become the wife of a millionaire living in South America, an unlikely but indubitable survivor, a comic, tragic, lost lady for whom Niel can now feel genuine affection (172). The news that she would "almost" make the trip to see her.

There is no clearer indication of Niel's achievement than in his final attitude toward Marian Forrester, for whom his earlier contempt has turned into a mature awareness of her two gifts to him: she has become both "a bright impersonal memory," a manageable ideal, and the woman who had helped in "breaking him in to life," his mentor and guide into the real world (170). If Niel has learned from Captain Forrester and the dreams of boyhood that the modern world has fallen from glory, he has learned from the captain's lady the equally powerful truth that it must nevertheless be lived in.

In *One of Ours* and *The Professor's House*, the two novels published on either side of *A Lost Lady*, the early deaths of Claude Wheeler and Tom Outland are commonly seen as assertions of Catherian despair. But it should be remembered that Cather is also compelled, with Tom the physicist-inventor as she was with architect Niel Herbert, to carry on her search for new possibilities, new symbols of meaningful work, to replace those which had departed with the frontier of her childhood. For Cather in 1925 as in 1912 "making something well," as she claimed, "is the principal end of education."[39] In the achievements of Tom Outland, who, as Professor St. Peter thinks admiringly, "had made something new in the world" (261), Cather concludes the procession of significant moderns who shape the natural wilderness of the western landscape, or the power of their own artistic energy, or the randomness of the physical world, into meaningful contemporary forms. After the brief *My Mortal Enemy* (1926), in which proud and selfish Myra Henshaw's decline in a shabby Pacific Coast city hotel room marks the bankruptcy of her fierce materialism, the emptiness of westering devoid of a dream, Cather turned, except for *Lucy Gayheart* (1935), to the distant past and to historical figures for the heroes and heronies of her final books. *Death Comes for the Archbishop* (1927) is set in the nineteenth-century Southwest, *Shadows on the Rock* (1931) in eighteenth-century Quebec, and *Sapphira and the Slave Girl* (1940) in pre-Civil War Virginia. Tom Outland's death prepares us for that shift to the past and suggests his creator's deeply felt rejection of the communal burden of an emerging new America. But Tom's life and the strivings of all his predecessors reveal that the obligation to accept the role of contemporary pioneering is no less central a concern of the essential Willa Cather.

With its close relationship to *Alexander's Bridge*, as was claimed at the opening of this chapter, *The Professor's House* reveals a remarkable and yet disturbing pattern of consistency in Cather's thinking between 1912 and 1925. Just as the propensity for withdrawal from society and heroic individualism is present in both works, and in those intervening, so is the recognition of Frederick Jackson Turner's later hope, in the face of a disappearing frontier, that the cyclic nature of the pioneering process would continue to present new horizons to challenge even industrialized and urbanized Americans. To place before us in 1925 as a "glittering idea" (*Professor's House*, 111), the most unreservedly heroic figure in all of her contemporary novels, a scientist and inventor, is a measure of Cather's stubborn obligation to hope. Still there is evidence — not limited to the titles of her framing books — that Tom Outland will be the last of his procession, that the optimistic outreaching of Alexander's bridge has withdrawn itself into the last refuge of the professor's house. Most noticeably there is the pejorative shift in the image of Bartley's occupation between the two novels. The engineer as modern western hero, Bartley, becomes, by the time of *The Professor's House*, the engineer as worldly Jew, Louie Marsellus.[40] Tom is a "pure" scientist, a researcher who, with his disinterested discovery of the Outland vacuum and engine, is carefully distinguished from Louie, the electrical engineer who "got the idea over from the laboratory to the trade" and reaped the attendant monetary rewards (41). This leaves Tom free to serve communal needs, so Cather implies, without actually participating in their dispensation on the destructive and degrading personal level, that level revealed in the private lives of Bartley Alexander and Louie Marsellus. Compared to Bartley, then, Tom Outland becomes Cather's last hope to define the social role of the archetypal new American, the scientist-inventor, in terms that would not sully his individual striving.

On a deeper level of meaning, there is a significant quieting of Bartley's churning energy in the calm self-sufficiency of Tom Outland, to the point where Tom comes to resemble in his unassailable repose, as the restless Bartley never did, the classic code hero of western myth. Tom's purity and honor are maintained until death; self-contained and invulnerable, untouched by the winds of moral uncertainty that sweep those about him, he goes his own way in the laboratory as he had in his cowboy days in the West, a kind of "last gentleman."[41] He serves society, but only by being what he *is*, and without compromising his distance from the prevailing social body. And he explores and discovers alone, whereas Bartley is tied to an army of workers and cost accountants, and Louie Marsellus requires a phalanx of experts to help him convert Tom's invention into commercial production. Finally, when the confrontation of war comes, Tom leaves unhesitatingly for the front, and Louie remains behind to marry the girl, Rosamond, St. Peter's daughter, who had loved Tom. The professor's reflection upon Tom might have served for all our mythic Westerners of fiction and film: "Fellows like Outland don't carry much luggage, yet one of the things you know them by is their sumptuous generosity — and when they are gone, all you can say of them is that they departed leaving princely gifts" (121).

But if it is possible for a last moment to follow Cather's lead by suggesting a fuller future scenario for Tom Outland had he survived the World War, it would have included more portentous activities than the writing of useless letters and false excuses, the managing of money, the placating of a demanding woman, that Professor St. Peter imagines burdening Tom in "the trap of worldly success" (260). We might imagine him working on in his laboratory at the university, or, should that institution continue tne downward slide that St. Peter complains of in the novel, moving to one of the country's major private research institutes.

In either case, by 1925, the year of the publication of *The Professor's House*, Tom Outland, as a theoretical physicist on the cutting edge of new research in his field, would probably have joined his colleagues in pursuing a fascinating new possibility, the splitting of the physical atom. And had Tom, that "glittering idea," that last Catherian heroic projection of modern science, been permitted to survive until 1945 (he would not yet have been sixty years old), he would have seen in the flash of Hiroshima, as Cather herself was to live to see, the ultimate revelation of the relationship of pure to applied science, the final impossibility of separating the scientist, even the scientist-as-artist, from his age.[42] The vacuum that was Tom Outland's original great discovery will not serve as emblem for his career or for the possibility of creative scientific individualism sealed off from public and social control. Like the older pioneers such as Captain Forrester, Tom Outland is the vanguard of the very forces his creator deplores, and the "princely gifts" that young Tom departs leaving must include the darker consequences of his heroic new pioneering.

NOTES

1. Bernice Slote, "Willa Cather," *Sixteen Modern American Authors*, ed. Jackson R. Bryer, (New York: W.W. Norton, 1973), pp. 39-57, offers an admirable overview of this pattern in Cather research and criticism.

2. Besides the essays in *The Art of Willa Cather*, ed. Bernice Slote and Virginia Faulkner (Lincoln: University of Nebraska Press, 1974), especially those by Eudora Welty, Marcus Cunliffe, James Woodress, Michel

Gervaud, Aldo Celli, Donald Sutherland, and Bernice Slote, see Slote, "Willa Cather," *Sixteen Modern American Authors*, pp. 42-43 et passim, for early studies that recognized Cather's international heritage, and Slote, "Introduction," *The Kingdom of Art*, ed. Bernice Slote (Lincoln: University of Nebraska Press, 1966). Further works emphasizing Cather's merging of Old and New World influences and her use of primitive and mythic materials include James E. Miller Jr., "*My Ántonia*: A Frontier Drama of Time," *American Quarterly* 10 (Winter 1958): 476-84; Robert L. Gale, "Willa Cather and the Past," *Studi Americani* 4 (1958): 209-22; Dorothy Van Ghent, *Willa Cather* (Minneapolis: University of Minnesota, 1964), p. 5; Don D. Walker, "The Western Humanism of Willa Cather," *Western American Literature* 1 (Summer 1966): 75-90; Evelyn T. Helmick, "Myth in the Works of Willa Cather," *Midcontinent American Studies Journal* 9 (Fall 1968): 63-69; Dorothy Tuck McFarland, *Willa Cather* (New York: Ungar, 1972); and David Stouck, *Willa Cather's Imagination* (Lincoln: University of Nebraska Press, 1975).

    3.   The treatment of *Alexander's Bridge* and *The Professor's House* that follows here was first read as a paper at the 1975 meeting of the Western Literature Association in Durango, Colorado. Reevaluations of *Alexander's Bridge*, in addition to Geismar's, are found in Edith Lewis's *Willa Cather Living* (New York: Alfred A. Knopf, 1953), pp. 78-79; E. K. Brown's *Willa Cather: A Critical Biography* (New York: Alfred A. Knopf, 1953), pp. 154-61; John H. Randall's *The Landscape and the Looking Glass* (New York: Houghton Mifflin, 1960), pp. 38-42; James Woodress's *Willa Cather: Her Life and Art* (New York: Pegasus, 1970), pp. 139-44; and David Stouck's *Willa Cather's Imagination* (Lincoln: University of Nebraska Press, 1975), pp. 12-19. Bernice Slote's new edition of *Alexander's Bridge* (Lincoln: University of Nebraska Press, 1977) contains in its introduction the fullest justification yet published of the novel's place within the Cather canon. A continuing tendency to disregard the novel, however, is demonstrated in Robert Edson Lee's *From West to East* (Urbana: University of Illionis Press, 1966), p. 131; Marion Marsh Brown and Ruth Crone's *Willa Cather: The Woman and Her Work* (New York: Charles Scribner's Sons, 1970), pp. 52-53; and Dorothy Tuck McFarland's *Willa Cather* (New York: Frederick Ungar, 1972), p. 12, which devotes only two or three sentences to *Alexander's Bridge*.

    4.   See *Alexander Bridge*, New Edition with a Preface (Boston and New York: Houghton Mifflin, 1922), pp. v-ix. All references to the novel are from this edition, and page numbers will hereinafter be incorporated into the text. For further disparagement by Cather, see her 1931 article "My First Novel (There Were Two)" in her *On Writing* (New York: Alfred A. Knopf, 1949), pp. 91-97.

    5.   See *The Song of the Lark* (Boston: Houghton Mifflin, 1943), p. 552; *My Ántonia* (Boston: Houghton Mifflin, 1949), p. 240; *My Mortal Enemy* (New York: Random House Vintage Books, 1961), p. 82; *The Professor's House* (New York: Random House Vintage Books, 1973), p. 272. Further references to the last work will be incorporated into the text. The poem

cited is Cather's misquoted version of the opening of Longfellow's "Grave." See E. K. Brown, *Willa Cather*, p. 244.

6. Brief mention is made of the central similarity between Bartley Alexander and Godfrey St. Peter by E. K. Brown, p. 155; Woodress, p. 141; Stouck, pp. 16-17; John P. Hinz, "A Lost Lady and *The Professor's House*," *Virginia Quarterly Review* 29 (Winter 1953): 83; and Bernice Slote, ed., *Alexander's Bridge* (Lincoln: University of Nebraska Press, 1977), pp. xxii-xxiii.

7. John P. Hinz describes the collapse of a great cantilever bridge in Quebec in 1907 that was the historical source for Cather's fictional incident. See his "The Real Alexander's Bridge," *American Literature* 21 (January 1950): pp. 473-76.

8. The setting is familiar to students of Cather. See e.g., her stories "The Enchanted Bluff" and "The Treasure of Far Island," in *Willa Cather's Collected Short Fiction, 1892-1912*, ed. Virginia Faulkner (Lincoln: University of Nebraska Press, 1965), the dedicatory poem in her *April Twilights* (Boston: Richard Badger, 1903), and *My Ántonia* (Boston: Houghton Mifflin, 1949), pp. 151-59.

9. *On Writing*, pp. 31-32.

10. "Plays of Real Life," *McClure's* 40, no. 5 (March 1913): 72.

11. "American Technology and the Nineteenth Century World, *"American Quarterly* 10 (Summer 1958): p. 130.

12. See E. K. Brown, *Willa Cather*, p. 43, and Elizabeth Shepley Sergeant, *Willa Cather: A Memoir* (Philadelphia: J. P. Lippincott, 1953), pp. 18-19.

13. John P. Hinz first explicated the epigraph in his "A Lost Lady and *The Professor's House*" (see n. 6).

14. "Charles H. Hoyt," a dramatic review, October 10, 1895, reprinted in *The Kindgom of Art*, p. 243.

15. The list of examples in Cather's work of "that joy of saluting what is far above one," as she describes it in the opening of *Lucy Gayheart*, can be extended indefinitely: for example, Lucy's star, Jim Burden's and Ántonia's plow against the sun, Jim's evening star, the eagles that inspire Thea Kronborg of *The Song of the Lark*, the various depictions of the moon in Cather's work. (On the latter, see Slote, *The Kingdom of Art*, pp. 97-103.) Conversely, oceans and rivers in Cather often suggest powerful and potentially destructive emotions and forces, as the water rushing underneath Bartley's train on the bridge "meant death" (p. 96).

16. See the Prefatory Note to her *Not under Forty* (New York: Alfred A. Knopf, 1936).

17. See Randall, pp. 41, 391, and Gelfant "The Forgotten Reaping-Hook: Sex in *My Ántonia*," *American Literature* 43 (March 1971): 61. For a fuller discussion of Gelfant and of Cather and sexuality, see n. 26.

18. That Cather was aware that Bartley was open to at least the traditional charge of immorality is indicated in Woodress's biography, pp. 143-44: "Apparently accused by her aunt of allowing moral flimsiness in

Bartley Alexander," she [Cather] admitted the charge and defended herself by asserting that one can not always write about what one most approves of." She went on to argue that what makes a character significant to a writer is the creator's ability to see deeply and sympathetically into his character.

19. Cather used the same incident, the death by drowning of an artist, pulled down by a lesser man, in her 1935 novel, *Lucy Gayheart* (New York: Alfred A. Knopf, 1966), p. 138.

20. "Willa Cather Talks of Work," *Special Correspondence of the [Philadelphia] Record,* New York, August 9[1913], in *The Kingdom of Art*, p. 447. See also Cather's preface to Sarah Orne Jewett's *The Country of the Pointed Firs* (London: Jonathan Cape, The Travellers' Library, 1927).

21. *O Pioneers!*, Sentry Edition (Boston: Houghton Mifflin, 1941), pp. 20, 22. Further references will be included in the text.

22. The name "Moonstone" may have been suggested to Cather by Wilkie Collins's famous novel, *The Moonstone* (1868), whose plot revolves around the theft of a fabulous jewel. Cather's further use of moon imagery in the novel is discussed by Bernice Slote in *The Kingdom of Art*, pp. 96-103. As Slote points out on p. 86, Thea in Keats's "Hyperion" is "the tender spouse of gold Hyperion" (1. 95). They were deities of the sun and the moon. The jewel imagery is extended to another work of Cather's with an operatic heroine, "The Diamond Mine" (1916), in which Cressida Garnet is the treasure trove for her acquisitive relatives and her various husbands.

23. *The Song of the Lark*, new edition (Boston: Houghton Mifflin, 1943), pp. 10, 12. Further references are included in the text.

24. "Kroner" is also the root word for various Scandinavian coins bearing the imprint of a crown. And "Thea" is the generic name of a tropical Asiatic tree or shrub with large white or red flowers, usually solitary.

25. *My Ántonia*, Riverside Edition (Boston: Houghton Mifflin, 1949), pp. 1, 2. Further references are included in the text. The original preface to the 1918 edition was revised in 1926, deepening Jim's attachment to his memories of Ántonia by making the decision to record them his own, rather than a result of the talk with narrator-Cather.

26. Three important, full-length interpretations of Antonia as the subject of Jim Burden's shaping influence are Terence Martin's "The Drama of Memory in *My Ántonia*," *PMLA* 84 (March 1969): 304-11; William J. Stuckey's "*My Ántonia*: A Rose for Miss Cather," *Studies in the Novel* 4 (Fall 1972): 473-83; and Blanche H. Gelfant's "The Forgotten Reaping-Hook: Sex in *My Ántonia*," *American Literature* 43 (March 1971): 61-82.

Gelfant's essay is particularly significant not only in its reading of *My Ántonia* but in its penetrating analysis of Cather's fear of sex as revealed in her life and her fiction. No careful reader of Cather can fail to find Gelfant's thesis provocative and deep-going. She maintains that Jim Burden is an unreliable narrator because he is afraid of sex, that his memories and the various apparently unrelated vignettes in *My Ántonia* are evidence of his susceptibility to sexual fears. But Jim's aversion to sex, his turning away from whatever is unpleasant in his memories, does not negate the importance of his worldly achievements, which are cited in the book's introduction, for which Jim is not responsible, and which are manifest in the creation of the book itself, a work which, even under Gelfant's searching reinterpretation emerges as, in her words, "exciting — complex, subtle, aberrant" (p. 61). What I find significant, in this regard, in the succession of Cather's heroes and heroines from *Alexander's Bridge to The Professor's House* is that while they may reveal Cather's determination to avoid marriage or sex or disintegrative social obligations — all threats to her personal autonomy — they also acknowledge an obligation to society that transcends their creator's private abhorrence of that obligation.

Gelfant's thesis that Cather is obsessed with the need for autonomy and that she denies sex as a threat to this autonomy suggests a further observation: that for Cather and her main characters the creative act takes the place of the sexual act, and is often described in unmistakably sexual terms. In her story "The Namesake" Cather writes:

It was the same feeling that artists know when we, rarely, achieve truth in our work; the feeling of union with some great force, of purpose and security, of being glad that we have lived. For the first time I felt the pull of race and blood and kindred, and felt beating within me things that had not begun with me. It was as if the earth under my feet had grasped and rooted me, and were pouring its essence into me. I sat there until the dawn of morning, and all night long my life seemed to be pouring out of me and running into the ground. (*Willa Cather's Collected Short Fiction* [1982-1912], p. 146.)

In *The Song of the Lark* Cather describes young Thea, on the floor of her bedroom in the moonlight, as possessing the body of the artist, "pulsing with ardor and anticipation" (p. 177). Later, Thea's love for music is described in terms that suggest her virginity, and she will yield it only to herself: a man accosts her as she leaves a concert and she imagines a kind of conspiratorial rape is being attempted against her by "some power," but she resists, and determines to have her ecstasy all to herself (254-55). Still later, as the opera star Kronborg, we learn that "all that deep-rooted vitality flowered in her . . . like a tree bursting into bloom" (p. 571). Similar statements may be found throughout her work, especially in the early materials collected in *The Kingdom of Art*. The substitution of creative art for full sexuality is aberrant, perhaps, but of course ultimately felicitous. To paraphrase Faulkner, *My Ántonia* is worth any number of successful love affairs.

27.   For Cather's early praise of the western railroads for their comfort and elegance, see Cather, *The World and the Parish* II, ed. William A. Curtin (Lincoln: University of Nebraska Press, 1970), pp. 836-39.

28.   Both John H. Randall (*The Landscape and the Looking Glass*, p. 10)

and Evelyn Hinz ("Willa Cather's Technique and the Ideology of Populism," *Western American Literature* 7 [Spring 1972]: 47-61) find Populism an important influence upon Cather. A revisionist study of Populism, Norman Pollack's *The Populist Response to Industrial America* (Cambridge, Mass.: Harvard University Press, 1962), argues that Populism was not a retrogressive but a progressive movement that accepted the principles of industrialism and social change while it attacked the subjugation of the individual that resulted from capitalistic exploitation of industrialism. Pollack's thesis thus supports the view of Cather and technology argued herein.

29. David Stouck (*Willa Cather's Imagination*, p. 84) points out that, despite Cather's public statements that the original for Claude Wheeler was a cousin of hers killed in the war, she revealed in a letter to Dorothy Canfield Fisher that she had thought of Claude as herself.

30. See *The Kingdom of Art*, pp. 211-13. It is worth noting that Cather wrote several very appreciative reviews of Norris's novels in 1899 and 1900. See *The World and the Parish*, pp. 605-8, 702-3, 745-49.

31. *One of Ours*, Vintage Edition (New York: Random House, 1971), p. 84. Further references are included in the text.

32. "Two Novels of Willa Cather," rpt. in James Schroeter, ed., *Willa Cather and Her Critics* (Ithaca, New York: Cornell University Press, 1967), p. 28.

33. That Cather's perspective is ironic is the assumption of David Stouck in *Willa Cather's Imagination*, pp. 58-72. Stouck perceptively notes the ironic framing of Niel's viewpoint in the story, and my reading of the opening chapter generally parallels his own. Beyond that point, my analysis differs from Stouck's, which is a generic study of the novel as a "pastoral of experience," in focusing upon the historical and cultural significance of Niel's actions and upon the extent and danger of his delusions. Dorothy Van Ghent, in her *Willa Cather*, questions whether Marian Forrester is "only the corruption of an image in Niel Herbert's mind?" (p. 28). Bruce E. Miller, in "The Testing of Willa Cather's Humanism: *A Lost Lady* and other Cather Novels," *Kansas Quarterly* 5, (Fall 1973): 43-50, notes that Niel is unreliable where Marian Forrester is concerned because he is in love with her, a point which I shall expand upon later. Since I delivered this section on *A Lost Lady* at the April 1976 meeting of the Pacific Northwest American Studies Association, several other treatments of Niel's unreliability have appeared, the most recent of which is Anneliese H. Smith's, "Finding Marian Forrester: A Restorative Reading of Cather's *A Lost Lady*," *Colby Library Quarterly* 14 (December 1978): 221-25. Susan J. Rosowski offers important insights into Cather's treatment of past, present, and future in the novel in her "Willa Cather's *A Lost Lady*: The Paradoxes of Change," *Novel* 11 (Fall 1977): 51-62.

34. For Cather's problems with point of view in writing *A Lost Lady*, see Edith Lewis, *Willa Cather Living* (New York: Alfred A. Knopf, 1953), pp. 124-25.

35. Willa Cather, *A Lost Lady,* Library Edition (Boston: Houghton Mifflin, 1938), p. 3. Further citations will be included in the text.

36. See John D. Hicks, *The Populist Revolt* (Minneapolis: University of Minnesota Press, 1931), pp. 60-75.

37. E. K. Brown, Maxwell Geismar, and Leon Edel briefly question the romantic conception of the railroad aristocrats as pioneers in their treatments of the novel. While Geismar suggests that this may be due to the fact that we are seeing the captain through a child's eyes, Brown and Edel attribute the flaw to Cather herself. See Brown, "Willa Cather," *Yale Review* (1946), rpt. in James Schroeter, ed., *Willa Cather and Her Critics,* p. 78; Geismar, *The Last of the Provincials* (Boston: Houghton Mifflin, 1949), pp. 182-83; and Edel, "Willa Cather," in *Literary Lectures* (Washington: Library of Congress, 1973), pp. 353, 360.

38. Ironically, the overbuilding of the railroads in the late 1800s was one of the principal causes of the sorts of ruinous panics to which the captain's bank falls victim.

39. Quoted in Edward A. and Lillian D. Bloom's *Willa Cather's Gift of Sympathy* (Carbondale: Southern Illinois University Press, 1962), p. 105.

40. Cather's treatment of Louie Marsellus as anti-Semitic is argued by James Schroeter in his "Willa Cather and *The Professor's House.*" See Schroeter's *Willa Cather and Her Critics,* pp. 363-81.

41. The phrase is from Robert Warshow, to whom I am indebted for his analysis of the western film hero. See his "Movie Chronicle: The Westerner," *The Immediate Experience* (Garden City, N.Y.: Doubleday, 1962), p. 141.

42. Although it was written prior to the dropping of the atom bomb on Hiroshima, Cather, in a 1944 letter, had come to blame the scientists for bringing us to the edge of ruin. See Philip Gerber, *Willa Cather* (Boston: Twayne Publishers, 1975), p. 163.

4

Sherwood Anderson: Stilling the Machine

We Americans had got into that great empire, the middle west, mid-America, the real body of America, the great fat land stretching from the Appalachian Mountains to the Rockies, and had built our towns and cities. The land had opened slowly at first and then had come what we now call the "industrial revolution." The pace of life had been set by the horse, the ox, and the plow and now it was being set by the locomotive. Great trains roaring through the Ohio towns. On to the west! New towns and cities still to be made, to the west. Thomas Jefferson had died thinking it would take two hundred years to settle America and he had been dead but little more than a hundred years. Look at us go, boy!

Sherwood Anderson, *Memoirs*[1]

I live in a wide valley of cornfields and men and towns and strange, jangling sounds, and in spite of the curious perversion of life here, I have a feeling that the great basin of the Mississippi River, where I have always lived and moved about, is one day to be the seat of the culture of the universe.

Anderson, letter to Paul Rosenfeld[2]

THE Chicago of Frank Norris's final novel, *The Pit*, a roaring vortex of the powerful and potentially destructive forces of modern industrial capitalism, was to become an even more pervasive and compelling representation of the technological present in the works of Sherwood Anderson.[3] And if the wall railway map of California gives us the central symbol of *The Octopus*, a figure whose tentacles reached out to all corners of that western state, one had only to look at

170

the nation's transportation network as a whole to find the center of all lines converging in the great city at the foot of Lake Michigan. There, in the low, ramshackle buildings on South Fifty-seventh Street that had been hurriedly erected for the 1893 Exposition, Anderson was first to meet, in 1913, the members of Chicago's artistic and intellectual community and to sense the possibilities of a writer's career for himself. There, to Chicago, with neither Norris's or Garland's enthusiasm nor Cather's level-eyed purposefulness, come Anderson's fictional seekers, not always young, often only vaguely motivated, but on their way somewhere, to something. While indefiniteness comes to typify his novelistic figures, Anderson himself is to exhibit a remarkable coherence of tone toward them, an acceptance and understanding that may be seen to emerge from his firm sense of himself as the prototypical mid-American, one capable of expressing both the private and communal essence of his great western heartland, "the real body of America."

Anderson's formative years, as he was to repeat so compulsively throughout his writing, spanned the watershed moment of our history, the swift transition from rural agrarian to urban industrial nation. He was to see the decline of country life, was himself to feel the pull of Chicago and to become part of the steady movement toward the raw, new western cities. He was to write poignantly of the smudging of the bright dream of progress that had infused his boyhood. "Where did America go wrong?" "What can be done?" The yearning questions recur constantly and in various forms throughout his imaginative fiction, his essays, and his letters. More than any of the novelists represented here, more than any of his contemporaries, Anderson is to find his life spent in the answering of these questions. In doing so, he both insists upon and courts the appellation of autochthonous mid-American artist and representative man of his generation. " 'If you say the real American is not yet born, you lie. I am the type of fellow.' "[4] "I believe myself and have always thought of myself as a very typical American."[5] Virginia Woolf, noting Anderson's tendency to mesmerize himself into this self-mythicized state, finds in his actions a strategy for survival; in a shrill and ugly America, the writer can survive only "by being resolutely and defiantly American."[6] This dual image of artist and American — spokesman for the private and public self, the voice of the cornfield and the factory — Anderson was to find troublesomely self-contradictory, as might be expected. Yet he could disregard neither role. The double sense of himself impelled him throughout his career to attempt to redeem American lives — no less his own — from the chaotic displacement wrought by the triumph of shrieking industrialism over the quiet fields and villages of his youth.

Anderson was to find his emerging sense of himself as an American artist, more particularly as a *western* American artist, sharpened and clarified by the eastern intellectuals Waldo Frank and Van Wyck Brooks, who had enthusiastically welcomed the early publications of this unknown forty-year-old from the provinces beyond the Alleghenies. In response to their attention, as Walter B. Rideout has shown, Anderson, while he was to admit something of his own lack of sophistication in deference to the eastern intellectual establishment, was also to sense and assert that his western achievements were nevertheless possessed of their own kind of validity.[7] It was a self-conception that Garland and Cather understood well. Like Basil March, Ohio-born William Dean Howells's fictional spokesman in *A Hazard of New Fortunes*, Anderson is unable to suppress, among the most civilized Easterners, a sense of pride in his western roots. For Anderson, the greater crudity of his West, the ugliness of its cities, the graceless and confused lives of its people, were their own curious vindications of the significance of mid-America. Trailing clouds of glory but culturally and aesthetically impoverished, it simply *counted*, as the crowds of shoppers on New York's Fifth Avenue did not, as Waldo

Frank recalled, *count* to Anderson.[8] And although Anderson admired Henry Adams's *Education*, he would also insist that Adams and New England could not speak for his Westerners: "Nothing about us is as yet so completely and racially tired."[9] Half-critical of his native region, half-defiant on its behalf, Anderson finds in the uneasy conjunction of its silent cornfields and rumbling cities the appropriate setting for his own version of the new American. There, reflecting Anderson's drive toward reconciliation between these perverse oppositions, his hope for himself and his country, we find his fictional figures fashioning a characteristic pattern of striving in cadence to an industrial machine which they must somehow both reject and embrace.

To Chicago come Sam McPherson and "Beaut" McGregor, the young protagonists of his first two novels, *Windy McPherson's Son* (1916) and *Marching Men* (1917), and in that setting Anderson's warring attitudes toward the technological present were first to reveal something of their force and complexity. Both Sam and McGregor are brooding villagers who rise in the city along divergent lines of achievement. Sam McPherson becomes one of the "western giants of finance,"[10] and McGregor a powerful labor leader, but their accomplishments are less important in themselves than as manifestations of the compelling need for meaningful work in modern America that drives both men. In their heroic attempts to interpret and control the chaotic forces of modern urbanism Anderson asserts their role as distinctive new Americans. At the same time, their dynamic venturings threaten to wall them off from a society that they realize they cannot and must not disregard.

Windy McPherson's Son is thickly sown with the elements of Anderson's life: the youth in a small town in the midwestern cornfields, the boastful, convivial father, the exhausted and silent mother, the nickel-hustling boyhood, the drift to Chicago, the rise to success, the marital problems, the

"walkout" on business life — these were to become familiar
elements in Anderson's later works about himself, including
A Story Teller's Story, *Tar*, and the *Memoirs*. The book's
pervasive autobiographical cast again suggests the pattern of
duality — shaping artist and representative American —
that was to form the basis of Anderson's struggle with the
machine age. Structurally, the novel's four major sections
mark not only the chronological stages in Sam's life, from
rural Iowa boyhood, to Chicago, to the road, to a village on
the Hudson, but also the pattern of acceptance and rejection,
yearning and disgust, that was to characterize Anderson's
own attitudes toward his times.

After early success as a buyer of farm products (a success
based upon shrewd and ruthless treatment of his competitors),
Sam McPherson rises in the Rainey Arms Company in
Chicago, marries Sue Rainey, the boss's daughter, and
reflects in the glow of his achievements that "his station, his
wife, his country, his end in life, when rightly seen, was the
very apex of life on the earth, and to him in his pride it
seemed that he was in some way the master and maker of it
all" (191). This innocent euphoria is, of course, destined to
be undercut. The couple's hope for children, which was also
to have brought Sam back within the social orbit, must be
given up after Sue's several miscarriages. In a subsequent
fight for control of the Rainey Company, Sue leaves Sam
and her father commits suicide. The discouraged and
confused Sam becomes a wanderer, going forth "to seek
Truth, to seek God" (244). Sam McPherson as Truth Seeker
may indeed, as Wright Morris claims, strike the modern
reader as a foolish and outmoded figure, a self-justification
for his forty-year-old creator, but it is also a measure of
Anderson's conviction that his hero's search for place and
meaning in modern America life would serve to excuse what
even Anderson must have recognized would be regarded
from a realistic viewpoint as a rather clumsy and romantic
pilgrimage.[11]

Through Sam's business career Anderson dramatizes the perversion of values during a time when no achievement in America is so highly prized as financial gain. Sam is a representative leader out of America's heartland, the man thrown up by an acquisitive society as its acknowledged leader. But he is also depicted by his creator as blind and ignorant, an untrained master in an unworthy system, one of a group of men "who became what they were because the world offered them no better outlet for their vast energies."[12] The energies themselves command Anderson's sympathies. Even on the road as a vagabond, Sam finds that he must seek consequential action, "real work that would demand of him day after day the best and finest in him'" (263). The lethargy and aimlessness of his fellow wanderers is abhorrent to him. He is urged on by a conviction that there is a worthwhile role somewhere for him, and that he must find it. During the course of the novel, Sam experiences and turns away from nearly every phase of contemporary life: moneymaking and spending of all varieties, working at many kinds of manual labor, practicing social philanthropy, intervening in a labor dispute, at the same time attempting to root some prodigious truth out of each person he meets in his wandering. On the road he follows the practice of testing out each new idea that comes to him by immediately living it. At one point he envisions creating a city, "built for people, . . . independent, beautiful, strong, and free," but the vision is dispelled by a deeper doubt that society could be moved to share his desire for such a creation. And he must further acknowledge to himself that it is not for the people that he desires such a city, but for himself, as a heroic task to be done with his own hands (263-64). Still, he feels at times that all men and women, at bottom, must desire, as he does, a purposeful life (294). " 'I will find work. I will find work. I will seek Truth,' " Sam repeats obsessively, and his equation of *work* with *Truth* — *Truth* is also linked with *God* — is an index of the transcendent importance of finding one's right career in the new America (265, 221, 268).

Like Van Wyck Brooks, for whom Anderson was "the essence of the West"[13] and a harbinger of new literary possibilities from the American heartland, Anderson calls, through the searchings of Sam McPherson, for a new spirit in America to match the country's early promise. Aimlessly wandering in a strange midwestern city, Sam reflects upon the brutality and sordidness of his urban countrymen, thinking that " 'American men and women have not learned to be clean and noble and natural, like their forests and their wide, clean plains." The profligacy of American cities has produced only " 'disease and ill health and poverty, and hard brutal faces and torn, greasy finery' " (294-95). At the same time, the Andersonian hero, unlike Brooks, would not dismiss the pragmatic achievements of American technology. Sam admires the makers of machines, for example, for their purposeful achievements. The lives of workers in steel and iron are successful because they have found freedom to create (231).

But the gospel of progress and success carries with it the fear of failure that Sam cannot shake even after his decision to return to his wife and surrender his dreams of momentous enterprise to the obligations of a husband and father to the three children, abandoned by their mother, whom he has brought with him. The novel closes uneasily with Sam wondering to the last if he can force himself back into the social role which he has earlier rejected. Sam's turning away from heroic aspirations in favor of the little life of home and family in a town on the Hudson is the very essence of Andersonian pastoral, with its characteristic pattern of reconciliation and harmony, but the solution is so tenuous (Anderson rewrote the ending for a 1922 edition, but was still unable to impart any sense of authorial confidence to Sam's decision) that little can be made of it. Sam's fear, at last, that he has unfairly shifted to his children the obligation of his own uncompleted seeking leaves matters hanging unresolved, a pattern which is to become familiar in Andersonian endings.[14]

"Beaut" McGregor — nicknamed by a townsman for his extraordinary homeliness, of course, by what must pass in this land for a stroke of wit — also attempts to order his life according to some discovered truth. But while Anderson's first novel follows a circular, if inconclusive, pathway leading the hero back to the limited life of family and town, *Marching Men* travels in a straight line away from such a resolution. In doing so it provides us with a work that, particularly in the suggestiveness of its images, takes us directly to the center of Anderson's conflict with industrialism. Unlike Sam McPherson, McGregor possesses almost from the beginning an intimation of what he seeks; it is a vision of men acting together in massed order, thus overcoming the random meaninglessness of modern life. McGregor's dream begins as a reaction to the sordid disorder of Coal Creek, the mining town of his youth. His conviction drives him to the heart and source of industrial disorder, Chicago, where he becomes the leader of an army of workmen. Throughout his quest he rejects the sort of personal alternative that claims Sam McPherson; a farm in a peaceful vally, a business career, the love of women — all are put aside by McGregor in the pursuit of his shadowy vision of concerted action.

Marching Men presents a powerful dramatization of the need for a pure release of expressive energy. McGregor forms his army (that is to say his *machine*, as Lewis Mumford's exhaustive studies have made clear)[15] without any definite objective in mind, but as a counterforce to the disorder which has blighted modern urban life. Anderson is said to have conceived the idea for the book from his drill experiences in the National Guard and the Spanish-American War.[16] But the love of order and the controlled play of raw power — the rhythm and discipline of the machine — that is the book's most insistent theme is offset by a number of other elements which indicate something of the ambivalence of Anderson's response. To begin with, there is the difficulty raised by the relationship between McGregor, the leader or general, and his machine army. Are they merely the extension of his heroic or anarchic will? Is he the hero of a romance or a social novel?

That the man-swarm deserves to be organized only to destroy itself, a victim of McGregor's hatred and destructive impulses, is suggested early in the novel. Like Mark Twain's Hank Morgan, who organized — and destroyed — armies in *A Connecticut Yankee*, McGregor reveals to us that an inevitable outcome of converting men into agents of a larger purpose, a machine, is that *their* condition and the fate cease to be of any consequence. At one point in *Marching Men*, the generals of armies are depicted gloriously for their boldness in using human lives "with the recklessness of the gods";[17] that is, they are cosmic artists. At another point, they are condemned for selling their men out, using their armies' collective power to serve their own ends. We are told that the impulse toward order is bigger and more important than individual expression. If this is so, then the attractions of godlike power for Anderson's hero, who "expressed perfectly that pure brute force, the lust for which sleeps in the souls of artists" should be less compelling in the novel than they are (161). If McGregor is simply the necessary catalyst by which the latent energy of his marchers is channeled to some purpose, then what is that purpose, and why do they do nothing but march back and forth, here and there?

Although McGregor's army raises these sorts of questions in the reader's mind, he senses something of Anderson's fascination with the idea of a powerful machine — a human machine, an organic machine — which can substitute for the noisy clamor of the industrial panorama a purposeful silence. For the wordless McGregor forms his wordless army to march in awesome silence through the streets of Chicago. He is a "poet of movement," not words, as Anderson conceived of him.[18] The image is a potent one for Anderson.

At the time of *Marching Men*'s publication in 1917, Anderson was writing to Waldo Frank of the clamor and stridency which he felt had come to typify American life. Recalling his own boyhood in Clyde, Ohio, Anderson remarked: "I can remember old fellows in my home town speaking feelingly of an evening spent on the big, empty plains. It has taken the shrillness out of them. They had learned the trick of quiet. It affected their whole lives. It made them significant."[19] Anderson's recollections of these still townsmen of a stiller town, his condemnation of verbosity and noise as somehow symptomatic of what had gone wrong with America, his equation of personal meaning with a kind of inner quietude — these are more than voice-from-the-cornfield pronouncements to an admirer from among the New York intelligentsia. To Anderson's reader, these judgments indicate a central tension revealed clearly in *Marching Men* and the works to follow. Consider Anderson's depiction of noise and silence as the mirror opposite of Frank Norris's, for whom silence signaled the absence of the life-force, as sound corroborated its presence. Anderson's misgivings about the drift of modern America, his concern about the isolation of man from nature and from his fellow man, his aversion to noise — from the roaring of cities and factories on one level to the chatter of words and talk on another — are imagistically contrasted with his reverence for the psychic states associated with the natural world, with pastoral life, and with silence as a measure of inner significance. This tension is to assume major proportions in Anderson's depiction of the industrial dilemma.

The wordslingers in *Marching Men*, an advertising agent, a soapbox socialist, a reporter, are reduced to insignificance by the cornfield stillness of McGregor and the menacing silence of his men. Curiously, McGregor struggles up from ignorance to become a lawyer and he achieves his greatest triumphs — successfully defending an innocent man in a murder trial, commanding the massed Labor Day multitudes, electrifying an audience of workers in a dingy labor hall — through human speech. It is as though his language, forced and inelegant as it is, proceeds from so utter a conviction that it is a crude kind of poetry, and thus is spared Anderson's characteristic contempt for human speech. McGregor's addresses to the workers, in which "he was themselves become expressive" (213), suggest his affinity with the *Winesburg* artist-to-be George Willard, and define a more defensible creative role for McGregor than that of the celestial general with his human playthings. Still, as McGregor's shrewd nemesis from the establishment, David Ormsby, notes at the conclusion of the novel, " 'talk kills dreams, and talk will also kill all such men as McGregor. Now that he has begun to talk we will get the best of him' " (222).

The role of women in the machine age, which Anderson was to address directly some years later in *Perhaps Women* (1931), also forces its way into Anderson's burgeoning technological equation. In that later work, woman will be advanced as the biological antidote to the machine. Stronger than man because of her procreative mission, she may become humanity's best hope for resisting the machine, whose power is reducing men to impotence. In *Marching Men*, where the machine army is heroically drawn, women are viewed suspiciously as a kind of competing machine, a procreation trap which must be avoided by the hero. McGregor's apprehension over becoming a reproductive tool, a pawn in the ancient and aimless biological process (a fear that Anderson had already dramatized in his first novel) — is suggestively expressed in Anderson's linking of references to women and marriage to images of the hated coal mines of McGregor's youth. McGregor fears that marriage will compel him into a hole like that into which the beaten and dispirited miners of his birthplace, Coal Creek, are forced each day as they descend into the mines.[20] If these images are revealing in a Freudian context,

Anderson's depiction of the machine in *Marching Men* may also express itself in a larger, archetypal framework, in his powerful evocation of the subterranean gods of coal and fire, and in the intrusion of the figure of the giant. Coal Creek is repeatedly depicted as an industrial inferno, a hell of smoke, blackness, glaring fires, shaking of the earth, rumbling of coal cars. As coal is the trapped sun, the ominous dark body of that ancient source of life, so it is the evil genesis of all mechanical power that fuels McGregor's machine civilization. Men burrow in the earth for the coal to raise up the industrial age, and are in turn brutalized and degraded by it, as is suggested by the broken and dirty little houses of Coal Creek, the spiritless miners, the cries of a woman being beaten by her drunken husband, and of course by the depiction of Chicago, to which young McGregor moves from his native Coal Creek, as merely a monstrous Coal Creek, a "vast gulf of disorder," a wasteland of clattering cheapness (113). From a mythic perspective, the city, essentially a religious phenomenon in its earliest development, was the home of a god, and its walls were the means of holding chaos at bay.[21] But Chicago is a travesty of this. The industrial god, whose home is Chicago, is chaos himself, and the only unity lies outside the city, as Anderson reminds us, in the long straight rows of corn, whose lesson Chicago has forgotten. Against all this, McGregor may be seen as a version of the modern Prometheus, whose sacred gift to mankind is the consciousness that men hold within the potentiality of their massed action the mightiest machine of all, the means by which the enslaving god of industrialism might be overcome and brought to human service.

As Paul Ginestier points out in his *The Poet and the Machine*, the machine often plays a role analogous to that of the wicked giant of folklore. That is, one slip with this creature means death. "In humanity's great effort to snatch its well-being from nature, human blood must pay the price."[22] Anderson's later works will project this image of the giant to suggest this unleashed and arrogant power of the machine. In *Poor White* (1920), the "giant, Industrialism" — again reflecting Anderson's ambivalence in its depiction as "half-hideous, half-beautiful in its possibilities" — awakens and turns upon those who have aroused it.[23] Later, in "King Coal," Anderson writes of a mining town,

> "In the darkness the rows of coke ovens were like the glistening teeth of a giant. Something sleeping in the ground under the hills was being troubled . . . and was ill. The giant was being made to spew forth coal. . . .
>
> The black giant, disturbed in his sleep, has set forth and conquered. We all breathe his black breath."[24]

The figure of the giant in *Marching Men* is possessed of no tonal simplicity. Anderson's need, in the novel, to affirm a collectivistic human force more powerful than industrialism itself, leads him to attempt to invest McGregor's worker army with the qualities of a heroic giant, a personification of "huge, crude Old Labor" (204). Although this giant inspires terror, he does so only in the hearts of the rich and powerful. He is blind, he sleeps away the centuries, he is even without a brain, but aroused and marching he can shake the earth's foundations. " 'When you have marched until you are one giant body,' " McGregor tells his followers, " 'then will happen a miracle. A brain will grow in the giant you have made' " (214). Judging from the failure of McGregor's army to effect a change in history, it must be assumed that the giant remains brainless, and thus ominous in its suggestion of power without purposeful direction.

McGregor, a physical giant of a man himself, is an objectification of this shadowy metaphor. He is perceived as a benevolent giant by Margaret Ormsby, who represents the attractions of love and beauty for McGregor, but who recognizes his higher obligations: " 'We are children in the hands of this giant,' " she thinks as she watches McGregor address a crowd of workers (215). But the frightening possibility that the virtuous giant will suddenly transform himself into a wicked tyrant lies just below the surface. Anderson himself realized some years later, and with some chagrin, that what *Marching Men* had called for in the figure of McGregor was nothing less than a Hitler or a Mussolini.[25]

Looking beyond the troubling figure of the giant McGregor, David Ormsby, the plow manufactuer and rival for his daughter's affections with McGregor, is closer to the characteristic hero of Anderson's novels. Ormsby is no doctrinaire robber baron but a sensitive and thoughtful man who combines the exercise of industrial power with an active pursuit of culture, doubtless such a representative of the modern Higher Business as Anderson himself wished to be considered during his years as manufacturer in Elyria, Ohio. But Ormsby is a larger figure than that, for he improves upon the groping, functionless Sam McPherson of Anderson's first novel, and he anticipates a major new American, Hugh McVey of *Poor White*, in several important respects. He pursues, like Hugh, technological innovations that lessen the toil of the workers. As his daughter proudly says of him, " 'He makes plows...makes them well — millions of them. He doesn't spend his time talking....He works, and his work has lightened the labors of millions while the talkers sit thinking noisy thoughts' " (148). Although the proletarian mold of *Marching Men* requires that McGregor effectively oppose the plow maker, Ormsby is a significant addition to the ranks of new Americans whom Anderson creates to carry forward the visionary hope of the older America into the machine age.

From still another viewpoint, that of narrative technique, the reader may sense the trepidation with which Anderson encounters the machine in *Marching Men*. The book's closing chapters are particularly suggestive. There are Anderson's obvious difficulties in ending the book, with one apparent conclusion following another. There is the curious intrusion of the narrator in the final pages, admitting that he is "of two minds about the manifestation now called, and perhaps rightly, 'The madness of the Marching Men.' " On the one hand, it is "something unspeakably big and inspiring" (198); on the other hand, there is the narrator's attraction to little things, to the lives of ordinary people, the commuter who stands musing in his radish patch in the evening. While Anderson was to turn, in *Winesburg, Ohio* and in much of his most memorable fiction away from the great big ideas of *Marching Men* and toward the little soul in his radish patch, he would be unable to ignore the larger social implications of industrialism, and would find himself drawn back to them again and again in his work.

The paradoxical qualities of the organic and industrial worlds presented in *Windy McPherson's Son* and *Marching Men* reveal the knotted contrarieties within which Anderson found himself, and predict what will become his lifelong struggle with the machine. The admirable qualities of the natural and the human-centered world, beauty, love, individualism, creativity, and self-expression, are opposed by its propensities toward inconsequentiality, eccentricity, blandness, and escape into mindless sensation. The mechanical world asserts its power, force, speed, accomplishment, order, and sometimes a cold kind of beauty; but in exchange it produces ugliness, noise, and the dislocation of the individual from his surroundings, his work, and his fellow creatures. Within this welter of conflicting views, Anderson may be seen in the following years repeatedly shifting his authorial stance in an effort to synthesize the machine into some harmonious relationship with man and earth.

The publication of *Mid-American Chants* in 1918 marks another of Anderson's attempts to record the sense of dislocation in industrial America, and to fashion an appropriate response to it. This collection of forty-nine loosely strung poems, intended to follow in the tradition of Whitman and Sandburg, distills the oppositions present in the two preceding novels between city and countryside, between industrialism and an earlier time of faith and brotherhood. Here for the first time Anderson strongly asserts his "mid-Americanism," not only to verify his bardic credentials but also to provide himself a suitable metaphor for his role as reconciler of a fragmented people. And in speaking to us as a *poet*, for the first time, Anderson obviously intended to tap a source of ultimate power that he consistently accords poetry and the poet. *Marching Men*, for example, should have been, as Anderson saw it later, "a great epic poem," and McGregor, "a man really inspired, a poet;"[26] and throughout his work Anderson attributes only to the poet the gift of infallible truth-telling. In his foreword, Anderson admits that his work may be premature: "I do not believe that we people of mid-western America,...hurried and harried through life by the terrible engine — industrialism — have come to the time of song. To me it seems that song belongs with and has its birth in the memory of older things than we know."[27] And yet, because the need and the desire for song is strong in the American midlands, the poems are offered as the introduction states: "Here we stand in roaring city streets, on steaming coal heaps, in the shadow of factories from which come only the grinding roar of machines. We do not sing but mutter in the darkness. Our lips are cracked with dust and with the heat of furnaces" (7-8).

The *Mid-American Chants* sharply focus their creator's attitudes toward the technological present, and unmistakably assert a strong impulse toward reconciliation among people, a desire to return to the old gods of fields and farms in order to carry their lesson to the suffocating city dwellers. Anderson's opening chant, "The Cornfields," expresses these themes:

In the darkness of the night I woke and the bands that
bind me were broken. I was determined to bring old
things into the land of the new. A sacred vessel I found
and ran with it into the fields, into the long fields where
the corn rustles.

All of the people of my time were bound with chains.
They had forgotten the long fields and the standing
corn. They had forgotten the west winds. (11)

Although the *Chants* generally fail to translate Anderson's
ideas into memorable language, they illustrate his continuing
experimentation with form and idiom, and his attempts to
heal those divisive dislocations caused by the industrial
juggernaut. As in *Marching Men*, a new American steps
forward to galvanize his countrymen into action against the
chaos that surrounds them. More so than McGregor the
taciturn general, the singer of *Mid-American Chants* expresses
the note of human brotherhood ("In the disorder and
darkness of the night, in the wind and the washing waves, I
shout to my brothers — lost in the flood. . . . We have to find
each other" [17-18]). But neither figure moves confidently
toward any recognizable goal.

The singer of the *Chants* who must return to the quiet
fields beyond Chicago to relearn the forgotten lesson of the
corn suggests the figure of the poet-as-youth, George Willard,
of Anderson's masterwork, *Winesburg, Ohio*, published in
1919, the year following the *Chants*. The "Revolt from the
Village" label which *Winesburg* wore during the years
following its publication is scarcely noticed today. A
characteristic 1919 review claimed that the book would
"shatter forever what remains of the assumption that life
seethes most treacherously in cities and that there are sylvan
retreats where the days pass from harvest to harvest like the
idylls of Theocritus."[28] It remained for V. F. Calverton,
Maxwell Geismar, and others to correct the book's early
reputation; and today it seems clear that Anderson turned

back, in *Winesburg*, to the cornfields and the village of his youth because it represented the only sort of ordered, natural world where love and communication were even possible. Throughout his career the return to the village, not the revolt from it, was to become the characteristic journey of Anderson's idealized self.

In the setting of *Winesburg*, the fields and farms and the simple round of town life, are to be found the sources of the book's undeniable evocation of lost goodness. Through the setting is expressed the essential unity of country life, linked to the natural cycle of crops, to the weather, and the slow turning of the seasons. Here is a world organic and yet impervious to time. Its calmness and stillness indicate the silence of self-sufficiency, full of promise and significance.

Balanced against this green world are threatening, disintegrative forces. Implicitly, there is the city, which stands on the horizon of Winesburg's scenes and events, an emblem of irresistible progress and of little-understood forces that threaten to alter forever the life of the town. Like Auden's personification of time, the city "watches from the shadows/ And coughs when you would kiss." It has attracted the smart young village boys like Ned Currie, and it has turned back queer souls like Enoch Robinson and Doctor Parcival, just as it has accepted only the perfect, uniform apples from the Winesburg orchards, which "have been put in barrels and shipped to the cities where they will be eaten in apartments that are filled with books, magazines, furniture, and people. On the trees are only a few gnarled apples that the pickers have rejected. . . . Only the few know the sweetness of the twisted apples."[29]

These grotesques, unfit for the city, provide an explicit counterforce to the natural self-sufficiency of the setting, from which they are cut off almost as completely as from the great world on the horizon. The silence of many of them, while it is a measure of their twisted "sweetness," their significance, is not the purposeful silence of their surroundings. Rather, it is a threatening muteness, stretched taut over a tremendous pressure to communicate. While they are likely to remain almost wordless until the moment at which they attempt to reveal their truth, a few, at the other extreme, sputter uncontrollably, talking feverishly to anyone who will listen, like Joe Welling, in "A Man of Ideas," who cannot restrain himself when caught up in one of his schemes: "Words rolled and tumbled from his mouth. . . . Pouncing upon a bystander he began to talk" (103). Doctor Parcival, in "The Philosopher," is another compulsive talker, who watches from his office window until George Willard is alone in the newspaper office where he works, then hurries in to tell the boy his tales. Later, in self-disgust he says, "What a fool I am to be talking" (154). Elizabeth and Tom Willard illustrate the two sorts of verbal aberration in uneasy conjunction; indeed, as in *Windy McPherson's Son*, the characterization of the young hero's parents parallels Anderson's published recollections of his own mother and father — the mysterious, dark-haired, silent mother and the boastful, pretentious father.

The common failing of all the grotesques is suggested in the plight of Enoch Robinson, in "Loneliness," who "wanted to talk, but he didn't know how" (169).[30] Thus both the mute grotesques and the sputtering grotesques manifest a sickness that is in conflict with the quiet benignity of the setting. The verbal incapacity of these figures who cannot love, who cannot draw sustenance from their surroundings, is suggestive of their crippling inner wound.

George Willard, in whom the grotesques find the opportunity for verbal release is, in a sense, the *genius loci* of the Winesburg landscape, the attendant spirit of the town. He is also a synecdoche for the village itself, standing expectantly between innocence and experience, youth and maturity, rural past and urban future. At the end of the book, filled with vague dreams, he is inevitably drawn to the city where, having finally immersed himself in that destructive element, he promises to become the hoped-for connector between the failed souls of forgotten America and the great world, the artist who, as Edwin Fussell says, will become the spokesman for all of the grotesques, whose "fragmentary wisdom" he now possesses.[31]

Anderson's faith in "the lesson of the corn," which led him, in *Winesburg*, to turn, for a time, from what he had come to regard as the shrillness and disorder of industrialism back to the country town of his youth, was, in an important sense, a valid apprehension. The book is, in terms of Anderson's conflict with the technological present, a portrait of a town in a condition of arrested preexperience personified in George Willard, a new American in the chrysalis stage. But although *Winesburg* delineated the qualities of village life against which the technological and urban present might measure itself, Anderson moved toward a less oblique commentary on his age in his formulation of *Poor White* (1920). "The new novel," he wrote to friends, "will, I hope, build up the country about Winesburg, sweep Winesburg into the modern industrial life." "We've got a new people now. . . .Our life in our factory towns intensifies. It becomes at the same time more ugly and more intense."[32] If *Poor White* seems to ignore the formalistic discoveries of *Winesburg*, to fall again into the trap of "thinking big" in its attempt to represent the entire technological revolution in the American Middle West, it is also further evidence of its author's compelling need to address the contemporary implications of industrialism. In whatever directions Anderson's artistic abilities lay, *Poor White* has nevertheless come to be recognized as one of the major novels of the period of the technological takeover, a work of primary cultural importance as well as a significant literary achievement.

The figure in whom Anderson embodies this age of transition, Hugh McVey, is partially drawn from among the makers of machines admired by Sam McPherson in Anderson's first novel and the taciturn, purposeful plow maker, David

Ormsby, of *Marching Men*. Like the three protagonists in
Windy, *Marching Men*, and *Winesburg*, McVey has something
of the dreamer and poet about him; like them he moves from
country to city in response to an insistent urge. At this point,
George Willard's story stops; and even were it to be carried
into his maturity there is the question with Anderson, as
with Norris and Sinclair Lewis, whether the artist-hero
possesses the worldly significance to shape or direct the
urban machine. The three "Macs," McPherson, McGregor,
and McVey — did Anderson mean to suggest the amalgam
of national types, doer and dreamer, as well as the hopeful
possibilities of a newer generation ("Mac" as "son of"), in
these Scotch-Irish surnames? — all move into maturity and
the new century. Sam McPherson is too closely involved
with the industrial machine to effect any more creative
response to its threatening rhythms than either surrender or
revolt. He fails to find "real work" in his own time, and his
personal compromise at the conclusion of the novel begs its
most insistent questions. McGregor possesses the requisite
vision and the quiet forcefulness to lead us out of the
mechanical muddle, but the sense of order to which he
aspires fails to define itself in objective action. The marching
goes nowhere, and the gigantic figure of McGregor dissolves
into fable at last, transubstantiated into mist as he prepares to
harrow the metropolis.

Hugh McVey, however, has McGregor's gifts of silence
and isolation and other virtues as well. He is, above all, a
technocrat, an inventor who understands and creates the
machinery that defines his age, although he is paradoxically
bewildered by the new forces unleashed by his creations. In
addition, he is possessed of a larger social conscience than
the labor giant. His period of roaming as a young man
through the Midwest is motivated by an insistent hunger for
community, a search for "the right place and the right
people."[33] The city does not attract him, as a young man. His
two hours between trains in Chicago, in which time he walks

the streets, are an Andersonian distillation of the city as nightmare: "a roaring, clanging place. . .thousands of people rushing about like disturbed insects. . .whirling churning mass of humanity. . . .men swore, women grew angry, and children cried. . .cab drivers shouted and roared. . . .the rush of people. . . .came in waves as water washes along a beach during a storm. . .a pall of black smoke covered the sky" (30-31). Frightened and bewildered, Hugh flees the city. But the town of Bidwell, Ohio, in which he settles with the belief that it offers the human companionship which he has sought, will be transformed by the "giant, Industry," that lengthened shadow of himself, into something closer to Chicago than to the peaceful village that has attracted him.

Even after reaching Bidwell, Hugh remains an outsider, his quiet shyness and reserve marking him among the townpeople as a "deep one." "His silence made it possible for the people. . .to let their minds take hold of something they thought was truly heroic" (118). In his loneliness and his wish to expunge what he has been taught to regard as his shiftlessness, a propensity for daydreaming, he turns to his innate mechanical and mathematical abilities and begins making drawings and plans for machines. There is no thought of conventional success or hopes for wealth in Hugh's tinkering. Rather, his efforts to overcome his tendencies toward brooding and idleness have combined with a compassionate wish to help free the farm hands, whom he has watched at their work in the fields, from their exhausting stoop labor. His first invention, a cabbage-planting machine, is born out of a moment of compassion for the workers, "stooped misshaped figures crawling slowly along. . . . wriggling. . .like grotesquely misshapen animals" (77). As George Willard promises to transfigure the grotesques of Winesburg through the medium of his art, thus rendering them human once again, Hugh McVey would lift the burden of physical labor from his distorted villagers, enabling them to rise erect as men and women. Hugh's inventions are thus a means of communication from their introverted, yearning creator to his fellows, an iron gift to humanity from an inarticulate lover.

But McVey's inventions do not break down the walls that separate him from the townspeople. Instead his creations are appropriated by sharp promoters, and Hugh is caught up in a series of bewildering changes that attend the mechanical age. A new force is abroad, "meant to seal men together, to wipe out national lines, to walk under seas and fly through the air, to change the entire face of the world in which men lived" (60). The obverse of these bright depictions of progress is acted out in the town of Bidwell, as factories are built, young men of the town and its surrounding farms are hired as workers, the town's shopkeepers greedily invest their savings into the new ventures, and a class of speculators and fast-talkers arises as the new controllers of Bidwell's destiny. The industrial "giant," "the terrible new thing, half hideous, half beautiful in its possibilities" walks the land, while "thought and poetry died" (60-61). Anderson's symbolic depiction of industrialism, when it is not the ambiguous giant, is openly malevolent. It is a "mad awakening," in which we are meant to question the disapprobation of Hugh's adolescent, dreaming state; it is a clamor of millions of voices, terrible and confusing; the industrial cities are dimly lit houses with dark walls separating the inhabitants; or the cities are lightless and colorless stones of drabness cast upon the land; the coming of industrialism is a flooding river that destroys towns and forests and drowns men and children; it is a storm, with blackened sky, black clouds of dust, and furious wind and rain (129, 62, 112, 358, 28-29, 109-12). Particularly in these latter images, we find industrialism represented in terms of a violent and far-reaching aberration in nature, a cosmic disharmony which reflects, as surely as the storm in *King Lear*, the chaotic disarray of right human relationships on earth.

The inventions by which Hugh McVey becomes a figure

of consequence in the new age, one who has found his role, who can "express himself wholly in work" (69), are also the means by which the town's craftsmen, such as Joe Wainsworth, the harness maker, are rendered useless, severed from any meaningful relationship to their work. Anderson, who saw the love of life as a product of honest materials lovingly wrought, repeatedly characterized himself in his autobiographical writings as a craftsman, also:

> I had accepted my passion for scribbling as one accepts the fact that the central interest of one's whole being lies in carving stone, spreading paint upon canvas, digging in the earth for gold, working the soil, working in wood or in iron. The arts are after all but the old crafts intensified."[34]

Never a systematic thinker, Anderson reveals himself most meaningfully in those images and words which characteristically cluster about his subjects, and it is significant that the terms that accompany his description of the machine (for example, *shrieking, whistling, screaming, roaring, clatter, whirl, screech, speed, flying, hurry, tension,* etc.) are esentially those for the city (*disorder, roaring, crowded, whirling, churning, clatter,* etc.). The likeness is not surprising considering that the modern city is the ultimate product of machine civilization. But what is striking is how these associations, so related to those Andersonian villains of noise and rapid activity, contrast with the words and images accompanying a subject such as craftmanship to which Anderson gives unwavering homage. There we find *surface, sensual, texture, smell, touch, eyes, ears, nose, fingers, world of nature, hesitatingly, lovingly, alive, feeling, natural, real, true, slow, glad, loved, religious, old, small* — terms grounded in the senses, in pleasurable emotions, and natural objects. The associations illustrate an important feature of Anderson's style: the tendency to link virtuous and admirable qualities, persons, events, with natural rather than artificial or mechanistic terminology.[35] And we understand again something of

Anderson's dilemma over his craft-destroying hero in *Poor White*. The sacrifice of Joe Wainsworth to Hugh McVey's new America was deeply troubling to Anderson and is so revealed not only in the ending of *Poor White* but in the jumble of conflicting attitudes toward industrialism that he was to exhibit in the years to come. Hugh McVey is himself, indeed, a craftsman of sorts, a designer and builder in the materials of the new age, but his artistry in technology differs in two crucial ways from the craftsmanship that Anderson praised. First, Hugh's work, by its very nature, is destructive of other crafts and craftsmen, a denial of the life and work of one's fellow artisans. Second, the craftsman of the machine must deny his own part in his creation, just as the worker who operates it must do. As Lewis Mumford points out,

> In handicraft it is the worker who is represented: in machine design it is the work. In handicraft, the personal touch is emphasized, and the imprint of the worker and his tool are both inevitable: in machine work the impersonal prevails, and if the worker leaves any tell-tale evidence of his part in the operation, it is a defect or a flaw.[36]

Anderson underscores this divorce of the technological craftsman from his creations in Hugh's inability to influence or control his machines once the original prototypes leave his hands. After that, they become as impersonal as money and are as freely bartered and "managed" by the promoters and bankers.

How can we know the dancer from the dance? Anderson faced serious artistic and personal difficulties in attempting to separate his sorcerer's apprentice Hugh McVey from the system which he has helped to pioneer. Hugh's consolation that he has relieved the field workers of their exhausting labors seems to lack real conviction, and does not appease the bone-wisdom within him that remains convinced of a primal fault somewhere within the giant Industry. And even the field-hands-turned-factory-hands mock his ameliorative conclusions when they are overheard by Hugh complaining about the drudgery and ugliness of their new jobs and lives. Uncomprehendingly, Hugh is pulled increasingly into the orbit of those opportunists like Steve Hunter and Tom Butterworth (whose rebellious daughter, Clara, Hugh marries) who use his inventions to exploit their townsmen, rather than being drawn closer to the craftsmen and workers with whom he had sought companionship. Authorial praise of McVey as a latter-day folk hero is similarly troublesome:

> All men lead their lives behind a wall of misunderstanding they themselves have built, and most men die in silence and unnoticed behind the walls. Now and then a man, cut off from his fellows by the peculiarities of his nature, becomes absorbed in doing something that is impersonal, useful, and beautiful....Men and women stop their complaining about the unfairness and inequality of life, and wonder about the man whose name they have heard. (221)

But the reign of wonder is brief. The walls of misunderstanding do not fall away; the unfairness and inequality go on. The figure of McVey, "something a little inhuman....a man almost gigantic in his bigness" (274), reaches its paradoxical apogee in the scene when, in the cabbage field at night, he attempts to translate the movements of the workers setting the plants into a problem of mechanical design, swinging his arms stiffly up and down and acting out the part of the new machine (80). As an Andersonian hero, McVey as Mr. Mechano is virtually impossible, and the necessity of humanizing him becomes more insistent as the novel progresses. Clara Butterworth reflects both Anderson's dilemma and his strategy for distancing Hugh from his machines. Clara is alternately attracted and repelled by the inventor hero. At first she accepts him for his silent, purposeful commitment to his goals. But after their marriage she rejects him for his part in the destruction of the old craftsmen like Joe Wainsworth. Then, when Wainsworth finally attacks Hugh in a murderous fit, Clara undergoes a sudden reversal of feeling — the maternal instinct, we are told; she is carrying their child — and springs to Hugh's defense, casting Wainsworth aside. The depiction does not go far in solving the larger problem with which Anderson was struggling. Clara's final acceptance of Hugh is made instinctive, as naturalistic as McTeague's inner beast — "within her arose the mother, fierce, indomitable" (360) — rather than rationally convincing.

Anderson's other technique for humanizing McVey is to submerge him, imagistically, into the natural world insofar as is possible. Clara, we learn, trusts Hugh because he is "like the things most grateful to her own nature, the sky seen across an open stretch of country or over a river that ran straight away into the distance. . . . He was, she decided, very like a horse; an honest, powerful horse" (248). Later, she thinks of Hugh's work in an organic metaphor of growth: "The figure of the farm hand Jim Priest working in a field of corn came to her mind. 'The farm hand works,' she thought, 'and the corn grows. This man sticks to his task in his shop and makes a town grow" (262). Near the conclusion of the novel, Hugh is moved to contemplation by some brightly colored stones that he has found and put into his pocket. For a moment, we are told, "he became not an inventor but a poet," and that a change within him, a rejection of the industrial world, had begun. But he cannot secede so easily from his age. His musings are set against the conversation of a man who plans to send his son to college to study mechanical engineering or business and who voices the truths that Anderson and his fictional hero must both painfully acknowledge for themselves: " 'It's a mechanical age and a business age. . . . I want him to keep in the spirit of the times' " (358). And as Hugh's mind plays with the image of the colored stones as a "poet," he also realizes that pleasing thoughts will not help him solve a patent problem with a rival inventor.

The concluding pages of *Poor White* deepen this ambivalence. As in *Windy McPherson's Son*, husband and wife are reunited in the promise of children; problems are set aside to allow for a tentative, closing domestic idyll, another characteristic pastoral resolution. Once again, Anderson's drive toward reconciliation led him to a hopeful rather than a despairing conclusion, a separate but troubled peace with the age. In the final sentences Hugh and Clara stand together late at night outside the Butterworth farmhouse when, above the sounds of the sleeping farm hand and the stirring of farm animals, "arose another sound, a sound shrill and intense, greetings perhaps to an unborn Hugh McVey. For some reason, perhaps to announce a shift in crews, the factories of Bidwell that were engaged in night work set up a great whistling and screaming" (363). Whistles shrieking in the middle of the night, overcoming the sounds of organic life, ring in Hugh's ears as a final reminder of a time-ridden age, a compelling new tempo of existence that responds to mechanistic rather than human impulses and that implacably resists integration into Anderson's scheme of things.

In the early and mid-1920s, the middle years of Anderson's career, his work has typically come to be characterized as primitivistic in theme and attitude. There are his famous short stories of the racetracks, collected in *The Triumph of the Egg* (1921) and *Horses and Men* (1923), and his novels, *Many Marriages* (1923), *Dark Laughter* (1925), and the autobiographical *Tar* (1926), all of which treat primitivistic materials, including the life of the senses, nature, childhood, sexuality, the unconscious, and, for Anderson and the 1920s, the Negro. But Anderson's use of these materials is, for the most part, uncharacteristic of primitivism, in which the crucial element is a total rejection of civilization, usually through escape from it. Rather, the writer's representative stance in these works continues to be a struggle toward resolution between the hero and a threatening society. If there is rejection or escape, it is typically undertaken so that the individual can somehow bring himself to cope with an inescapable and complex urban present. The central meaning of Anderson's track stories "I Want to Know Why," "I'm a Fool," and "The Man Who Became a Woman" is an awareness of a certain disillusionment not with the natural life of the track, the sights, sounds, and smells, the thoroughbreds, the trainers, and the "niggers," but with the first-person narrator's *place* in such a life. The racing world, caught in its own sensual music, is lost to the narrator and his audience. The direction of all of these stories is toward a letting go of the dream of escape. The autobiographical *Tar: A Midwest Childhood*, also concerned with the gulf between childhood innocence and later maturity, similarly recreates the sensations and feelings of an earlier world while dramatizing the impossibility of remaining within it.

But if the racetrack stories and *Tar* correct the notion that one can hope to linger forever in fields of clover, *Many Marriages* and *Dark Laughter* reject the opposite view that one must deny the sensual life entirely while upholding respectable appearances. Both novels concern a familiar Andersonian situation, men in their mid-thirties, one an ex-reporter turned factory hand, the other a manufacturer of washing machines, disillusioned with marriages and seeking a more honest and instinctive love relationship. In *Dark Laughter*, the principal figure, Bruce Dudley, learns from a fellow worker, "Sponge" Martin, who manages to assert a sense of individuality in his personal life and to practice a kind of craftsmanship even at his wheel-varnishing job in the factory, how to keep industrial pressures at bay. Although gestures of revolt are at the center of each work, both heroes assert the need for *purpose* in life, and both move toward a more hopeful future with their new mates. It is an escape in each case, but an escape to, as well as from. The first destination in both cases is Chicago, not Tahiti, and a dominant imagistic figure in both works is that of cleansing, purifying, rebuilding one's *house*, which suggests not a mindless pursuit of sensations for both men but a purposeful, *Walden*-like response to the examination of their own lives. "This isn't pagan world. It is a world of machines," wrote Anderson later,[37] as if in answer to the specious appeal of pure escape, nut-brown maidens, and fingers instead of forks. As in all of Anderson's heroes, there is in both men, but especially in the dreaming manufacturer of *Many Marriages*, an essential buried self, a figure of worth, of true potentiality, which demands release and expression. Before these new Americans can find their appropriate work, Anderson seems to be saying, their repressed selves must be released, and having seen this accomplished both novels stop.

During this same period in the early and middle 1920s, Anderson was to reveal some of his darkest antagonisms toward the machine. In *A Story Teller's Story* (1924), he predicted a victory of the workers against their machine oppressors,[38] a notion perhaps suggested earlier in Joe Wainsworth's attack upon the mechanists in *Poor White*. In his *Notebook* (1926), Anderson is again the occasional Luddite, quoting approvingly Gilbert Cannan's foreboding prediction: " 'Befoul the workman's tools and materials long enough . . . and in the end the workman will turn on you and kill you.' "[39] Anderson's second volume of poems, *A New Testament* (1927) includes a bitter excoriation of the "Half-Gods," those caught up in the mechanical age who have allowed it to turn them into subhuman automata.[40] And yet these same works often indicate his characteristic unwillingness to remain at odds with the prevailing experience of his time, his refusal to yield to the forces that would alienate him from his country. A *Notebook* passage, for example, calls for an acceptance of industrial life, however ugly:

> There is something approaching insanity in the very idea
> of sinking yourself too deeply into modern American
> industrial life. . . . But it is my contention that there is no
> other road. If a man would avoid neat slick writing he
> must at least attempt to be brother to his brothers and live
> as the men of his time live. He must share with them the
> crude expression of their lives. (200)

Here again Anderson acknowledges that his direction as an
American artist must lie along the common road.

Anderson's life in the American South, where he moved in
the mid-1920s, is marked by a new series of attempts to
assimilate the machine. He was attracted to the South for a
variety of personal reasons, not the least of which was his
need to search out a region indifferent to frenzied commerce.
But while agrarian values and ways were still evident in the
hill country, in the valley towns great cotton mills were
drumming a new pulse into their workers' lives. Indeed, the
presence in the South of pastoral hill life concurrent with a
recently emerging industrialism may have been particularly
stimulating to Anderson in these later years, when the
machine had already long since won the day in his native
Midwest.

Anderson had no part in the group led by John Crowe
Ransom, Allen Tate, Robert Penn Warren, and Donald
Davidson which became the Southern Agrarians, but he
shared similar attitudes with them on some issues. The
Agrarians claimed in their 1930 manifesto, *I'll Take My Stand*,
what Anderson had established earlier, that industrialism
had given neither pleasure nor security to the worker: "his
labor is hard, its tempo is fierce, and his employment is
insecure."[41] What Anderson had praised in the honest
relationship between the old craftsman and his materials,
the Agrarians extolled in the South's disappearing intrinsic

arts — "in ballads, country songs and dances, in hymns and spirituals, in folk tales, in the folk crafts of weaving, quilting, furniture-making."[42] The Agrarians' description of the ceaseless attempts by southern chambers of commerce to import blighting industries recalls Anderson's personification of King Coal with his "vanguard of Rotary Club members . . . breathing his black breath over greater and greater stretches of green country."[43] But above all, Anderson and the Agrarians shared a spiritual vision of modern man's need for a harmonious relationship with the earth. Unwilling to turn his back upon the industrial present, Anderson could nevertheless accept the conclusion of Donald Davidson of the Agrarians who wrote that "only in an agrarian society does there remain much hope of a balanced life, where the arts are not luxuries to be purchased but belong as a matter of course in the routine of . . . living."[44] Anderson wrote to a friend of his interest in *I'll Take My Stand*, shortly after its publication, but his plebian assumptions, he later reveals, ran counter to what he saw as reactionary tendencies in many Southerners, including Ransom. "He [is] so damned softly and gently superior that it makes me want to shout, 'Balls.' "[45]

If it was the easy pace of the Southern hill country that attracted Anderson to begin with, it was the South's recent industrialization to which he responded most fully as an artist during the 1930s. And his responses are to reveal still different accents and attitudes toward technology than have been evident in the past. Anderson's early works, as has been seen, present a range of tentative but uneasy responses to the machine age: the bewilderment of *Windy McPherson's Son*, the authoritarian appeal of *Marching Men*, the cry for brotherhood of *Mid-American Chants*, the threatened pastoralism of *Winesburg, Ohio*, the attempted humanizing of the machine maker in *Poor White*, the rejection of the dream of escape in the 1920s. Anderson's continuing attempt to posit still new responses to the technological present during the thirties is convincing testimony to the seriousness with which he accepted his role as communal artist, as well as to his unending ordeal with the machine, his inability to either accept it or leave it alone.

Most notable among these new attempts to encompass the machine are Anderson's experiments in celebrating it as a new aesthetic experience, allowing its characteristics to determine and shape a new style, in the manner of the European Futurists and Dadaists and of Hart Crane's innovations here in America. Anderson's letters during the early months of 1930 are full of enthusiasm for his new efforts to feel and reproduce the "whirl and wonder of modern high-speed machinery and...what it is doing to people." He speaks of the "beauty and poetry of the machine" and believes that this field is "vast and full of strange poetry and significance. I believe I have got hold of something that will keep me happy and busy the rest of my life."[46] A product of this new enthusiasm is his "Machine Song" ("Written at Columbus, Georgia, in a moment of ecstasy born of a visit to a cotton mill") in which Anderson chants a rather frenzied paean to the mill, to "the song of it, the clatter of it, the whurrr, the screech, the hummmmm, the murmur, the shout of it,"[47] as he attempts to find an appropriate new vehicle to express the technological marvels of the new age, to pump new and propitious meanings into those old Andersonian atrocities — noise and ceaseless activity. Perhaps the more sophisticated technology of the modern cotton mills, something of an advance over the roar and grind of the primitive heavy industry of the past, would allow itself to be shaped into a "song," into "the singing machines, the shouting dancing machines!" of a new vision.[48] At the same time, Anderson confesses that the poet in him is sick of his former self that rejected the machine and his own times.[49]

This newfound resolution to celebrate the machine is accompanied by increased interest in the daily lives of the men and women who tend them. Magazine pieces such as "Factory Town," as well as his two final novels, *Beyond Desire* (1932) and *Kit Brandon* (1936), and the essays collected in *Perhaps Women* (1931) and *Puzzled America* (1935), reveal Anderson's attempts to humanize the machine not, as in *Poor White*, through a depiction of the life of its creator but through a sympathetic study of the lives of its workers.[50] During this time Anderson will even attempt to revive the deflated dream of *Poor White* that the machine will free people from toil. In a letter to two dramatists Anderson tentatively outlines a projected play, what would be a new *Poor White*, about man's hope for the machine, opening with the figure of a jerky, mechanistic, McVeylike man in a potato field planning his potato-digging machine while the field workers, fascinated and repelled by this strange figure, alternately move toward and away from him. (The play is to open, inevitably, with "a grey blanket of sound . . . .maybe factory whistles, . . .police sirens, etc.") But to all of this familiar Andersonian ambivalence is to be added a more hopeful conclusion: "With this start might not we go on and develop the whole thing as the story of man's making of the machine, then his struggle with it, the coming victory proclaimed?"[51] Still, one notes wryly the assured strokes with which Anderson sketches out the early action depicting the machine dilemma, while the victory is advanced only as a question.

At the heart of Anderson's new determination to acclimate himself to the technological present is the necessity, recognized most insistently in *Perhaps Women*, for the acceptance of a new mythology, in brief, a machine-God. The image of the machine as new God, a final apotheosis of the ambivalent machine-giant or King Coal metaphor of the earlier works, is explored tentatively in *Poor White*, wherein the old farmers who raised their arms "supplicating the gods for fair days" are replaced by the townsman who has an urge to kiss the legs of Hugh McVey's new machine, or like

Henry Adams before the dynamo, to kneel before it and say a prayer.[52] In *Perhaps Women*, Anderson faces the problem squarely:

> Will you take the new life? Will you take the factories, the inside and the outside of the factories, as once you took rivers, fields, grassy slopes of fields?
> Will you take the blue lights inside of factories at night as once you took sunlight and moonlight? . . .
> Will you live, or die?
> Will you accept the new age?
> Will you give yourself to the new age?   (17)

Unable, like Adams, to hold off the dilemma with a kind of sardonic irony, Anderson can only occasionally muster even a tentative acceptance, and then in terms that nevertheless deny the surface assertions. Except for the opening selection, "Machine Song," *Perhaps Women* may be summarized as a record of the writer's continuing dismay and despair over the effects of modern industrialism. The attributes of the machine, its power, its strength, its order and discipline, are indeed those of a god (hence the difficulty of "humanizing" it), but of what sort of a god? In the selection "Life Up Thine Eyes," Anderson grimly parodies the 121st Psalm in describing the new god, the assembly-line belt, from whence cometh our fear.

> The belt controls me.
> It moves.
> It moves.
> I've tried to keep up.
> I tell you I have been keeping up.
> Jointville is God.
> Jointville controls the belt.
> The belt is God. (25-26)

Later in *Perhaps Women*, Anderson will reassert the need for a return to the old gods: "It may sound childish, but men will have to go back to nature more. They will have to go back to the fields and the rivers. There will have to be a new religion, more pagan, something more closely connected with fields and rivers." (57)

Although *Perhaps Women* finds Anderson at several points in moments of machine worship, "on my knees before the new god, the American god" (125), there is no sustained evidence in *Perhaps Women* or the works to follow that Anderson could translate the act of will he felt required of him to an act of belief capable of motivating and informing any significant artistic achievement. There can be no true acceptance for Anderson of a god which usurps the potency of the male, as do the machines of the southern mills in *Perhaps Women*, when maleness is closely knitted to the creativity of the artist and craftsman, as it is for Anderson. There can be no genuine affirmation of a system which inverts all of the earth-centered values with which he associated personal sanity and artistic integrity. Even the occasional machine celebrations of *Perhaps Women* are contradicted by Anderson's announced intention in the book's introduction to "arouse a real fear and perhaps respect for the machine," and to help "save man from the dominance of the machine before his potency, his ability to save himself, is quite gone." The machine-god is finally no god at all, for Anderson. Rather, the machine is ironically humanized, becoming an extension of man's most ignoble attributes, his destructive will to pride and power, his ugly attempt to rise out of his own flesh, to deny the saving ties to his fellow creatures and to the earth.

Anderson searches the mills in *Perhaps Women* for suitable new Americans in whom he can invest hopeful belief. They are not to be found among the male workers, eunuchs who stand bewildered before their great machines, taunted in their impotence by the women workers. And, although the factories are no Tartarus for Anderson's maids, the women in the mills are in Anderson's view essentially passive guardians of biological life, not the imaginative adventurers whom his vision of salvation would require. While the inwardness of women may insulate them from the stress and tension of the machines, Anderson does not conceive of them in roles of significant action. They may prevail, but they do not lead.

The writer is unable to work up any genuine enthusiasm for those logical new heroes of the technological age, the young engineers and superintendents who preside with cool Veblenian precision over the whirling mills. Anderson finds little to interest him behind their clear untroubled eyes, "clean young men without vices," who "studied hard, did things well" (101). He see himself separated from them by a great gulf, and although he admits curiosity about them since Lindbergh fixed the type in our national mind he repeatedly characterizes them as aloof, impersonal, shallow in their nonquestioning acceptance of technology, and thus finally brothers to the callous financiers who control the industrial juggernaut. The Hugh McVey figures, the creators and builders of the new machines, are once again alluded to admiringly in *Perhaps Women*, but only briefly so. The modern machine builders are artists of our time, Anderson says, just as much as the builders of the Chartres Cathedral were in theirs, but appreciation of these successful moderns quickly fades before thoughts of the human failures associated with their achievements, the dominant note of *Perhaps Women* as it was of *Poor White*.

Anderson's two final novels, published during the early and mid-1930s, reflect his experiments with machine-ecstasy and his attempts to assimilate the machine through sympathetic portrayals of the lives of mill workers. Both have as their central figures young people who are initiated, through the mills, into the new rhythms of industrial life, but whose responses to these forces are characteristically troubled, uncertain, and finally negative. The machines resist assimilation and Anderson's characters turn toward each other to find solace from the fearful symmetry of the industrial design.

Red Oliver of *Beyond Desire* is not really a mill worker, but a college student looking for a way to fill his summer vacation, and to answer his curiosity about the new life in the mills. He is introduced to the ordered life of the mills, "the path of American genius," and becomes "exultant" at his work in the great, light rooms with their marvelous arrays of machines, which "knew what they had to do" and "all day...went singing and humming to their tasks."[53] The cleanliness and purposefulness of the mill stands in sharp contrast to the disordered town outside its walls, and even to the random world of nature, of forests and rivers. Red comes to admire the mill superintendent, the quiet, impersonal human ally of these machines, and to note with wonder an affinity between the girls who tend the giant spinning machines and their charges. Still, there is a tenseness in the air of the mill, and "queer little moments of fright" at the speed and power of the equipment (53). And as the novel proceeds, Red's early conception of a wondrous technology is set aside for a series of portraits of the lives and backgrounds of individual mill girls, and for Red's confused love affair with the town librarian. Anderson is once again unable to integrate successfully the lives of his characters with the social and technological setting. There is a proletarian cast to the novel — the picture of working conditions in the mills, the mistreatment of workers by the mill owners and foremen, the initiation of the young hero into class warfare and violence, and finally his death during a strike — but these are blurred by Anderson's inability to project just what *is* worth fighting for in the new America. Stylistically, the work is characterized by evidence of such uncertainty: "He had been in it. He wasn't in it. He was. He wasn't"; "It's nice. It's terrible."; "You want it. You don't. You do."; "Ned Sawyer liked it. He didn't like it." ' " 'I am of them and not of them.' "; "it's the struggle of all men...it is...it isn't...."[54]

The vision of sublime technology is not pursued with any conviction in the novel beyond Red's initial sense of fascination, and by the conclusion the machine has become recognized as the destroyer of Jeffersonian democracy.

If technology fails to emerge as a bright promise, so too does the struggle of the workers. Red Oliver is less the sacrificial martyr than the bewildered young man who has wandered into the proletarian struggle almost by mistake. As he steps forward to face the guns of the National Guard, sent to put down the strikers, he can only think, " 'I'm a silly ass' "; and his counterpart across the firing line, the young leader of the Guardsmen, says to himself as he raises his pistol, " 'Why'd I want to get myself into such a hole?...A damn fool, that's what I am' " (356). In place of a confrontation between the fervent spirit of labor and the entrenched power of capitalism there is the dismal spectacle of one confused young man being shot by another.

Kit Brandon, Anderson's final novel, is innovative in combining the figure of the woman — more capable than man, in Anderson's view, of surviving the dislocations of industrialism — with that of the adventuresome seeker of a new destiny, a role heretofore reserved by Anderson for the male. The novel traces the life of a young Southern hill girl who leaves her impoverished family in their upland shack to find work in the cotton mills of the new South. Eventually she becomes a driver for an organization of bootleggers carrying moonshine whiskey out of the hills to be sold in the cities, later leaving this life to search out other opportunities.

In some respects, the work is an updated *Poor White*, mirroring in the life of its young striver, the transition of a region from bucolic to industrial. There is the recitation of the rape of a once fair country: great hardwood forests logged from the steep Southern hillsides, coal ripped from the ground, the consequent washing away of the topsoil, a process of waste and destruction that swept westward across the South leaving an impoverished land and people behind it. Upon the denuded and barren hills, people like Kit's family scratch out a miserable living. It is an old American story, says Anderson; " 'We are after the money. Let the land and the people of the land go to hell.' "[55] Given the choice to stay on the land and starve or go to work in the new mills, Kit chooses the mills. There is no sense of eviction from the Garden in the exodus of Kit and thousands of young people like her from their hillside pockets of rural poverty. They want the mill life. It is clearly preferable to the hills. With their parents it is different; " 'the hills had them,' " Kit says of the inability of those older ones like her father to make the transition into the mills and towns (p. 5). But the hills do not have her, and, like Dreiser's Sister Carrie, she accepts the pulse of the new age immediately and with hardly a backward glance.

There is the same pattern of Kit's initial attraction to the mill life and celebration of its dancing, spinning wonders that was seen in *Perhaps Women* and *Beyond Desire*, except that Kit is more fully a modern, one who has "the feel of machinery down into her veins, into all of her body," a quality that explains her later success as a driver but that is not, of course, without its ominous overtones (23). (Once again Anderson is unwilling to carry this comparison over to the realm of metaphor. Kit is never depicted in mechanistic imagery. On the contrary, she is "like a young tree in a vast forest, a blade of grass in the spring" [56-57].) Still, answering to the call of the machine and eventually becoming a top driver among the whiskey-runners of Tom Halsey, Kit seems, also like the emotionally incomplete young Hugh McVey, incapable of responding with genuine sentiment or full sexuality to others. Her car becomes the only lover capable of stirring her, and she talks to it, cries out for more prodigious performance by it, as she drives (261).

Kit's early attraction to the factory life diminishes as she learns something of the human costs involved: the contempt for the workers by the mill owners and the town's middle class, the perversion of values in the mills by which the machines are hooded and ventilated to protect them from the fine cotton lint that floats everywhere in the air, while the workers are allowed to breathe the substance into their lungs, or by which the mill air is saturated with a fine mist to keep the cotton thread pliable, leaving the workers wet and miserable. In the mills she finds, too, a predatory world in which a young woman must choose between the factory life and wearing herself out with children and drudgery in marriage. Although Kit soon leaves the mills, the rest of her story reflects to some degree the credo of callousness that they taught her: " 'If you don't put it over on them, they'll put it over on you.' " (166). This hardness, together with her native nerve and intelligence, might have made her, in other circumstances, a leader in industry or business. No proletarian revolutionary like her friend in the mills, Agnes, Kit seeks power in her relationships with others, and quality and style in her surroundings. Once out of the mills she puts her trust in fast cars, money, and fine clothes, in anything well-made. Although Anderson gives evidence in narrating *Kit Brandon* of sympathy with the collectivist themes inherent in his material, he allows the heroine to go her apolitical way.

Weighing her opportunities carefully, Kit marries Gordon Halsey, the weak son of the powerful and rich bootlegger Tom Halsey. She wins the respect of the elder Halsey and rises to become one of his best drivers. Tom Halsey, although a criminal, is presented as native American success story. The son of a lumberjack father who revered the great Appalachian forests even while cutting them down, Tom is possessed from childhood with natural talents for action and organization. He is seen as "an earlier American, one of our pioneers, a pioneer of business, of industry...like a man building a railroad across the continent in an earlier day...stealing land along the railroad as he went...

corrupting legislatures as he went" (46). Like Kit, he might have been a Gould or Rockefeller or Harriman. There is little to choose from between a Halsey and a Rockefeller; the acquisitive business instinct, in all cases, legal or illegal, Anderson sees as the perversion of some finer aim (122). Tom Halsey's strength, his purposeful quietness, his Svengalilike power over men and women, mark him as a potent figure for Anderson. But his greed prevents him from carrying out his grand plan. Like Faulkner's Thomas Sutpen, he dreams of achieving the facade of Southern culture: wealth, respectability, and the founding of a great family name. Through Tom Halsey's story Anderson depicts the hollowness of the first-I'll-get-rich-then-I'll-do-something-worthwhile mentality in America. Tom is mistakenly shot at last, during a federal raid on his illegal liquor operations, by his worthless son, Gordon, upon whose inadequacies the father's grand design ironically depended. The elder Halsey also exemplifies, however, a more pervasive failing revealed in the lives of the novel's characters: the waste of spirit, the perversion of human effort which attends the pursuit of ignoble goals. Again, as in Anderson's earlier novels, there seems to be no opportunity for worthwhile and satisfying *work* in the America of *Kit Brandon*. Talented and attractive young people — not only Kit, but the well-born college men from the cities who join the rum-runners — act out over and over again gestures of rebellion at the boredom and frustration fostered by a culture that seems merely acquisitive. And the existence of Prohibition, the main motivation for most of the novel's action, is, of course, a monstrous hypocrisy, a papering over of reality with a respectable illusion of national rectitude.

Faced once more with his old ambivalence toward the machine age, trying to sing that for which he lacked essential conviction, Anderson nevertheless is able to make of uncertainty itself a compelling kind of plea, as he had done so often before. In Kit Brandon's story he gives us an analogue of a national yearning for new beliefs. Her fascination with the automobile and the open road — "there was a kind of ecstasy in that....The American roads,... twisting their ways through states, over mountains, over rivers, at night through sleeping towns" (267) — is finally not enough. The whiskey-running, the fast, powerful cars, the expensive clothes, the excitement, leave Kit nevertheless lonely and unfulfilled, as on the larger level our national devotion to mechanical and material goals has left us still reaching out with unplenishable hunger:

> " 'I want....I want.'...science gone a little insane. 'Let's go to the moon or to Mars.' O.K. Go on child-man. We'll see what you get out of that." (214)

Kit leaves the rum-running life at the book's conclusion, and her disavowal of it (" 'I want something new now, I don't want to buy and sell. I want to do work that has some meaning' " [344]) Anderson still intends to stand as the credo for a generation of new Americans. The fixed idea of progress, the polestar of the American consciousness, must realign itself with more meaningful human aspirations and national enterprises. In his closing paragraph, Anderson, in a characteristic scaling down of these ideas, follows Kit's thoughts as she remembers appreciatively an earlier scene, a young farmer, with his wife, beside their hill cabin, and from this remembrance fashions a worthier hope for her own future. Out of this image from her rural past, Anderson suggests, Kit may find the means by which to stay herself against the modern ruin. Anderson is led once again in *Kit Brandon* to the dilemma in which he praises the machine itself and the genius that created it, calls for new poets to sing of the factory life, hesitantly attempts such songs himself, but is finally silenced by the human costs which industrial technology exacts, and turns from it toward vague but more hopeful alternatives.

One of the important contributions of the proletarian novel of the 1930s, as suggested in Walter B. Rideout's study of the genre, was the affirmation that the novelist also was a citizen.[56] It was a function that Anderson had always assumed instinctively and not merely from the peripheral acquaintance with radicalism reflected in *Beyond Desire* and *Kit Brandon*. One finds this role represented in Anderson's final book of the decade and of his life. It was the pattern of his career that he was, at its end, to draw closer to the American small town again, and to find in it a new opportunity for pastoral synthesis between the natural and the great worlds. In *Home Town* (1940), a long essay on the resurgence of town life as a result of industrial dislocation and urban unemployment during the Great Depression, Anderson is characteristically hopeful for the future of American towns, "halfway between the cities whence we get the ideas and the soil whence we draw the strength."[57] Unable to make himself or his fictional characters over in the image of the new industrial America, to turn the act of will into an article of faith, he nevertheless ends his career still searching for the means to reconcile the machine and the cornfield.

Sherwood Anderson's rejection of either escape from or submission to modern industrialism drove him to create a group of ambiguous new Americans who, if they cannot project an imperial selfhood upon the mechanical age, are not, on the other hand, to be sacrificed to it. What seems apparent in retrospect is that Anderson's long struggle to lift the machine into some harmonious relationship with his conception of a worthwhile life is, from the start, an impossible task for him. For his vision of a richly poetic agrarian past the machine promised an endless repetition of standardized todays; for the silence and slow, purposeful growth of the organic world it answered with a blur of speed, a cacophony of shrieks and whistles, and instant creation — washed, sealed, and untouched by human hands. For moods, feelings, the grotesqueness and wonder of life, it held forth a stultifying sameness; for his search for love and brotherhood, it promised only emotionless indifference.

Despite his best intentions, Anderson was never able to transcend the machine, to cease regarding it self-consciously, as a troublesome subject for reform or ingratiation. The psychic costs were too great for him to allow it to shape his figures into new metaphors of modernity. Nowhere in his fiction does there emerge the hero or heroine capable of recreating the noted photographer Alfred Stieglitz's achievement, about which Anderson had written admiringly in 1919, of "make[ing] machinery the tool and not the master of man."[58] While Anderson might assent, in principle, to Hart Crane's lines in *The Bridge*, "sustained in tears, the cities are endowed / and justified conclaimant with the fields," he could not, like Crane, translate that affirmation into memorable expression. Unable or unwilling to sacrifice the communal side of himself to the demands of a truly recreative artistic vision, Anderson sought what perhaps no American artist ever achieved, or could achieve: a public voice that was also a personal voice. Given the refractory materials of his America, he came as near to this as perhaps any artist of his time. For Anderson, as Alfred Kazin has said, "writing was not just a means of personal expression, but a search for salvation; it was the way he saved his own life, every day her wrote, in the hope that he was also helping to save his country."[59] The confrontation within Anderson of obligations and dreams, the citizen and the poet, finds expression not only in the hopefully tentative figures who people his novels but also in the unmistakable tone of understanding and reconciliation which remains constant in his work from beginning to end.

Writing in his *Memoirs* during the last decade of his life, Anderson recalls his own search for a career during his younger years, having to admit to himself that the mechanical and inventive genius which was expressing itself in the

Midwest of that time had not been given to him.[60] Instead —
and here we nod in recognition of the familiar recitation —
he became a salesman and a manufacturer of the products of
the new technology until sickening of his life, he found
himself at last as an artist. Only in this often-told tale of
himself do we sense the figure who never quite takes shape
in his novels: only here do we find the material for that
supreme novel that lies behind all his published fictions.
Out of his struggle with industrialism, both as representative
man and as expressive artist, may be said to come Sherwood
Anderson's most memorable creation: the Andersonian
artist himself, the sayer of these books, who, in his unyielding
determination to encompass the divisive forces of his times,
in his refusal to deny the age he cannot accept, emerges as
the only assuredly heroic figure from among all his new
Americans.

NOTES

1. *Sherwood Anderson's Memoirs: A Critical Edition*, ed. Ray Lewis White
(Chapel Hill: University of North Carolina Press, 1973), pp. 241-42.
Herein abbreviated *Memoirs*.
2. *Letters of Sherwood Anderson*, ed. Howard Mumford Jones and Walter
B. Rideout (Boston: Little, Brown and Company, 1953), p. 79. Herein
abbreviated *Letters*.
3. The only study of Sherwood Anderson and industrialism, aside
from my unpublished doctoral dissertation, "Sherwood Anderson's American
Pastoral" (University of Washington, 1964), is in Thomas Reed West's *Flesh
of Steel: Literature and the Machine in American Culture* (Charlotte, N.C.:
Vanderbilt University Press, 1967), pp. 21-34. West finds in industrialism
the opposed qualities of energy and discipline and treats these ideas in
brief chapters on Anderson and other twentieth-century American writers,
including Sinclair Lewis. West's discussion is perceptive in its larger
outlines and frequently insightful, but his limited treatment of Anderson's
work and the fact that West's book is not, as he points out, intended to be
primarily a literary study, invite further consideration of Anderson's
responses to technology. In addition, West, I would suggest, underestimates
Anderson's continuing antipathy to the machine, beneath the surface level
of acceptance and celebration during the decade of the 1930s.
4. Quoted in Robert F. Almy, "Sherwood Anderson: the Non-Conforming
Rediscoverer," *Saturday Review of Literature* 28 (January 6, 1945): 18.

5. *Memoirs*, p. 243.

6. Virginia Woolf, "American Fiction," *Saturday Review of Literature* 2 (August 1, 1925): 2.

7. Walter B. Rideout, "Sherwood Anderson's 'Mid-American Chants,' " in *Aspects of American Poetry*, ed. Richard M. Ludwig ([Columbus]: Ohio State University Press, 1962), pp. 154-56.

8. Waldo Frank, "Sherwood Anderson: A Personal Note," *Newberry Library Bulletin*, Second Series, no. 2 (December 1948), 41. Quoted in Rideout, ibid., p. 156. Further evidence of Anderson's self-conscious westernness is found in the *Letters*, pp. vii-x, 7, et passim.

9. *Letters*, p. 43.

10. *Windy McPherson's Son* (Chicago and London: University of Chicago Press, 1965), p. 220. Page references to this and other works, following the initial citation, will normally be included in the text.

11. See Morris's introduction to *Windy McPherson's Son*, ibid., pp. x-xi.

12. *Windy*, p. 220; see also pp. 131, 142, 148.

13. See Brooks's introduction to Anderson's "Letters to Van Wyck Brooks," *Story* 19 (September-October 1941): 42-43.

14. This pattern is explored in Nancy L. Bunge, "The Ambiguous Endings of Sherwood Anderson's Novels," in *Sherwood Anderson Centennial Studies*, ed. Hilbert H. Campbell and Charles E. Modlin (Troy, N.Y.: Whitston Publishing Company, 1976), pp. 249-63. Walter B. Rideout, in correspondence with me, argues that *Windy's* ending is clearly pressimistic, as does J. R. Scafidel in "Sexuality in *Windy McPherson's Son,*" *Twentieth Century Literature* 23 (February 1977): 98-100.

15. See, e.g., Mumford's *The Myth of the Machine* (New York: Harcourt, Brace and World, 1967-70).

16. See *Memoirs*, pp. 185-87. Another possible source is the "industrial army" described in Bellamy's *Looking Backward*, which Anderson cited in his *Memoirs* as an influential book in his youth.

17. *Marching Men: A Critical Text*, ed. Ray Lewis White (Cleveland and London: Case Western Reserve Press, 1972), p. 91.

18. *Memoirs*, p. 186.

19. *Letters*, p. 23.

20. The novel's attack upon women reflects Anderson's growing discontent with his own first marriage. See William A. Sutton, *The Road to Winesburg* (Metuchen, N.J.: Scarecrow Press, 1972), pp. 378-79.

21. See Lewis Mumford, "Utopia, the City and the Machine," *Daedalus* 94 (Spring 1965): 281.

22. Translated from the French by Martin B. Friedman (Chapel Hill: University of North Carolina Press, 1961), p. 35.

23. (New York: Viking Press, 1966), p. 61.

24. In *Sherwood Anderson's Notebook* (New York: Boni and Liveright, 1926), pp. 206, 216. Walter B. Rideout points out in a letter to me that "King Coal" was actually first published as "My Fire Burns" in *Survey* 47 (March 25, 1922): 997-1000.

25. *Memoirs,* p. 187.

26. *Memoirs,* p. 186.

27. *Mid-American Chants* (New York: John Lane Company, 1918), p. 7.

28. M. A., "A Country Town," *New Republic* 19 (June 25, 1919): 257.

29. *Winesburg, Ohio,* ed. Malcolm Cowley (New York: Viking Press, 1960), p. 36.

30. The theme of human communication in *Winesburg* is examined closely in three articles: John J. Mahoney, "An Analysis of *Winesburg, Ohio,*" *Journal of Aesthetics and Art Criticism* 15 (December 1956): 245-52; Edwin Fussell, "*Winesburg, Ohio*: Art and Isolation," *Modern Fiction Studies* 6 (Summer 1960): 106-14; and my "*Winesburg, Ohio* and the Rhetoric of Silence," *American Literature* 40 (March 1968): 38-57, from which the present discussion is taken. Mahoney's essay, while making the valuable observation that the speeches in *Winesburg* are essentially soliloquies, seems to me to misinterpret George Willard's role, seeing him as only a "good listener." Fussell's article is an excellent treatment of the nature of the artist as revealed in the characterization of George Willard; Fussell's essay differs considerably, however, in its emphasis, from my interpretation, which is concerned with the implications of silence and communication beyond those linked to the young hero's development as an artist.

31. Fussell, p. 110.

32. *Letters,* pp. 58, 31.

33. *Poor White* (New York: Viking Press, 1966), p. 37.

34. *A Story Teller's Story* (Garden City, N.Y.: Garden City Publishing Company, 1924), p. 327.

35. This trait, says Leo Marx, is "a characteristic legacy of agrarian experience." See "The Machine in the Garden," *New England Quarterly* 29 (March 1956): 40.

36. Quoted in West, *Flesh of Steel,* p. 109.

37. *Letters,* p. 196.

38. *A Story Teller's Story,* p. 295.

39. *Sherwood Anderson's Notebook,* p. 154.

40. *A New Testament* (New York: Boni and Liveright, 1927), p. 37.

41. Twelve Southerners, "Introduction: A Statement of Principles," *I'll Take My Stand* (New York: Harper and Brothers, 1930; Harper Torchbooks, 1962), p. xxii.

42. Donald Davidson, "A Mirror for Artists," *I'll Take My Stand,* p. 55.

43. *Notebook,* p. 216.

44. *I'll Take My Stand,* pp. 51-52.

45. *Letters,* pp. 226, 389. Later, in his *Memoirs,* Anderson would speak disparagingly of Allen Tate as a respresentative of the old, aristocratic South: "Our Stark Youngs and Allen Tates are our ultimate vulgarisms" (p. 555).

46. *Letters,* pp. 209, 211, 215.

47. Anderson, *Perhaps Women* (New York: Horace Liveright, 1931; Mamaroneck, N.Y.: Paul P. Appel, 1970), p. 9.

48. Anderson, *Beyond Desire* (New York: Liveright, Inc., 1932), p. 50.

49. See "Machine Song," *Perhaps Women*, p. 14.

50. Still stubbornly attempting to organicize the machine, Anderson would claim, in *Puzzled America* (New York: Charles Scribner's Sons, 1935), p. 114, "I like machines. They won't stand being neglected, being made to live dirty, neglected lives." The terms are reminiscent of Anderson's praise of the thoroughbred in "The Man Who Became a Woman," in *Horses and Men* (New York: B. W. Huebsch, 1923), p. 204: "A race horse isn't like a human being. He won't stand for it to have to do his work in any rotten ugly kind of a dump the way a man will, and he won't stand for the smells a man will either."

51. *Letters*, pp. 282-85.

52. *Poor White*, pp. 130, 135. The subject of a machine-god had been given wide currency by Eugene O'Neill's *Dynamo*, produced in 1929. Anderson mentions the play in a letter to Horace Liveright, *Letters*, p. 209.

53. *Beyond Desire* (New York: Liveright, Inc., 1932), pp. 49-50.

54. *Beyond Desire*, pp. 258, 286, 345, 354, 355.

55. *Kit Brandon: A Portrait* (New York: Charles Scribner's Sons, 1936), p. 28.

56. Rideout. *The Radical Novel in the United States, 1900-1954* (Cambridge, Mass.: Harvard University Press, 1956), p. 287.

57. "The American Small Town," in *The Sherwood Anderson Reader*, ed. Paul Rosenfeld (Boston: Houghton Mifflin Company, 1947), p. 744.

58. *Notebook*, p. 159. See also Waldo Frank, *Our America* (New York: Boni and Liveright, 1919), p. 181.

59. "The Letters of Sherwood Anderson," in Kazin's *The Inmost Leaf* (New York: Harcourt, Brace, 1941), p. 225.

60. *Memoirs*, p. 243.

5

Sinclair Lewis:
New Pioneering on the Prairies

> "It's just that I have some kind of an unformulated idea
> that I want to be identified with Grand Republic — help
> in setting up a few stones in what may be a new Athens.
> It's this northern country — you know, stark and clean
> — and the brilliant lakes and the tremendous prairies to
> the westward — it may be a new kind of land for a new
> kind of people, and it's scarcely even started yet."
>
> Sinclair Lewis, *Cass Timberlane*

WHEN Sherwood Anderson described Sinclair Lewis in
1922 as "a man writing who, wanting passionately to love the
life about him, cannot bring himself to do so,"[1] he expressed
what has become a characteristic judgment, for perhaps no
American writer of modern times has so insistently presented
an ambivalent and divided artistic self to his readers and
critics as has Lewis. Participant and enthusiast as well as
observer and critic, the scourge of American villages,
doctors, preachers, businessmen, as well as — so Lewis later
assured us — their heartiest well-wisher, he remains a
compelling figure for the student of our culture. T. K.
Whipple, in his well-known essay in *Spokesmen* fifty years
ago, concluded that "Lewis is the most successful critic of
American society because he is the best proof that his
charges are just."[2] And more recently, Mark Schorer, Sheldon
Grebstein, D. J. Dooley, and Martin Light, in their books on
Lewis, all demonstrate convincingly that he was a writer
possessed of eternally warring qualities, that on almost any
level of personal or artistic performance he reflected a

continuing split in sensibility: lonely introvert versus mad exhibitionist, coy romancer versus satiric realist, defender versus derider of intellect and art, alternately ridden by, and rejecting, material success.[3] From this welter of contrarieties hopelessly yoked emerges what Schorer calls "the real enigma of his novels, a persistent conflict of values that clashed no less within him" (4).

In this opposition of values, it is Lewis the nay-sayer, the tormentor of middle America, who has received the most attention. "The fact is," one typical judgment runs, "that Lewis is dull when being positive but delightful when being negative."[4] Yet in attempting to understand more clearly the paradox that Schorer describes we are driven back to a fuller consideration of the other Lewis, the Lewis who would seem to claim a place in the main current of American idealism, who with Emerson and Whitman would project upon a native landscape the values of democratic individualism and a sublime conception of the future, and who would present in his fiction idealized alternatives to the society whose chronicler he was. This is the Lewis who scored the "contradiction between pioneering myth and actual slackness" in America, and who wrote of himself that he "mocked the cruder manifestations of Yankee Imperialism because he was, at heart, a fanatic American."[5] This is the Lewis who in 1938 called Willa Cather the greatest living American novelist because "no other has so preserved our frontier . . . . yet no one has more lucidly traced the post-pioneer American than she. . . ."[6] While these counterforces of affirmation in Lewis's work have received some recognition, their function as a compelling, and at best controlling, set of ideas in the body of his novels is, I believe, open to further examination.[7] Such examination may not only clarify our understanding of the main strands of Lewis's idealism and their interrelationships, but may also reveal how these patterns of affirmation pervade Lewis's fiction, emerging in his early novels, shaping his major books of the 1920s and finally slipping toward incoherence and frustration in his later works.

Cass Timberlane's speech, above, serves as illustration and starting point.[8] It presents the reader with a unique cluster of images and ideas that may be seen to function prominently in Lewis's novels: an exalted midwestern natural landscape, against which is set forth a visionary future (objectified as a modern creation, often a city), and a figure indigenous to this landscape — appropriate here even to his name — who stands as a harbinger or creator of this future. Associated with this grouping — idealized natural setting, city of the future, and creative new American — are revealing aspects of style. Most notable is the metaphorical cast of the speaker's utterance, "setting up a few stones in what may be a new Athens." Even the actual name, "Grand Republic," calls up the utopian rhetoric of earlier Cass Timberlanes. And although Lewis may mock such Founding Father manifest-destinyism elsewhere in this novel (as well as in setting *Kingsblood Royal* in a racist "Grand Republic" and *Babbitt* in "Zenith") he is clearly sympathetic here to his speaker's conception. Related to this metaphorical distancing of subject is the tentativeness of the entire statement: "Some kind of an unformulated idea…what may be…you know…it may be…." From what we come to know of the speaker, his lack of specificity suggests not a casual disregard for what he is saying, but rather the opposite. As with a Hemingway hero, the speaker's avoidance of a more precise articulation of his ideas is a measure of their potency to him, an appeal to the listener for a psychic response, an assumption of agreement below the word-surface. Even the use of dashes rather than conventional punctuation or transitions which would clarify the logical progression may be seen as a stylistic device to emphasize both the interrelatedness of these notions within the speaker's mind and the urgency behind them. Setting aside for the moment considerations of *Cass Timberlane* as a novel, what Lewis provides in this passage is a prototype whose development and significance may be profitably examined.

This characteristic pattern of images and ideas emerges falteringly in the five early Lewis novels that antedate the publication of *Main Street* in 1920. Lewis's treatment of nature and landscape in these works, to begin with, seems to offer little opportunity for development. Despite his claim that *Walden* was the chief influence upon his formative years, and his high praise of Thoreau, Lewis's early version of pastoral is often, unlike Thoreau's, merely the sentimental countryside rapture that has always flourished in our popular literature, to which category the early works may, on the face of it, be consigned.[9] Nature in these novels is commonly simply an escape, albeit a beneficial and restorative one, and the urbanite ennobled and revivified by an Arcadian interlude is to become a stock figure for Lewis. The milquetoast, citified hero of his early novel, *Our Mr. Wrenn* (1914), is, for example, propelled into self-reliance partly as a result of his walking trip through the English countryside. Similarly in *The Innocents* (1917) an elderly New York couple set out on a walking trip across the country, and en route are rather incredibly transformed from shy nonentities into aggressive and successful go-getters.[10] City girls like Ruth Winslow of *The Trail of the Hawk* (1915) and Claire Boltwood of *Free Air* (1919) change, through contact with nature, from eastern, or "indoor," to western, or "outdoor," women, thus completing a required rite of passage for Lewis heroines. As Lewis's sympathetic treatment of them prepares us for his later favorable view of "outdoor" women like Carol Kennicott in *Main Street*, Edith Cortright in *Dodsworth*, and Ann Vickers, so his dismissal of the "indoor" Gertie Cowles of *The Trail of the Hawk* presages his later unsympathetic treatment of "indoor" women like Joyce Lanyon of *Arrowsmith*, Fran Dodsworth and Jinny Timberlane, Cass's young wife, whose moral lapse accom-

panies her transition from "outdoor" to "indoor" woman.
Alert to the worst excesses of sentimental pastoral in these
early works, Lewis tempers his treatment of nature by the
inclusion of realistic or even satiric detail. For example, a
country-engendered euphoria mistakenly causes Una Golden
of *The Job* (1917) to succumb to "the thwarted boyish soul
that persisted in Mr. Schwirtz's barbered, unexercised,
coffee-soaked, tobacco-filled, whiskey-rotted, fattily-
degenerated city body."[11] In *The Trail of the Hawk* Lewis at
one point spoofs the clichés of popular wilderness fiction at
the same time that he repeats its basic values:

> "If this were a story," said Carl, knocking the crusted snow
> from dead branches and dragging them toward the center
> of a small clearing, "the young hero from Joralemon
> would now remind the city gal that 'tis only among God's
> free hills that you can get an appetite, and then the author
> would say, 'Nothing had ever tasted so good as those trout,
> yanked from the brook and cooked to a turn on the
> sizzling coals.' " She looked at the stalwart young man, so
> skillfully frying the flapjacks, and contrasted him with the
> effeminate fops she had met on Fifth Avenue.[12]

This alternate milking and mocking of the conventions of
the wilderness novel is a practice that Lewis carries on
throughout *Free Air* as well as in the later *Mantrap* (1926). In
Free Air Lewis includes realistic treatments of the primitive
roads, temperamental automobiles, the occasional filthy
hotel and backroad degenerate, the debunking of Milt
Daggett's pulp-fiction stereotype of aggressive lumberjacks
wooing and winning reticent maidens. Nevertheless, the
larger conception of nature and the West that emerges from
the novel is not Claire Boltwood's early impression of "rocks
and stumps and socks on the line," but rather is that familiar
mythic territory for which Milt serves as emblem.[13]

Indeed, Lewis has a firmer grasp on these early characters
whose linkage with nature is the result not of escape but of
birthright. Carl Ericson of *The Trail of the Hawk* and Milt

Daggett of *Free Air* are presented as authentic native heroes, clear-eyed rural Midwesterners who have absorbed the sources of strength and vitality in the land itself. Such origins will be the means of legitimizing the aims and ennobling the character of later Lewis figures like Martin Arrowsmith, Sam Dodsworth, Cass Timberlane, and Neil Kingsblood, as well as such minor but significant characters as Bone Stillman of *The Trail of the Hawk* and Miles Bjornstam of *Main Street,* both of whose association with wilderness — rather than simply rural — images is an index to their more radical individualism.[14] Still it is not merely in their origins but in their futures that Carl Ericson and Milt Daggett emerge as the most prophetic of Lewis's early heroes. Ericson, in particular, typifies Lewis's new American:

> Carl was second generation Norwegian; American-born, American in speech, American in appearance save for his flaxen hair and china-blue eyes. . . . When he was born the "typical Americans" of earlier stocks had moved to city palaces or were marooned on run-down farms. It was Carl Ericson, not a Trowbridge or a Stuyvesant or a Lee or a Grant, who was the "typical American" of his period. It was for him to carry on the American destiny of extending the western horizon; his to restore the wintry Pilgrim virtues and the exuberant, October, partridge-drumming days of Daniel Boone; then to add, in his own or another generation, new American aspirations for beauty. (6)

Once again the problem with Lewis's characterization of this first of his visionary Westerners is that his validity as an archetypal figure is weakened by an occasionally effusive romantic overlay. For the young Carl Ericson, we are told, for example,

> it was sheer romance to parade through town with a tin haversack of carbons for the arc-lights, familiarly lowering the high-hung mysterious lamps, while his plodding acquaintances "clerked" in stores on Saturdays or tended

furnaces. Sometimes he donned the virile — and noisy — uniform of an electrician: army gauntlets, a coil of wire, pole-climbers strapped to his legs. Crunching his steel spurs into the crisp pine wood of the lighting-poles, he carelessly ascended to the place of humming wires and red crossbars and green-glass insulators, while crowds of two and three small boys stared in awe from below. (26)

Still, despite his tendency to veer off into cuteness, Lewis has discovered a figure of potentiality for him in a young Westerner who reads *Scientific American*, finds inspiration in his high school laboratory, and lusts after an automobile. Both in *The Trail of the Hawk* and in *Free Air* Lewis begins to turn his treatment of nature and the West — virtual synonyms for Lewis, as for Thoreau — away from a simplistic celebration of its potentialities for escape and toward an alliance with scientific progress.

Carl Ericson and Milt Daggett are more than just two more in a procession of nature's noblemen; in addition to their irreproachable natural credentials they are both creative technologists, "new" men. Milt not only wins Claire Boltwood out west but prepares himself there for accession into the technological age, as represented by his study of engineering at the University of Washington. Beyond that lies what he envisions as a challenging careeer as a builder in Alaska. Carl becomes not only a famous pioneer aviator but also the inventor of a camping automobile called the Touricar, and an early version of the more substantial later designer and industrialist, Sam Dodsworth. Lewis had earlier demonstrated knowledge of the new science of aviation in his first published novel, a boy's book called *Hike and the Aeroplane* (New York: Stokes, 1912) in which the adventure centers upon a new "tetrahedral aeroplane."[15] And Carl Eriscon, in appearance and accomplishment, is a remarkable anticipation of Charles Lindbergh, whose Swedish immigrant family had settled near Lewis's home town of Sauk Centre, Minnesota. The same symbolic unity of man and machine which

troubled Sherwood Anderson in the figure of Lindbergh
and his 1927 flight — Lindbergh even called his published
autobiographical account *We*, himself and the plane as one
— was for Lewis simply an affirmation and justification of
his earlier fictional hero.[16]

Both Milt Daggett and Carl Ericson, then, emerge as
seminal heroes for Lewis, figures whose alliances both to the
land and the technological future might qualify them as new
American pioneers. Like all those other new Americans,
these Lewis heroes cross the threshold from an agrarian past
into an industrial future. And, like a succession of figures
from Twain's Connecticut Yankee to Norris's Bennett and
Annixter, to Cather's Bartley Alexander and Tom Outland,
to Anderson's Hugh McVey, the ability of Lewis's young
men to mechanize successfully serves to demonstrate their
claim to an appropriate role in the new age. Nature by itself
was irrelevant, and the Westerner bound to the soil an
anachronism. If "the American destiny of extending the
western horizon" was to be advanced, as Lewis believed, it
would be by the native Westerner who had grasped the new
tools of science. Thus, Lewis joins the earlier writers treated
here in his belief that the old stalemate between machine
and garden might be transformed into a progressive synthesis.
And in this important sense, Lewis is not merely lavishing
exquisite praise upon nature, as T. K. Whipple accused him
of doing (227). Rather, Lewis reaches toward the awareness
of his culture hero Thoreau that nature exists most
meaningfully in relationship to the civilization of its time
rather than apart from it.

As novels, however, neither *The Trail of the Hawk* nor *Free
Air* can be taken as seriously as their controlling theme
would seem to require. Both are mired in the excesses of
popular romance, and while *Free Air* ends before Milt
Daggett's new pioneering actually begins, *The Trail of the
Hawk*, instead of engaging seriously Carl Ericson's proposed
archetypal role, diffuses it into a series of "adventures." It

remained for *Main Street*, published in 1920, the year following *Free Air*, to manifest these early ideas in an imaginative work of primary importance, and to open a decade in which Lewis's new pioneers would occupy the center of most of his major works.

Although *Main Street* represented a critical and popular advance over the earlier novels, it bears important similarities to them in the figure of Carol Milford Kennicott. Like Milt Daggett, Carol sees great work to be done in the future and eagerly anticipates her own part in it. Like Carl Ericson she is depicted as a representative new American: "The days of pioneering, of lassies in sunbonnets, and bears killed with axes in piney clearings, are deader now than Camelot; and a rebellious girl is the spirit of that bewildered empire called the American Middlewest."[17] And once again the heritage of the young seeker is an America still in the process of becoming, "bewildered" by the speed of its cultural change. The hill upon which Carol stands in the novel's opening sentences, "where Chippewas camped two generations ago," now looks out upon flour mills and the skyscrapers of Minneapolis and St. Paul. It is a land, she realizes later, whose work has scarcely begun, "the newest empire of the world. . . . They are pioneers, these sweaty wayfarers . . . and for all its fat richness, theirs is a pioneer land. What is its future? she wondered. . . . What future and what hope?" (28-29) Carol, in her eager hopefulness, owes much to the earlier figure of Rose Dutcher in Hamlin Garland's 1895 novel; in an earlier tribute to Garland, Lewis wrote that it was in Garland's books "that the real romance of that land [the upper Midwest] was first revealed to me."[18]

Like both Carl and Milt, as well as Garland's Rose Dutcher, Carol is a Midwesterner who is closely identified with the natural world. In the opening she stands beside the Mississippi, "in relief against the cornflower blue of Northern sky," and although Lewis playfully diminishes her pose by listing the random contents of her mind, he consistently identifies her eagerness of spirit with the potentiality for hope and beauty in the wide midwestern landscape. Even when Gopher Prairie's ugliness and pettiness threaten to overwhelm her she can find in the land itself, as she does after a day spent hunting and walking with her husband, Will, "the dignity and greatness which had failed her in Main Street" (61). She is first attracted to Will by those qualities of his personality closest to her own: his fondness for tramping and the outdoors, his sense of the heroic midwestern past, his occasional awareness of its possibilities for the future. His proposal of marriage is presented in the only terms which Carol would have accepted: " 'It's a good country, and I'm proud of it. Let's make it all that those old boys dreamed about' " (22), and it is his failure to recognize the seriousness of this vow for Carol that lies at the base of their later misunderstandings. Failing to take Carol seriously, as Daniel Aaron has pointed out, is also a mistake for those, like H. L. Mencken, who see Carol only as a featherbrained romantic.[19] It is, of course, just the visionary propensity that made her ridiculous to Mencken and others that defines her as an appropriate Lewis heroine.

What had begun for Carol during college as a reading assignment in a sociology class — a text on town improvement — and a resolution to " 'get my hands on one of these prairie towns and make it beautiful' " (11), seems to offer itself as actual opportunity through Will's proposal.[20] But she soon finds that what Will and the townspeople have in mind by town improvement is cosmetic rather than surgical. One exception and possible ally for Carol is Guy Pollock, the lawyer, who can imagine the progressive disappearance of the small town as swift monorails carry the country residents each evening into cities as captivating as those in a William Morris utopia (153). Pollock, however, almost immediately disqualifies himself, as a victim of that paralysis of the will which he calls the Village Virus, from any active part in this social pioneering. Another possible kindred spirit, Vida Sherwin, the schoolteacher who has long campaigned for a new school building for Gopher Prairie, moves too slowly to suit Carol's visionary ambitions.

Carol's ideas for social amelioration extend beyond that of rebuilding prairie towns (Will complains that she is "always spieling about how scientists ought to rule the world" [381], an idea straight out of Veblen, and she espouses other typical Progressivist concerns), but it is primarily as a thwarted builder that she is presented to the reader. In the famous passage in which she walks down Main Street for the first time, only The Farmer's National Bank ("An Ionic temple of marble. Pure, exquisite, solitary" [40]) escapes her catalog of the town's ugliness, "planlessness," and "temporariness," where "each man had built with the most valiant disregard of all the others" (41).[21] Later when she analyzes more carefully the town's appearance it is with the eye of the architect and planner:

> She asserted that it is a matter of universal similarity; of flimsiness of construction, so that the towns resemble frontier camps; of neglect of natural advantages, so that the hills are covered with brush, the lakes shut off by railroads, and the creeks lined with dumping grounds; of depressing sobriety of color; rectangularity of buildings; and excessive breadth and straightness of the gashed streets, so that there is no escape from gales and from sight of the grim sweep of land, nor any windings to coax the loiterer along, while the breadth which would be majestic in an avenue of palaces makes the low shabby shops creeping down the typical Main Street the more mean by comparison. (260)

This indictment of the ubiquitous American gridiron plan would be echoed by Lewis Mumford in his 1924 study of American architecture, *Sticks and Stones*, as he described a nation of Gopher Prairies which "acquired the framework of a metropolis before they had passed out of the physical stage of village," and which announced unabashedly to the world that they had no other desire than to grow, attract business, and increase land values.[22]

Another credulous western innovator like Carl Ericson and Milt Daggett, Carol is a more compelling figure than either of her predecessors because of the extraordinary tension between the eager expectancy of her hopes and the forces of dullness and smugness which oppose her. Shut off from any meaningful work by her position as woman and wife, by her shallow education, by her own sentimentalism and flightiness, and by her sense of inadequacy to her task, she can bring her dreams to no real end. Vida Sherwin's judgment against Carol that she is "an impossibilist. And you give up too easily" (263), seems to have been shared by Lewis to some extent, if we consider external evidence in the form of a "sequel" to the novel, a visit by the author, after a lapse of four years, to his imaginary town, which Lewis published in *The Nation* in 1924. In Gopher Prairie, a new school building "with its clear windows, perfect ventilation, and warm-hued tapestry brick," stands as testimony to Vida's effective gradualist tactics.[23] The Carol of the sequel, dumpy and defeated, has no such memorial to mark her fitful efforts at town improvement. And so Carol is resigned to her failure at the end of the novel:

> She looked across the silent fields to the west. She was conscious of an unbroken sweep of land to the Rockies, to Alaska; a dominion which will rise to unexampled greatness when other empires have grown senile. Before that time, she knew, a hundred generations of Carols will aspire and go down in tragedy devoid of palls and solemn chanting, the humdrum inevitable tragedy of struggle against inertia. (431)

At the end, no longer even the potential creator, she remains a frustrated figure living under a self-imposed truce in a community that she might have transformed into something distinctive and beautiful, had she possessed the technical skill and the nerve to match her idealism. Technical skill and nerve are, of course, the attributes of her doctor husband, Will, but without vision he remains merely the severed half of her incomplete self. What is called for in the wider design of *Main Street* is a sublime architect, a figure whose pragmatic technological mastery and courage to innovate are equal to the force of his, or her, dream.[24]

If *Main Street* shows us the incipient builder deprived of the realization of her goal — a new town on the prairie — *Babbitt* (1922) reverses the presentation to reveal the shining midwestern city achieved, but without an appropriate creator to shape or interpret its destiny. Both novels are concerned with defining humane life for the citizens of a community; both ask at what point in the process of development this humane life can best be realized. Zenith has clearly gone beyond that point, as Gopher Prairie has failed to reach it. Instead of *Main Street*'s heroic natural landscape blighted by human incompetence and pettiness, *Babbitt* presents a man-created world of immense technological dazzle, but finally devoid of meaningful relationships, not only among its inhabitants, but between man and landscape and between man and the products of his technology. It is a kind of upside-down *Walden*, where the buildings, houses, porcelain and tile bathrooms, and electric cigar lighters overwhelm the human figures and reduce their actions to insignificance. As he did in *Main Street*, Lewis was dramatizing, in *Babbitt*, Lewis Mumford's contemporary observation that "architecture and civilization develop hand in hand: the characteristic buildings of each period are the memorials to their dearest institutions."[25] Lewis establishes the pattern at once as the novel opens: "The towers of Zenith aspired above the morning mist; austere towers of steel and cement and limestone sturdy as cliffs and delicate as silver rods. They were neither citadels nor churches, but frankly and beautifully office-buildings."[26]

From this panoramic view of a city "built — it seemed — for giants," the camera eye moves down, in a characteristically ironic Lewis juxtaposition, to focus upon the helpless figure of George F. Babbitt, asleep in his Dutch Colonial house in Floral Heights, and from there down to the alarm clock, the bathroom gadgets "so glittering and so ingenious that they resembled an electrical instrument-board," the eyeglasses, the suit, the contents of Babbitt's pockets — all of the wares by which the new city asserts its mastery over its inhabitants (6, 8). As the opening chapter ends, Lewis turns his reader's attention back to the encompassing city as Babbitt stands looking out his window over the city, where his attention is drawn to the Second National Bank Tower:

> Its shining walls rose against April sky to a simple cornice like a streak of white fire. Integrity was in the tower, and decision. It bore its strength lightly as a tall soldier. As Babbitt stared, the nervousness was soothed from his face, his slack chin lifted in reverence. All he articulated was "That's one lovely sight!" but he was inspired by the rhythm of the city; his love of it renewed. He beheld the tower as a templespire of the religion of business, a faith passionate, exalted, surpassing common men; and as he clumped down to breakfast he whistled the ballad "Oh, by gee, by gosh, by jingo" as though it were a hymn melancholy and noble. (14-15)

Lewis is of course satirizing that form of technological progress that is born of inadequate goals, that masks the emptiness and confusion of its inhabitants with a facade of gleaming limestone. Integrity, decision, strength — the proper qualities of the shapers of this new city — are possessed only by its commercial buildings. Whereas in *Main Street* we are shown the dream of a new civilization without the reality, in *Babbitt* we have the reality without the dream, a humming dynamo of a modern city whose external intimations of heroic accomplishment mock the meager-hearted citizens who inhabit it.

The city seems to offer great freedom and myriad opportunities for human achievement. At several points in *Babbitt* Lewis holds up his narrative flow to scan the entire city of Zenith, giving us a montage of simultaneous events, vignettes of character and scene, ranging from low life to high, from urban despair to joy, from mindlessness to intellectual brilliance. Seneca Doane, the Darrowlike liberal lawyer whose opinions mark him as something of an authorial spokesman, defends Zenith against his European guest's charge of standardization in one of these vignettes, anticipating Sam Dodsworth's support of his country against the complaints of cynical Europeans. Doane's forthright and unslavish admiration for Zenith's dynamic power, his enthusiasm for the city's future, " 'so unknown that it excites my imagination' " (85), closely resembles Cass Timberlane's visionary hopefulness for his region. And both are revealed as essential beliefs of Lewis himself when he echoes that sense of great expectations at the conclusion of his Nobel acceptance speech. There he spoke of his joy in joining with other American writers in a "determination to give to the America that has mountains and endless prairies, enormous cities and lost farm cabins, billions of money and tons of faith, to an America that is as strange as Russia and as complex as China, a literature worthy of her vastness."[27] Lewis's satire in *Babbitt*, then, is placed against an urban landscape of great hope, a metropolis of boundless possibilities for accomplishment.

George F. Babbitt instinctively responds to these visionary intimations; "he loved his city with passionate wonder" (178). He palpitates in sympathetic response to its complex systems. Driving through its downtown streets he feels "like a shuttle of polished steel darting in a vast machine" (45). In his speeches to the Booster's Club he loftily portrays the "realtor" as a far-sighted visionary, functioning as " 'a seer of the future development of the community, and as a prophetic engineer clearing the pathway for inevitable changes' " (38).

But of course Babbitt is unable to translate this vision beyond its grossest private meaning, as Lewis underscores it for us, "that a real-estate broker could make money by guessing which way the town would grow." Lewis puts Babbitt's ill-defined reverence for his metropolis into perspective by detailing his ignorance of its civic life, its social needs, its architecture, and his inability to *do* anything of a constructive or purposeful nature on its behalf. Nimble only in the petty business of buying and selling houses, Babbitt, with his monumental incompetence, is a perversion of Lewis's progressive dream. In a city built for giants, the midget Babbitt, its representative man, can only barter its structures; he cannot create them.

Lewis clearly expects something more from his main figure. For George F. Babbitt is more than just the typical American businessman. He is also a Westerner, and the distinction, as the earlier works have demonstrated, is an important one for Lewis. As he explained it elsewhere, the Westerners may look like Easterners; "both groups are chiefly reverent toward banking, sound Republicanism, the playing of golf and bridge, and the possession of large motors. But whereas the Easterner is content with these symbols and smugly desires nothing else, the Westerner, however golfocentric he may be, is not altogether satisfied . . . . secretly, wistfully he desires a beauty that he does not understand."[28] Hence Babbitt's vague but insistent yearnings: "Wish I'd been a pioneer, same as my grand-dad' " (75), he muses at one point; at another, the outcast Seneca Doane touches Babbitt's secret, better self when he recalls their college days when Babbitt was " 'an unusually liberal, sensitive chap . . . .you were going to be a lawyer, and take the cases of the poor for nothing, and fight the rich. And I remember I said I was going to be one of the rich myself, and buy paintings and live at Newport. I'm sure you inspired us all' " (244). Both men had graduated from college in the class of 1896, in the heady, early days of Progressive reform. But while Doane had gone on to live out Babbitt's dream, Babbitt had succumbed to the young Doane's meretricious visions of wealth. In this reversal of roles is to be found Babbitt's private admiration for Doane, and the basis for the realtor's transformation into a temporarily independent thinker near the novel's conclusion.

And Babbitt is not alone in his western longings for a lost ideal, because the theme of having failed one's own dreams of personal fulfillment, of having falsified one's hopes of worthy *becoming*, rings through the characterizations of many of Babbitt's fellow mid-Americans. Paul Riesling, Babbitt's best friend, whose sense of having betrayed his own self-worth is the glue that holds Babbitt to him, has forsaken his love for the violin for a life selling tar-paper roofing. Chum Frink, the Eddie Guest doggerel-poet, admits boozily that he has perverted his talents, and might have been a real poet, " 'maybe a Stevenson' " (220). Ed Overbrook, the dismal insurance salesman, is another poet slipped off Parnassus (164). A salesman from Sparta whom Babbitt meets at the realtors' convention, "a grave, intense youngster," tells of his early hope to become a chemist (141).

To these admitted closet idealists may be added those whose failure to acknowledge the perversion of their own talents does not excuse them from Lewis's scorn. Babbitt's neighbor, Howard Littlefield, is one of these, a Ph.D. in economics who has reduced his scholarly and professional gifts to sanctifying the low trade cunning of the business class. (" 'The guy that put the con in economics,' " chirps Babbitt brightly of Littlefield, whose field is little indeed [98].) Then there are the ranks of bored and useless wives in the novel, women like Lucile McKelvey, Louetta Swanson, and Zilla Riesling, with nothing to do but vent their dissatisfaction in flirtation or nagging, their inner resources so flaccid that they may fall victim, as does Zilla, to a barking religious hysteria. Finally, in the novel's continuing inter-jection of marvelous counterfeits of contemporary magazine journalism and mail-order advertising, Lewis extends his gallery of dreamers to include an entire nation of upward-seekers, their tawdry pursuit of self-renewal unerringly mirrored in their mass media: manicure girls turned into movie stars, bootblacks become celebrated authors overnight, weak bodies transformed magically into strong, instant new careers in oratory, in banking. Improve Your Memory! No Special Education Required! Errant visions of the might-have-been and the might-be are thus projected into the larger social consciousness, and present the reader with an enormous Riesmanian lonely crowd, a veritable army of underachievers, marching to the same drummer while unable to deny the seductive private rhythms of their own dreams, beating within their own skulls.

As a Westerner, Babbitt is strongly drawn, like all of Lewis's main characters, to nature. Even his romantic fantasies with the "faery child" of his dreams occur in a series of natural settings — groves, gardens, moors, the sea. But more striking are those occasions when, seeking the balms of nature and male camaraderie, Babbitt heads off to the Maine woods to repeat the familiar American gesture of nonurban renewal. Even in Maine, of course, he cannot shake off the city which claims him. His dress and behavior in the woods are absurdly out of place: "[Babbitt] came out...in khaki shirt and vast and flapping khaki trousers. It was excessively new khaki; his rimless spectacles belonged to a city office; and his face was not tanned but a city pink. He made a discordant noise in the place. But with infinite satisfaction he slapped his legs and crowed, 'Say, this is getting back home, eh?' " (124)

His conception of his Maine guide, Joe Paradise, as an incorruptible Leatherstocking and an appropriate model for his own revivification is destroyed when Joe reveals himself as a backwoods Babbitt, one who will walk or canoe in to the best fishing places if the sports insist, but who prefers a flat-bottom boat with an Evinrude, and who looks forward to the

day when he can open a shoe store in town. Thus Babbitt —
too addled by his Zenith existence to absorb the regenerative
silence of the woods, bereft by the loss of his friend Paul
Riesling, and deprived, by Joe Paradise's abdication, of an
appropriate model of conduct toward nature — finds himself
drawn back to his city as one who "could never run away
from Zenith and family and office, because in his own brain
he bore the office and the family and every street and
disquiet and illusion of Zenith" (242). Babbitt's retreat into
nature fails as do his escapes into bohemianism and liberalism
because his Zenith preoccupations have drained him of the
values of hope and freedom which are his western birthright,
and he is thus incapable of grasping the terms of his
dilemma. The call of the wild is indubitably real to Babbitt,
as it has perhaps always been to Americans, but his
fragmentary and childish conception of it ("moccasins — six-
gun — frontier town — gamblers — sleep under the stars —
be a regular man, with he-men like Joe Paradise — gosh!"
[238]) renders him vulnerable to confusion and failure. The
novel ends, as did *Main Street*, with a chastened rebel, but
Babbitt remains at last a more pathetic figure than Carol
Kennicott, for unlike her he is never able to formulate
coherently the dream which he is finally forced to deny.
Still, Babbitt's son Ted, Theodore Roosevelt Babbitt, whose
name resonates with his father's not quite forgotten aspirations
toward Progressive action and the manly western virtues,
emerges at the end as an intimation of the hopeful future.
Ted, the rebellious would-be inventor, "a natural mechanic,
a maker and tinkerer of machines," who "lisped in blueprints"
(18), is the potential new technocrat who may rise out of
Babbitt's ashes.

   In *Arrowsmith* (1925) Lewis for the first time in a major
novel presents a main character whose consequence as an
agent of cultural progress matches his technical mastery and
his dedication to his goals. Martin Arrowsmith, the doctor

turned researcher, is an amalgam of the earlier Doc Kennicott and the visionary Carol. "I desired," Lewis recalled later, "to portray a more significant medico than Kennicott — one who could get beneath routine practice into the scientific foundations of medicine; one who should immensely affect all life."[29] " 'That's what I want to do!' " says Martin Arrowsmith as young country doctor listening to Gustaf Sondelius, the great epidemic fighter: " 'Not just tinker a lot of worn-out bodies but make a new world!' "[30] Although *Arrowsmith* exposes a great many charlatans and hypocrites within the medical profession, there are many competent and admirable doctors in the novel. Indeed, it is one of the book's ironies that an Olympian scientist like Max Gottlieb, an M.D. as well as a renowned pathologist, is incapable of diagnosing or treating his own wife's illness and must helplessly call upon "Dad" Silva, the despised medical school dean, for an accurate assessment of her condition. Still, Lewis most admires those like Gottlieb whose personal failures are rendered insignificant by the magnitude of their scientific achievements. Actually, the true great ones are to be recognized by their innocence of conventional success. Gottlieb, for example "had never dined with a duchess, never received a prize, never produced anything which the public could understand. . . .He was, in fact, an authentic scientist" (121).

Along with his scientific credentials, Arrowsmith possesses in his midwestern roots the requisite benisons of nature. The book opens with the scene of a wagon carrying his pioneer forebears through the Ohio wilderness, and with his great-grandmother-to-be saying portentously, " 'Nobody ain't going to take us in. . . .We're going on jus' long as we can. Going West! They's a whole lot of new things I aim to be seeing!' " (5). Heavy-handed as it sometimes is, the novel's frequently noted pioneering theme is appropriate to Arrowsmith in the realistic as well as archetypal sense: that is, as a heroic explorer of unknown frontiers, he is not quite the perfect social being. In this sense, nature has a double function in the novel, not only to ennoble the hero but to humanize him, as is seen in the description of his early summer spent stringing telephone lines in Montana: "The wire-gang were as healthy and as simple as the west wind; they had no pretentiousness; though they handled electrical equipment they did not, like medics, learn a confusion of scientific terms and pretend to the farmers that they were scientists. They laughed easily and were content to be themselves, and with them Martin was content to forget how noble he was" (33). From the linemen, admirable rustic technologists, Martin's cold idealism receives a lesson in humanity.

That lesson comes to fruition in the plague episode late in the novel where, on an Edenic island in the Caribbean, nature seems not the characteristic and familiar American restorative but the mask of a cosmic malevolence. The tropics, says Sondelius, dying of the plague, are the " 'jest of God. . . . God planned them so beautiful, flowers and sea and mountains. He made the fruit to grow so well that man need not work — and then He laughed, and stuck in volcanoes and snakes and damp heat and early senility and the plague and malaria. But the nastiest trick He ever played on man was inventing the flea' " (365). In this case, then, it is the scientist who must save his fellow creatures from a Creator's deadly joke concealed beneath the natural lushness of the tropics. More precisely, for the agnostic scientist, the plague, malaria, snakebite, sleeping sickness are not God's jests but natural calamities eradicable through rational thought and action. The scientist hero, then, is the ultimate humanist, working to reorder those conflicting aspects of the natural world so as to harmonize with human needs. True, humanity may not deserve the favor. There is a dark strain of Robinson Jeffers's inhumanism that surfaces occasionally in the thoughts of Gottlieb and Arrowsmith, when they are tempted to admire, more than the human swarm, the beautiful, fatal pathologies against which they war. But these notions are cerebral rather than actual challenges to their function as benefactors of mankind.

In the book's ending, Lewis provides the highest moral vindication of Martin's rejection of conventional society by presenting his action as a form of heroic new endeavor for "those of us who are pioneers" to escape the trap of becoming only "a machine for digestion and propagation and obedience" (425). Martin's destination is a laboratory in the Vermont woods established by his fellow scientist Terry Wickett, a Thoreauvian retreat complete with rough shack, pond, woodland neighbors, even a latter-day Thoreau himself in the abrasively individualistic Wickett. (Arrowsmith's cabin laboratory recalls the earlier shack of Miles Bjornstam in *Main Street*, where potbellied stove and bare pine floor share the scene with a workbench and assorted volumes, including a manual on gasoline engines and one by Thorstein Veblen [117].) Improbable as this conclusion may seem after the careful realism of the earlier sections, Martin Arrowsmith's cabin laboratory is an unmistakable projection of Lewis's linked themes of scientific progress, creative individualism, and nature.

It should be added, however, that in its apparent denial of the possibilities for reconciliation between the questing individual and society, the ending of *Arrowsmith* is uncharacteristic of Lewis. With this exception, it is not the wilds but the middle landscape between raw nature and the city that comprises the appropriate terrain for the Lewis hero. It is worth noting that Lewis, in a 1941 mock obituary about himself entitled "The Death of Arrowsmith," in *Coronet* for July 1941, suggests a softening of Martin's denial of society. After the title, Lewis uses his own name in the obituary but refers to himself in terms synonymous with Arrowsmith. We are told that for the last ten or fifteen years of his life, Lewis-Arrowsmith has lived in a modest country estate in northwestern Connecticut, with his cats, his garden, and his work. Thus we are left with a pastoral rather than a primitive landscape and with, in this bit of external evidence, the suggestion of synthesis rather than alienation. And it is true that Lewis's hero will not again be a scientist. Rather, Lewis will return to the more pragmatic designer, builder, and architect as his representative hero. Even Arrowsmith, of course, resists classification as a "pure" scientist in the category of a Max Gottlieb or Terry Wickett. Arrowsmith's humane impulses prevail over his scientific duties in the plague episode, and the experiment is, technically, a failure. Nevertheless, Arrowsmith remains as Lewis's only new American who may justifiably be termed radical.

Mention should be made at this point of Lewis's intervening "big" book, *Elmer Gantry* (1927). It stands as a kind of negative pole for all of Lewis's motivations toward social progress and heroic individualism. Without even the vague yearnings and abortive attempts of a Babbitt to invest his life with meaning, Gantry is the ultimate parasite, and Lewis's satire is correspondingly relentless. The book's only true Christian antithesis to Gantry is a backwoods cleric who finds his God — predictably — in nature. But the Rev. Pengilly is a minor character whose forest mysticism remains etherealized and private, useless in any combat of ideas. Even a more vital and significant foil for Gantry like Frank Shallard offers Lewis no model for a hero. An honest doubter like Shallard is to be preferred to a thorough hypocrite like Gantry, to be sure, but the genus is not promising for Lewis. The preachers, like the practicing physicians and the businessmen, are Lewis's second-class citizens, functionaries and servants of the social order rather than its designers and creators.

If *Arrowsmith* is the high point of Lewis's radical in-dividualism, *Dodsworth* (1929) presents the fullest treatment of the more characteristic figure toward whom the earlier novels have been pointing. In the opportunities for self-examination afforded by a trip to Europe with his wife, Fran,

Sam Dodsworth, fifty-year-old industrialist, decides that he wants to return to America and do something more with the rest of his life than build automobiles. Fran, conversely, selfishly worries over the loss of her youth and is increasingly attracted to aimless travel and superficial Europeans. After their separation, Sam meets Edith Cortright, a sympathetic widow whom, after various rebounds to Fran, he is finally to marry. During the course of the novel he has become interested in the garden suburb movement, as typified historically by Forest Hills on Long Island and its more flamboyant imitations, as represented by Zenith's "Sans Souci Gardens":

> To the north of Zenith, among wooded hills above the Chaloosa River, there was being laid out one of the astonishing suburbs which have appeared in America since 1910. So far as possible, the builders kept the beauties of forest and hills and river; the roads were not to be broad straight gashes butting their way through hills, but winding byways. . . .
> It came to him that now there was but little pioneering in manufacturing motors; that he hadn't much desire to fling out more cars on the packed highways. To create houses, . . .noble houses that would last three hundred years, and not be scrapped in a year, as cars were —
> "That'd be interesting," said Sam Dodsworth, the builder.[31]

In pursuing this venture, Dodsworth prepares to become Lewis's most significant and characteristic new pioneer: a western idealist who has mastered the technology necessary to achieve his goal, a goal that is sanctioned by its associations both with cultural progress and with nature. Dodsworth the automobile manufacturer is, in an age of automobiles, merely serving the social order without guiding or ameliorating its destiny. He cannot "immensely affect all life." The anticipated shift of his role to that of designer and builder of wooded suburbs promises to elevate him from mechanic to creator. A materialist who can yield to the dream that is his western inheritance but who nevertheless retains his mastery of the industrial technology, a searcher who has weighed his native values against the soft sophistication of Europe, Dodsworth, more than any other of Lewis's heroes, seems both properly qualified and properly motivated to move society along the path toward its appropriate future.

It should be emphasized at this point that if Arrowsmith is Lewis's Thoreauvian hero, Dodsworth is his Emersonian hero, and the latter figure, despite Lewis's stated praise of Thoreau and disparagement of Emerson, is the more typical of Lewis's work.[32] In his commitment to technological progress here and elsewhere Lewis comes into sharp conflict with Thoreau, who stood grimly on the side of nature in what he often depicted as a virtual state of warfare between country and city. Lewis, on the other hand, can hardly restrain his enthusiasm in the presence of advancing civilization:

> My delight in watching the small Middle Western cities grow, sometimes beautifully and sometimes hideously, and usually both together, from sod shanties to log huts to embarrassed-looking skinny white frame buildings to sixteen-story hotels and the thirty-story bank buildings, may be commented on casually. There is a miracle in the story of how all this has happened in two or three generations. Yet, after this period, which is scarcely a second in historic time, we have a settled civilization with traditions and virtues and foolishness as fixed as those of the oldest tribe of Europe. I merely submit that such a theme is a challenge to all the resources a novelist can summon.[33]

It is not Thoreau but Emerson who was Lewis's predecessor and who might have provided Lewis with a shock of recognition had he read Emerson more carefully. Lewis precisely echoes Emerson's belief that a civilization is to be judged by the extent to which it draws the most benefit from its cities. Like Emerson, Lewis sees nature and the city as ultimately reconciled through the city's being related more closely to its natural environment. Like Emerson, he envisions this reconciliation as the role of a heroic man of action who will fulfill his own destiny and that of the nation in carrying out this synthesis. Like Emerson, Lewis conceived of this figure as a western "cosmopolitan," one who would combine within himself natural and urban attributes. Finally, like Emerson, Lewis's emblem for the American future is what Michael Cowan, in his study of Emerson, calls a "City of the West," a combining and reconciling of industrial and Arcadian values.[34]

Although *Dodsworth* is the culmination of Lewis's efforts to bring forth a visionary western technologist, the work reveals a troublesome lessening of intensity toward the implications and consequences of his theme, an inability or unwillingness to follow it through to its novelistic conclusions. *Dodsworth* closes with the promise of a new life for Sam, but he has now bounced from wooded estates to travel trailers, which he has imagined as carrying urbanites in comfort into the forest. (" 'Kind of a shame to have 'em ruin any more wilderness. Oh, that's just sentimentality,' he assured himself" [27]). And houses or trailers, we are never witness to their creation, nor do they quite qualify for their role, however much they might widen the vistas of nature-hungry Americans. The earlier dream of a Carol Kennicott, hazy as it was, embraced the entire community in a gesture of democratic inclusiveness, rather than just that comfortably well-off portion of it to which Sam Dodsworth has limited himself.

In such curiously diminished forms, western builders will continue to appear in Lewis's later novels. Myron Weagle of *Work of Art* (1934), for example, actually achieves his version of a city in the West, but the reader has difficulty in taking it seriously. A New England hotelkeeper whose career is devoted to the creation of "the Perfect Hotel Inn," Weagle moves through a frustrating career, heads west, buys a small

hotel in a Kansas town, and turns it into a "work of art," as
opposed to the cheap and meretricious books turned out by
his writer brother. But after the larger design of Lewis's
earlier works, an innkeeper, however proficient, scarcely
qualifies as a pioneer of progress, nor does his western inn
begin to fill the expansive canvas which Lewis has prepared.

The same sorts of truncated dreamers and deflated visions
are found in Lewis's four final novels. *Cass Timberlane* (1945)
first establishes a panoramic West and a properly idealistic,
if middle-aged, Westerner and then reverts almost entirely
to domestic affairs. For Neil Kingsblood (*Kingsblood Royal*,
1947), the hopeful western horizon has shrunk to his suburban
home in Sylvan Park, a disquieting version of Sam
Dodsworth's earlier dream suburb. Here, according to the
brochure of Mr. William Stopple, realtor, "gracious living,
artistic landscaping, the American Way of Life, and up-to-
the-minute conveniences are exemplified in 'Dream o' Mine
Come True'...," while at the same time Mr. Stopple
privately advises that Sylvan Park "is just as free of Jews,
Italians, Negroes, and the exasperatingly poor as it is of
noise, mosquitoes, and rectangularity of streets."[35] While
Neil Kingsblood and his wife jeer at the rhetoric of the
Stopple brochure, they nevertheless unabashedly regard
Sylvan Park as "a paradise and a highly sensible paradise"
(10); and while they come to reject the racist values of
suburbia, they finally take up guns to preserve their place
within it. In *The God-Seeker* (1949), Lewis exchanges new
pioneering for old, but the pattern of reduction remains.
Aaron Gadd abandons the larger dream which has sent him
west to the Minnesota frontier and returns to his trade of
carpentry: " 'There are many things I don't ever expect to
know, and I'm got going to devote myself to preaching about
them but to building woodsheds so true and tight that they
don't need ivory and fine gold — straight white pine, cedar
shingles, a door that won't bind — glorious!' "[36]

Finally, in Lewis's last novel, *World So Wide* (1951), the

hopeful western horizon has simply turned into blank wall. Once again, Lewis posits his familiar builder hero, but here his dream does not survive even the opening chapter. Hayden Chart, an architect of the western city of "Newlife," Colorado ("that big, huge place where you look up to the horizon") decides on page nine that, after his wife's accidental death, he must turn from the task that was to have been his life's work: "now he would never build that prairie village which was to have been housed in one skyscraper: the first solution in history of rural isolation and loneliness."[37] Lewis had first advanced the idea of the office building as a new kind of village and community nearly thirty years earlier in the third chapter of *Babbitt* (30). And the plans for an actual skyscraper community were to be found on the desk of Frank Lloyd Wright, in another of those striking parallels between the thinking of Lewis and that visionary midwestern architect (see n. 24). Wright's towering skyscraper, "The Mile-High Illinois," a cantilevered shaft of 528 stories, was to have been a "sky-city," another attempt, like Lewis's, to redefine human relationships through the projection of bold new architectural forms upon the clean, mid-American landscape.[38] Both designs still await their builder.

As Chart's prairie skyscraper village diffuses into a world so wide, his life peters out into aimless travel, a pathetic following after Meaningful Experiences. In a final stroke, Lewis revives the figures of Sam and Edith Dodsworth, who befriend Chart in Europe. The Dodsworths, we learn have left America after returning there for only a short time, having found, as Sam confides, that Europe has "spoiled" them for life in America (46). Even offstage Lewis's American dream cannot sustain itself.

These reformed visionaries of his later works demonstrate Lewis's difficulty in engaging fully the concept of new pioneering that engrossed him throughout his career as novelist. In one respect, these western pilgrims, forever diverting themselves from the shining city on a prairie that is their professed destination, may dramatize their creator's misjudgment of his own abilities: although Lewis's impulses were often romantic and idealistic, his talents did not extend beyond the rendering of the actual. He may thus be seen as the victim of an idea that compelled him even as its formulation resisted his efforts to bring it to fictional life. In another respect, the half-hearted builders may suggest a collapse of will on Lewis's part, another manifestation of a familiar American failure, as Frederick I. Carpenter describes it: "The idealist, recognizing that his vision of perfection is impossible, renounces his vision and 'returns to reality.' "[39] Yet it is not Lewis's renunciation of his vision that is most striking, but rather that he clings to it long after it has ceased to be a working force in his fiction, that he finally *cannot* renounce the vision. While the dream goes slack or is vulgarized in the later works, we are nevertheless left with an assertion of, or preoccupation with, a basic belief that remains consistent throughout Lewis's novels and that seems to transcend the divided self that Schorer and others have portrayed. Whether Lewis defines the good life explicitly in the idealistic hopes of his characters, or implicitly in the objects he selects for attack, the satirist and idealist in him merge in the moral basis from which both modes proceed.

From what we know of the man it is difficult not to speculate that Lewis who could write of himself that "there never was in private life a less attractive or admirable fellow," and who, in reality, never revealed a deep appreciation of nature, sought in the visionary plans and pastoral associations of his main characters the means of legitimizing himself as an artist and a man.[40] His tendency to identify himself publicly with his fictional creation (e.g., Carl Ericson, Carol Kennicott, Martin Arrowsmith) suggests strongly that we may find in the novels fictional surrogates for this restless and unattractive loner.[41] Ridden all of his life by a deep sense of inferiority to the doctors in his family, his father and his brother Claude, Lewis, through his western builders, may have sought the means to vindicate himself as a creator, to authenticate his own personal worth and dignity, something that he felt his family never accorded him in his career as a writer. Perry Miller, in his account of his friendship with Lewis at the end of the author's life, tells of Lewis's blowup when he, Miller, facetiously suggested in the presence of Lewis and his brother, Dr. Claude Lewis, that Claude would doubtless prefer visiting medical facilities in Leiden the following morning to hearing Lewis's lecture. Later, Miller says, Lewis apologized, saying, " 'It's been that way from the beginning. . . .I wanted to write, and I've worked like hell at it, and the whole of Sauk Center and my family and America have never undersood that it is work, that I haven't just been playing around, that this is every bit as important as Claude's hospital. When you said that Claude did not want to hear my lecture, . . .you set up all the resentments I have had ever since I can remember.' "[42] If the speculation is valid, it cannot have escaped Lewis that in his Arrowsmiths and Dodsworths he possessed a potent challenge to the superiority of the Lewis family doctors, who, unlike the creators, had not the power to "immensely affect all life." Nor was it likely that he could overlook, in the impotence and failure of his later fictional heroes, the evidence of his own inability, at last, to validate his vision as a creator.

Seen thus, the Lewis canon offers itself as an ironic affirmation of Leon Edel's claim, in writing of Willa Cather, that an artist's works constitute a kind of supreme biography of their creator. As a writer, Lewis shared with many of his later characters an impatience with long-range goals even as he was driven to project them, a propensity for being too easily diverted, a tendency, like the historical pioneer, to move on, leaving disordered and unfinished landscapes behind him, without pondering the consequences. In this sense do Lewis's inadequacies constitute a kind of sardonic tribute to his superb gifts of mimicry and photographic realism, an ultimate stamp of corroboration upon his own, self-proclaimed "fanatic" Americanness.

Nevertheless, preoccupation with the long downward slope of Lewis's career in the years from the publication of *Dodsworth* to his death in 1951 should not, as Sheldon Grebstein reminds us, divert attention from his lasting achievements. Like Frank Norris, Sinclair Lewis attempted the great survey of American life as it passed swiftly into its modern phase. And Lewis's high praise of Cather, at the end of his career, as the greatest living American novelist for her having preserved the frontier at the same time that she treated the lives of postfrontier Americans is surely as much a judgment and vindication of his own career as of Cather's. In *Main Street, Arrowsmith,* and *Dodsworth,* and in the brilliant inversions of *Babbitt,* Lewis demonstrated his rightful claim to a place among those writers who have examined the sources of validity in American idealism, and who have created in their works new emblems of possibility to be measured against the failures of the present. While it may be objected that we search almost without success for those changes actually wrought by Lewis's western creators, the same criticism might be applied to many of the visionary designs in our literature. Fragmentary and resistant to close scrutiny they may still propose fresh possibilities to the imagination while they miscarry in actuality.[43]

A more formidable objection has been that Lewis's new pioneering fails not because it emphasizes the disparity between the real and the ideal but because it insists upon the possibilities for their reconciliaton. To a generation of critics and readers fashionably beyond innocence and accustomed to the assumption that a closed frontier and the presence of the machine in the garden must cause the serious artist to turn inevitably in the direction of alienation and tragedy, Lewis's idealistic technologists must seem to have either naively misjudged the realities or sold out to them. In Lewis's defense it must be questioned whether such judgments are not too narrowly conceived if they rule out a figure of his cultural and literary significance. Somewhere, Lewis believed, between the sod shanty and the asphalt parking lot we had missed civilization, but perhaps it was still not too late. Like the older Progressives of the turn of the century, with whom he finally belongs, he saw the historical process as a means of transcending the old paradox of industrial civilization destroying the American garden. Through his novels he continually asserts the prodigious speed with which the country was growing and changing, and his belief that the culture that emerged from this ferment of growth and change could be shaped and heightened by such fictional heroes and heroines as he created, and by such a writer as he himself wished to be. Thus we have his revealing assertion to Perry Miller that, " 'I love America. . . . I love it, but I don't like it,' " and his repeated claim that he wanted to raise the cultural maturity of America by mocking its "cruder manifestations."[44] When he complained of and satirized the pioneer myth, he did so only when it became an empty memorializing of the past and an apology for present mediocrity, rather than an impetus toward advancing our cultural possibilities.

To participate in the formulation and direction of this emerging culture was Lewis's aim as a writer. Hence his characteristic version of pastoral calls for the cultivation rather than the rejection of progressive human aspirations, and his best works project a new industrial mythology in which the rising leaders of a modern America search out their appropriate roles, as he had sought out his own. In his new pioneers he found a unique means to combine the diverse aims of personal freedom and social obligation. The fundamental Lewis hero hopes thus, through the discovery of his role and the achievement of his creative endeavors — invention, building, town, city, medical discovery — to assert not only his own individuality but also his participation in the social order and his commitment to help shape the emerging new America.

NOTES

1. "Four American Impressions," *The New Republic* 32 (October 11, 1922): 172.
2. *Spokesmen: Modern Writers and American Life* (New York: Appleton, 1928), p. 228.
3. Mark Schorer, *Sinclair Lewis: An American Life* (New York: McGraw-Hill, 1961); Sheldon Grebstein, *Sinclair Lewis* (New York: Twayne Publishers, 1962); D. J. Dooley, *The Art of Sinclair Lewis* (Lincoln: University of Nebraska Press, 1967); Martin Light, *The Quixotic Vision of Sinclair Lewis* (West Lafayette, Ind.: Purdue University Press, 1975). Another assessment, however, James Lundquist's *Sinclair Lewis* (New York: Frederick Ungar, 1973) argues that the "melodramatic" aspects of Lewis's career have been overstated.
4. Maurice Kramer, "Sinclair Lewis and the Hollow Center," *The Twenties: Poetry and Prose*, ed. Richard E. Langford and William E. Taylor (Deland, Fla.: Everett Edwards, 1966), p. 69.
5. The "contradiction..." statement is from Lewis's unpublished "Introduction to *Babbitt*," in *The Man from Main Street: Selected Essays and Other Writings: 1904-1950*, ed. Harry E. Maule and Melville H. Cane (New York: Pocket Books, 1963), p. 26. Hereafter cited as *MMS*. Lewis's self-description is from "The Death of Arrowsmith," *Coronet* 10 (July 1941): 108.
6. Sinclair Lewis, "The Greatest American Novelist," *Newsweek* 11 (January 3, 1938): 29.
7. Two important earlier studies that treat aspects of Lewis's idealism are Frederick I. Carpenter's "Sinclair Lewis and the Fortress of Reality," in his *American Literature and the Dream* (New York: Philosophical Library, 1955), pp. 116-25, and Maxwell Geismar's "Sinclair Lewis: The Comic Bourjoyce," in his *The Last of the Provincials* (Boston: Houghton Mifflin, 1949), pp. 69-150. I have also found stimulating the final chapter of D. J. Dooley's work (n. 3), as well as passing references in Grebstein and Schorer, especially pp. 810-11 in the latter's monumental critical biography. James Lea's "Sinclair Lewis and the Implied America," *Clio* 3 (October 1973): 21-34, provides another analysis of Lewis's idealism by examining seven novels that span the years 1830 to 1946 and that record American promise and failure.
8. *Cass Timberlane* (New York: Random House, 1945), p. 28.
9. For Lewis's praise of Thoreau and *Walden* see "Introduction to *Four Days on the Webutuck River*," *MMS*, pp. 169-70, and "One Man Revolution," *Newsweek* 10 (November 22, 1937): 33.
10. The wilderness rehabilitation at its most strained is found in Lewis's later work, *The Prodigal Parents* (1938), where Fred Cornplow rescues his dull-witted son from sloth and dissipation by forcing him into a canoe trip through the Canadian wilderness. With greater restraint, however, Lewis (himself an inveterate walker) will portray, in *Main Street* and *Dodsworth*, the hike through the countryside as a convincing effort by

his characters to break away from destructive and inhibiting social pressures.

11. *The Job* (New York: Harcourt, Brace, 1917), p. 203.

12. *The Trail of the Hawk* (New York: Harcourt, Brace, 1915), pp. 316-17.

13. *Free Air* (New York: Grosset and Dunlap, 1919), p. 190.

14. In *Kingsblood Royal* (1947), Neil Kingsblood's discovery of his black ancestor, Xavier Pic, is cushioned for the hero (and, one suspects, for Lewis and his audience) by Pic's having been an intrepid *voyageur* and explorer of the northern wilds.

15. See Schorer, p. 203.

16. For further treatment of the cultural significance of the Lindbergh flight see John William Ward's, "The Meaning of Lindbergh's Flight," *American Quarterly* 10 (Spring 1958): 3-16.

17. *Main Street* (New York: New American Library, 1961), pp. 7-8.

18. Schorer, p. 230.

19. Daniel Aaron, "Main Street," in *The American Novel*, ed. Wallace Stegner (New York: Basic Books, 1965), p. 171.

20. In attempting to find whether Lewis had an actual book in mind as the source for Carol's textbook, one is drawn back to Ebeneezer Howard's influential *Garden Cities of Tomorrow* (1902), first published in 1898 as *Tomorrow: A Peaceful Path to Real Reform*, and to the many books and periodicals that it spawned. (Howard's book itself was inspired by Bellamy's *Looking Backward*.) Professor Walter Creese, Department of Architecture, University of Illinois, Urbana, a student of this and related town-planning movements, has suggested, in answer to my inquiry to him, that Carol's text is probably a blend of these. Carol's college years (approximately 1904-7, according to Schorer's chronology) were the period in which the Garden City movement was flourishing. Lewis's frequent references to town planning and beautification in *Main Street* (see, e.g., pp. 129-30) and to garden suburbs and their historical development in *Dodsworth* demonstrate his familiarity with these movements.

21. In excepting the classical bank from Carol's catalog of Main Street's unrelieved ugliness, Lewis again reveals his architectural awareness. Every town was likely to have such a bank at the time, a tribute to ascendant capitalism; but, further, innovative architects like Louis Sullivan were building in bold, new designs, many small-town banks across the Middle West. Perhaps most noteworthy of these, judging by the prominence it is given in architectural histories, is the National Farmer's Bank (the name a reversal of Gopher Prairie's bank) in Owatonna, in Lewis's home state, constructed in 1907-8, on Sullivan's design. See, e.g., Vincent Scully, *American Architecture and Urbanism* (New York: Praeger, 1969), pp. 126-29, and Christopher Tunnard and Henry Hope Reed, *American Skyline* (Boston: Houghton Mifflin, 1955), pp. 210, 222-23.

22. Lewis Mumford, *Sticks and Stones* (New York: Boni and Liveright, 1924; Second Revised Edition New York: Dover, 1955), p. 87.

23. "Main Street's Been Paved!," *The Nation* 119 (September 10, 1924): 257.

24. Although the Lewis biographies (and a letter from Mark Schorer in response to my inquiry) indicate no direct evidence of Lewis's knowing Frank Lloyd Wright or his work, it is difficult to believe that Lewis, in whose works architecture is so often emphasized, would not be aware of Wright, or of the fact that Wright meets Lewis's requirements so admirably here, not only in Wright's radical innovativeness and technical skill, but in the extent to which, as the originator of "Prairie Architecture" at the turn of the century, he gave architectural expression to the middle western landscape. See his *Writings and Buildings* (New York: Horizon, 1960), pp. 37-55. See also the Wisconsin-born Wright's self-description as "grown up in the midst of a sentimental family planted on free soil by a grandly sentimental grandfather...the Welsh pioneer," and his claim that "the real American spirit, capable of judging an issue for its merits, lies in the West and Middle West, where breadth of view, independent thought and a tendency to take common sense into the realm of art, as in life, are characteristic. It is alone in an atmosphere of this nature that the Gothic spirit of building can be revived." (Quoted in Wayne Andrews, *Architecture, Ambition and Americans* [New York: Harper's 1955], p. 230.) David Noble's depiction of Louis Sullivan as another and complementary version of the architect as new American leader out of the heartlands is also instructive. See Noble's *The Progressive Mind* (Chicago: Rand McNally, 1970) pp. 119-21.

25. *Sticks and Stones*, p. 193.

26. *Babbitt* (New York: New American Library, 1962), p. 5

27. *MMS*, p. 17.

28. "Minnesota, the Norse State," *The Nation* 116 (May 30, 1923): 626.

29. Quoted in Schorer's "Afterword," *Arrowsmith* (New York: New American Library, 1961), p. 432.

30. *Arrowsmith*, p. 175.

31. *Dodsworth* (New York: New American Library, 1967), p. 182.

32. See n. 9. For Lewis's disparagement of Emerson, see Lewis's Nobel acceptance speech (*MMS*, p. 15); and "One Man Revolution," *Newsweek* 10 (November 22, 1937): 33.

33. "A Note about *Kingsblood Royal*," *MMS*, p. 37. Compare this, for example with Emerson: "The history of any settlement is an illustration of the whole — first the emigrant's camp, then the group of log cabins, then the cluster of white wooden towns...and almost as soon followed by brick and granite cities, which in another country would stand for centuries, but which here must soon give way to enduring marble." (*Uncollected Lectures*), quoted in Michael Cowan, City of the West: *Emerson, America, and the Urban Metaphor* (New Haven: Yale University Press, 1967), p. 26.

34. I am indebted to Cowan's *City of the West* for my understanding of Emerson in this context.

35. *Kingsblood Royal* (New York: Random House, 1947), p. 10.

36. *The God-Seeker* (New York: Popular Library, 1949), p. 307.

37. *World So Wide* (New York: Random House, 1951), p. 9.

38.   Frank Lloyd Wright, *A Testament* (New York: Horizon Press, 1957), 238-48.

39.   Carpenter, *American Literature and the Dream*, p. 124.

40.   The quotation is from "Self-Portrait (Berlin, August 1927)," *MMS*, p. 47. For the account of a calamitous actual encounter between Lewis and nature, see Claude Lewis's description of a trip with his brother into the Canadian wilds: *Treaty Trip*, Donald Green and George Knox, eds. (Minneapolis: University of Minnesota Press, 1959).

41.   For Lewis's identification of himself with Ericson and other of his characters, see "Self-Portrait," *MMS*, p. 46. For Lewis's admission that he was Carol, see Schorer, p. 286, and Grebstein, pp. 71, 171. His identification with Arrowsmith is the basis for his mock obituary, "The Death of Arrowsmith" *Coronet* 10 (July 1941): 107-110.

42.   Miller, "The Incorruptible Sinclair Lewis," *Atlantic*, 187 (April 1951): 34.

43.   The conception of this fragmentary but nevertheless potent visionary design is suggested by, and explored in, A. N. Kaul's *The American Vision* (New Haven: Yale University Press, 1963).

44.   Miller, p. 34. For Lewis's conception of his role as an agent of cultural progress, see n. 5, and also Alexander Manson, "The Last Days of Sinclair Lewis" (as told to Helen Camp), *Saturday Evening Post* 223 (March 31, 1951): 110. See also Lewis's disparaging of the false myth of pioneering quoted in Schorer, p. 300.

Afterword

> Art offers substitutive gratifications for the oldest and
> still most deeply felt cultural renunciations, and for that
> reason it serves as nothing else does to reconcile a man
> to the personal sacrifices he has made on behalf of
> civilization.
>
> Freud, *The Future of an Illusion*[1]

A homemade scrapbook of pictures of skyscrapers that
Frederick Jackson Turner kept in the years before his death
in 1932 expresses, as do the architectural dreams of Sinclair
Lewis, the persistence of the obligatory western vision of the
urban and industrial future that the White City had first
projected nearly forty years earlier: Across the cover of his
scrapbook Turner had written, "Vertical replacing horizontal
with the end of the era of expansion," an assertion of that
insistent need represented by his fellow Westerners, the
novelists studied here, to posit hopeful alternatives and to
formulate new social ideals for the nation which had arisen
so disturbingly out of the closed frontier.[2]

For Turner, according to his biographer, Ray Allen
Billington, the scrapbook and its inscription were, while an
overt declaration of Turner's faith in the continuing pattern
and process of American pioneering, a covert recognition of
the drift of his civilization into a frontierless and forbidding
future. For all of Turner's determination to accept the new
America, his skyscraper enthusiasm, says Billington, must
have been a kind of whistling in the dark, a forced
hopefulness in the face of a time to come that included the
threats, all addressed by Turner in his later years, of
overpopulation, mass starvation, the depletion of vital
mineral supplies, and worldwide warfare, even the possibility
of a "chemist's bomb" that might consume the entire planet.[3]

Turner's apprehensions about a saturated earth and a
nation whose physical frontiers had ended may, in retrospect,
be applied to the eventual dimming of faith in the western

progressive synthesis experienced by most of the novelists considered here, and reflected in the individual and collective lives of their fictional new Americans. Conceived out of an original impulse that contemporary western and nature-sanctioned figures of arresting urban-industrial identity might somehow transcend the chaotic disunity of their time and thus chart a hopeful direction for the nation's future, the new Americans groped for a center that could not hold. A brief review of each writer's ménage of fictional figures, set against their creators' own careers, underscores a fairly consistent final inability to shape the urban-industrial hero into assured and durable form.

Frank Norris's early death, like Tom Outland's, provided its own emancipation from the downward curve of his survivors. But while his career closed at its midpoint and thus precludes any estimate of ultimate directions and achievements, it may be claimed both that he established the western urbanite as the appropriate candidate for significant modern life and that he had yet, at his death, to discover the proper balance between their protean energies and the opportunities which a technological society made available to them. Hamlin Garland's own life etched itself into the pattern of his questing new Americans, liberated from the drudgery and boredom and failure of farm life and brought into the city or into new rural western careers in government and scientific conservation. But even in the Progressivism of his middle years, Garland also began publishing unrelievedly stereotyped Rocky Mountain scenic romances and novelistic excursions into the occult. And after the reform impetus of the Roosevelt presidency in the first decade of the century had diminished, he turned increasingly to the past, to family history and autobiography. In a West in which, as he once said, "nothing endures for more than a generation,"[4] his commentary upon the present came finally to occasional outbursts against what he saw as the old immorality of the New Morality which followed the Great War. As an instance of his latter-day misjudgments, he saw in Willa Cather's Lost Lady, Marian Forrester, only a concession to the contemporary appetite for "female libertines."[5]

Willa Cather's struggle to integrate her western strivers — engineer, artist, railroader, warrior, architect, scholar, scientist — with the new age was followed, like Garland's, with a resolute march toward the past during her later years. After three historical novels she was, at her death, writing a book set in medieval Avignon. Sherwood Anderson's searching businessmen, his unfulfilled factory workers, his yearning industrial giants like Beaut McGregor and Hugh McVey, reflect their author's inability to overcome his deeply felt antipathy to machine civilization. He was at last never able to create the essentially confident and enduring new Americans he believed his country deserved. The vigorous tradition of Sinclair Lewis's early makers and builders dissipated, in his later works, into a series of feeble charades — *et in Suburbia ego* — that bottomed out in a final novel in which his western architect hero, Hayden Chart, decides that there is for him simply no work left worth doing. Wandering abroad like some enervated parody of Norris's strapping, globe-circling Anglo-Saxons on their Great March of conquest, Chart points the way nowhere, except to his own creator, who guarded his westernness and his democratic optimism to the end and yet who died in Rome, among strangers.

This pattern of historical and fictional decline mirrors the generic recession of the novel itself as a literary form during the twentieth century, according to the postmodernist critic Mas'ud Zavarzadeh in the introduction to his *The Mythopoeic Reality*.[6] The novel as a genre, claims Zavarzadeh, is the essential literary form of an industrializing society, providing to a large readership the sense of an ordered and integrative response to a bewildering new mode of life. The "total answers" provided by the conventional novel serve as secular replacements for the lost cohesion once provided for the agrarian-centered community by religious — and, one might add for our figures, frontier-inspired — absolutes. Furthermore, the conventional integrative novel is supported by the ascendancy of traditional linear and rational patterns of thought necessary to an ordered industrial system. The waning of our figures, then, may, according to such an interpretation, be found in the congruent decline of the traditional novel, which has proved incapable of maintaining its grip upon an increasingly complex technological culture as it evolves from an industrial toward a postindustrial state.[7] The new Americans, with the totalizing novel itself, finally become the victims of a social machine more powerful than their visions of order.

But the dying fall of all these latter-day leave-takings should not obscure the larger meanings of the best and most vigorous works of those novelists studied here, and their more lasting contributions to the understanding of American life. If the western progressive legacy of their new Americans was unable to withstand either the cooling of the individual creative force that Emerson had lamented as the greatest human failing, or the historic shock waves of world war, economic upheaval, and a chaotically proliferating technology, it nevertheless had left its imprint upon our collective experience. While the forces of urbanism and industrialism finally proved less than responsive to those dreams of social and personal affirmation in America which existed, like Charles Eliot Norton's ideal Chicago, "not only in the brain, but in the heart of some of her citizens," the new Americans still showed us, even in diminished form, how we might live here. Whatever portion of Americans today that still seek to live lives of individual meaning and promise within a cohesive democratic community may return to these earlier figures with a sense of recognition. Their peculiarly American brand of pragmatic idealism was perhaps best described by its philosophical spokesman, William James, when he claimed that "the solid meaning of life is always the same eternal thing, the marriage, namely, of some unhabitual ideal, however special, with some fidelity, courage, and endurance; with some man's or woman's pains. — And, whatever or wherever life may be, there will always be the chance for that marriage to take place."[8]

Less important, of course, for the reader of literature than any of these summary statements about the novelists studied in the preceding pages is the sense of having dealt rightly and freshly with their individual accomplishments. As their own chapters here reveal, each of these writers sought the urban-industrial hero in different forms and with varying degress of success. But it may be suggested, at this point, that their contributions come together in describing a pragmatic union of hope and reality that, as the historian Daniel Boorstin claims, has characteristically distinguished American cultural experience.[9] Still threatened by the problems and challenges of our cities and our technology and yet unannihilated by them, we live out, as did the new Americans, a continuing effort to impose a sense of individual and social coherence upon our disordered surroundings. Whatever we have learned from the intervening depiction of the modern consciousness in our literature, we may look back to these figures to find that nihilism and despair are not the necessary sum total of our experience. What is left, as the present-day heir of these earlier western progressives, Wallace Stegner, reminds us, is what keeps us alive.[10] While we may no longer expect with any sort of assurance to encompass the threatening conflicts that challenged the novelists studied here, we survive, as they and their fictions helped to teach us to do, in doubt and failure and hope.

American literature, often criticized for its compulsive Manicheanism, its rigidity of reaction (in comparison with British and Continental literature) to the complexities of society, may reveal in such figures as those studied here evidence of a national literary response to such complexities other than through the classic American gestures of rejection and subsequent flight into the realms of sensation or metaphysics. The vestigial frontier heritage that might have inclined these figures toward such characteristic acts of denial and alienation was checked by their incontrovertible sense of a complex urban-industrial future in which deliverance was no longer to be found in escape but, paradoxically, must be sought in exposure, in participation. Keep up with the procession — in the terms of Henry Blake Fuller's novel — lead it if you can, or join with others to lead it, as the only assurance that it would go somewhere. Without denying the radical innocence and reigning wonder of many of our greatest books, then, the works discussed here, many of them, indicate the presence of a lesser but significant parallel tradition, an exploration of the middle range of national life, but in the terms of a new social mythology to which the traditional standards of Howellsian realism do not really apply. Working within the characteristic range of the realists yet stubbornly visionary, fully possessed of the unremitting American myth of individual self-creation yet determined to shape that energy into agents of hopeful communal leadership rather than of social alienation, these writers extend our sense of the richness of our literature and the continuing possibilities for its revaluation.

Willa Cather, in her later career, once likened a backward look at the novels published since the early 1890s to a walk through a World's Fair grounds years after it has closed: "Palaces with the stucco peeling off, oriental villages stripped to beaver-board and cement, broken fountains, lakes gone to mud and weeds. We realize that whatever it is that makes a book hold together, most of these hadn't it."[11] In these images of the White City fallen into decay, Cather scored the mass-produced shoddiness of the best-selling novels, historical and sentimental romances, of the nineties and early 1900s. If we are allowed to reverse the comparison, then her own best works and those of the other novelists studied here have bodied forth another White City of the imagination, built of more enduring artistic materials and yet no less significant for its attempt, as Turner had anticipated it in 1896, of working out "the problem of the West," the discovery of new social goals and possibilities for a radically changing nation.

NOTES

1. Trans. W. D. Robson-Scott; revised and newly edited by James Strachey (Garden City, New York: Anchor Doubleday, 1961), p. 18.
2. Ray Allen Billington, "Frederick Jackson Turner and the Closing of the Frontier," in *Essays in Western History in Honor of T. A. Larson*, ed. Roger Daniels, University of Wyoming Publications, 37:1-4 (October 1971): 55-56.
3. Billington, 47-53.
4. *A Daughter of the Middle Border* (New York: Grosset and Dunlap, 1921), p. 347.
5. See A. C. Ravitz, "Willa Cather under Fire: Hamlin Garland Misreads *A Lost Lady*," *Western Humanities Review* 9 (Spring 1955): 182-84. Garland's obtuseness here recalls Cather's early lack of patience with his work: "Art is temperament and Hamlin Garland has no more temperament than a prairie dog." Cather, *The Kingdom of Art: Willa Cather's First Principles and Critical Statements, 1893-1896*, ed. Bernice Slote (Lincoln: University of Nebraska Press, 1966), p. 331.
6. (Urbana: University of Illinois Press, 1976), pp. 5-6.
7. Zavarzadeh, pp. 5-6.
8. James, *Talks to Teachers on Psychology: and to Students on Some of Life's Ideals* (New York: Henry Holt, 1899), p. 299.
9. Boorstin, *The Americans: The National Experience* (New York: Random House, 1965).
10. Stegner, "Born a Square," in *The Sound of Mountain Water* (Garden City, N.Y.: Doubleday, 1969), p. 182.
11. Cather, "Miss Jewett," in *Not under Forty* (New York: Alfred A. Knopf, 1936), pp. 91-92.

Bibliography of Works Cited

INTRODUCTION AND AFTERWORD

Adams, Henry. *The Education of Henry Adams*. 1918. Boston: Houghton Mifflin Sentry Edition, 1961.

Barnett, F. L. "The Reason Why." In Ida B. Wells, *The Reason Why the Colored American Is Not in the World's Columbian Exposition*. Chicago: n.p., 1893.

Bellamy, Edward. *Looking Backward*. 1888. New York: Random House Modern Library Edition, 1942.

Billington, Ray Allen. "Frederick Jackson Turner and the Closing of the Frontier." In *Essays in Western History in Honor of T. A. Larson*, edited by Roger Daniels. Laramie: University of Wyoming Publications, no. 37 (1971).

Boorstin, Daniel. *The Americans: The National Experience*. New York: Random House, 1965.

Cather, Willa. "Miss Jewett." In her *Not under Forty*. New York: Alfred A. Knopf, 1936.

Clemens, Samuel L. [Mark Twain]. *A Connecticut Yankee in King Arthur's Court*. 1889. New York: New American Library Signet Edition, 1963.

Croly, Herbert. *The Promise of American Life*. New York: Macmillan, 1909.

Emerson, Ralph Waldo. *The Conduct of Life*. Boston: Ticknor and Fields, 1861.

Freud, Sigmund. *The Future of an Illusion*. 1928. Translated by W. D. Robson-Scott; revised and newly edited by James Strachey. Garden City, N.Y.: Doubleday, 1961.

Howells, William Dean. *April Hopes*. New York: Harper and Brothers, 1888.

———. *The Landlord at Lion's Head*. New York: Harper and Brothers, 1897.

———. *Letters of an Altrurian Traveller*. 1893-94. Reprint. Gainesville, Florida: Scholars' Fascimiles and Reprints, 1961.

———. *A Modern Instance*. 1882. Introduction and notes by George N. Bennett. Bloomington: Indiana University Press, 1977.

———. *The Son of Royal Langbrith*. 1904. Introduction and notes by David Burrows. Bloomington: Indiana University Press, 1969.

James, Henry. *The American*. 1877. Boston: Houghton Mifflin Riverside Edition, 1962.

———. "The Jolly Corner." 1908. In *Henry James: Seven Stories and*

Studies, edited by Edward Stone. New York: Appleton-Century-Crofts, 1961.

James, William. *Talks to Teachers on Psychology: and to Students on Some of Life's Ideals.* New York: Henry Holt, 1899.

Kasson, John F. *Civilizing the Machine: Technology and Republican Values in America, 1776-1900.* New York: Grossman, 1976.

Lévi-Strauss, Claude. *Totemism.* Boston: Beacon Press, 1963.

Lewis, R. W. B. *The American Adam.* Chicago: University of Chicago Press, 1955.

Marx, Leo. *The Machine in the Garden.* New York: Oxford University Press, 1964.

Noble, David W. *The Progressive Mind, 1890-1917.* Chicago: Rand McNally, 1970.

Simonson, Harold P. *The Closed Frontier.* New York: Holt, Rinehart and Winston, 1970.

Smith, Henry Nash. *Mark Twain's Fable of Progress.* New Brunswick, N.J.: Rutgers University Press, 1964.

Stegner, Wallace. *The Sound of Mountain Water.* Garden City, N.Y.: Doubleday, 1969.

Tate, Cecil F. *The Search for a Method in American Studies.* Minneapolis: University of Minnesota Press, 1973.

Turner, Frederick Jackson. "The Problem of the West." *Atlantic Monthly* 78 (1896): 289-97.

_____. "The Significance of the Frontier in American History." 1893. In his *The Frontier in American History.* New York: Henry Holt, 1920.

Vanderbilt, Kermit. *The Achievement of William Dean Howells.* Princeton: Princeton University Press, 1968.

_____. *Charles Eliot Norton: Apostle of Culture in a Democracy.* Cambridge, Mass.: Harvard University Press, 1959.

Westbrook, Max. *Walter Van Tilburg Clark.* New York: Twayne Publishers, 1969.

Wiebe, Robert. *The Search for Order, 1877-1920.* New York: Hill and Wang, 1967.

Zavarzadeh, Mas'ud. *The Mythopoeic Reality.* Urbana: University of Illinois Press, 1976.

SHERWOOD ANDERSON

Works by Anderson

Beyond Desire. New York: Liveright, 1932.

Dark Laughter. New York: Boni and Liveright, 1925.

Home Town. New York: Alliance Book Corporation, 1940.

Horses and Men. New York: B. W. Huebsch, 1923.

Kit Brandon: A Portrait. New York: Charles Scribner's Sons, 1936.

Letters of Sherwood Anderson. Edited by Howard Mumford Jones and Walter B. Rideout. Boston: Little, Brown, 1953.

Many Marriages. New York: B. W. Huebsch, 1923.

Marching Men. 1917. Critical text edited by Ray Lewis White. Cleveland: Case Western Reserve Press, 1972.

Mid-American Chants. New York: John Lane, 1918.

A New Testament. New York: Boni and Liveright, 1927.

Perhaps Women. 1931. Mamaroneck, N.Y.: Paul P. Appel, 1970.

Poor White. 1920. New York: Viking Press Compass Edition, 1966.

Puzzled America. New York: Charles Scribner's Sons, 1935.

The Sherwood Anderson Reader. Edited by Paul Rosenfeld. Boston: Houghton Mifflin, 1947.

Sherwood Anderson's Memoirs. 1942. Critical edition edited by Ray Lewis White. Chapel Hill: University of North Carolina Press, 1973.

Sherwood Anderson's Notebook. New York: Boni and Liveright, 1926.

A Story Teller's Story. Garden City, N.Y.: Garden City Publishing Company, 1924.

Tar: A Midwest Childhood. New York: Boni and Liveright, 1926.

Windy McPherson's Son. 1916. Chicago: University of Chicago Press, 1965.

Winesburg, Ohio. 1919. Edited by Malcolm Cowley. New York: Viking Press Compass Edition, 1960.

Other Works

Almy, Robert F. "Sherwood Anderson: the Non-Conforming Rediscoverer." *Saturday Review of Literature* 28 (January 6, 1945): 17-18.

Brooks, Van Wyck. "Introduction" to Sherwood Anderson's "Letters to Van Wyck Brooks." *Story* 19 (September-October 1941): 42-43.

Bunge, Nancy L. "The Ambiguous Endings of Sherwood Anderson's Novels." In *Sherwood Anderson Centennial Studies*, edited by Hilbert H. Campbell and Charles E. Modlin. Troy, N.Y.: Whitston Publishing Company, 1976.

Crane, Hart. *The Bridge*. New York: Horace Liveright, 1930.

Davidson, Donald. "A Mirror for Artists." In *I'll Take My Stand*, by Twelve Southerners. 1930. New York: Harper Torchbooks, 1962.

Frank, Waldo. *Our America*. New York: Boni and Liveright, 1919.

————. "Sherwood Anderson: A Personal Note." *Newberry Library Bulletin*, Second Series, 2 (1948): 39-43.

Fussell, Edwin. "*Winesburg, Ohio*: Art and Isolation." *Modern Fiction Studies* 6 (1960): 106-14.

Ginestier, Paul. *The Poet and the Machine*. Translated from the French by Martin B. Friedman. Chapel Hill: University of North Carolina Press, 1961.

Kazin, Alfred. "The Letters of Sherwood Anderson." In his *The Inmost Leaf*. New York: Harcourt, Brace, 1941.

Love, Glen A. "Sherwood Anderson's American Pastoral." Ph.D. dissertation, University of Washington, 1964.

————. "*Winesburg, Ohio* and the Rhetoric of Silence." *American Literature* 40 (1968): 38-57.

M. A. "A Country Town." *New Republic* 19 (1919): 257 59.

Mahoney, John J. "An Analysis of *Winesburg, Ohio*." *Journal of Aesthetics and Art Criticism* 15 (1956): 245-52.

Marx, Leo. "The Machine in the Garden." *New England Quarterly* 29 (1956): 29-42.

Morris, Wright. "Introduction" to Sherwood Anderson's *Windy McPherson's Son*. Chicago: University of Chicago Press, 1965.

Mumford, Lewis. *The Myth of the Machine*. New York: Harcourt, Brace and World, 1967-70.

————. "Utopia, the City and the Machine." *daedalus* 94 (1965): 271-92.

Rideout, Walter B. *The Radical Novel in the United States, 1900-1954*. Cambridge, Mass.: Harvard University Press, 1956.

————. "Sherwood Anderson's 'Mid-American Chants.'" In *Aspects of American Poetry*, edited by Richard M. Ludwig. Columbus: Ohio State University Press, 1962.

Scafidel, James R. "Sexuality in *Windy McPherson's Son*." *Twentieth Century Literature* 23 (1977): 94-101.

Sutton, William A. *The Road to Winesburg*. Metuchen, N.J.: Scarecrow Press, 1972.

Twelve Southerners. *I'll Take My Stand*. 1930. New York: Harper Torchbooks, 1962.

West, Thomas Reed. *Flesh of Steel: Literature and the Machine in American Culture*. Charlotte, North Carolina: Vanderbilt University Press, 1967.

Woolf, Virginia. "American Fiction." *Saturday Review of Literature* 2 (1925): 1-3.

WILLA CATHER

Works by Cather

Alexander's Bridge. 1912. New edition with preface. Boston: Houghton Mifflin, 1922.

April Twilights. Boston: Richard Badger, 1903.

The Kingdom of Art: Willa Cather's First Principles and Critical Statements, 1893-96. Edited by Bernice Slote. Lincoln: University of Nebraska Press, 1966.

A Lost Lady. 1923. Boston: Houghton Mifflin Library Edition, 1938.

Lucy Gayheart. 1935. New York: Alfred A. Knopf, 1966.

My Antonia. 1918. Boston: Houghton Mifflin Riverside Edition, 1949.

My Mortal Enemy. 1926. New York: Random House Vintage Books, 1961.

"Nebraska: The End of the First Cycle." *The Nation* 117 (1923): 236-38.

Not under Forty. New York: Alfred A. Knopf, 1936.

O Pioneers! 1913. Boston: Houghton Mifflin Sentry Edition, 1941.

On Writing. New York: Alfred A. Knopf, 1949.

One of Ours. 1922. New York: Random House Vintage Editions, 1971.

"Plays of Real Life." *McClure's* 40 (March 1913): 63-72.

"Preface" to Sarah Orne Jewett's *The Country of the Pointed Firs*. London: Jonathan Cape, The Travellers' Library, 1927.

The Professor's House. 1925. New York: Random House Vintage Books, 1973.

The Song of the Lark. 1915. Boston: Houghton Mifflin, 1943.

Willa Cather's Collected Short Fiction, 1892-1912. Edited by Virginia Faulkner. Lincoln: University of Nebraska Press, 1965.

The World and the Parish, vol. 2. Edited by William A. Curtin. Lincoln: University of Nebraska Press, 1970.

Other Works

Bloom, Edward A. and Lillian D. *Willa Cather's Gift of Sympathy*. Carbondale: Southern Illinois University Press, 1962.

Brown, Edward Killoran. *Willa Cather: A Critical Biography*. New York: Alfred A. Knopf, 1953.

Brown, Marion Marsh, and Crone, Ruth. *Willa Cather: The Woman and Her Work*. New York: Charles Scribner's Sons, 1970.

Edel, Leon. "Willa Cather." *Literary Lectures Presented at the Library of Congress*. Washington: Library of Congress, 1973.

Gale, Robert L. "Willa Cather and the Past." *Studi Americani* 4 (1958): 209-22.

Geismar, Maxwell. *The Last of the Provincials*. Boston: Houghton Mifflin, 1949.

Gelfant, Blanche H. "The Forgotten Reaping-Hook: Sex in *My Ántonia.*" *American Literature* 43 (1971): 61-82.

Gerber, Philip. *Willa Cather*. Boston: Twayne Publishers, 1975.

Helmick, Evelyn T. "Myth in the Works of Willa Cather." *Midcontinent American Studies Journal* 9 (Fall 1968): 63-69.

Hicks, John D. *The Populist Revolt*. Minneapolis: University of Minnesota Press, 1931.

Hinz, Evelyn. "Willa Cather's Technique and the Ideology of Populism." *Western American Literature* 7 (1972): 47-61.

Hinz. John P. "A Lost Lady and *The Professor's House*." *Virginia Quarterly Review* 29 (1953): 70-85.

———. "The Real Alexander's Bridge." *American Literature* 21 (1950): 473-76.

Lee, Robert Edson. *From West to East*. Urbana: University of Illinois Press, 1966.

Lewis, Edith. *Willa Cather Living*. New York: Alfred A. Knopf, 1953.

Martin, Terence. "The Drama of Memory in *My Ántonia*." *PMLA* 84 (1969): 304-11.

McFarland, Dorothy Tuck. *Willa Cather*. New York: Frederick Ungar, 1972.

Meier, Hugo A. "American Technology and the Nineteenth-Century World." *American Quarterly* 10 (1958): 116-30.

Miller, Bruce E. "The Testing of Willa Cather's Humanism: *A Lost Lady* and Other Cather Novels." *Kansas Quarterly* 5 (Fall 1973): 43-50.

Miller, James E., Jr. "*My Ántonia*: A Frontier Drama of Time." *American Quarterly* 10 (1958): 476-84.

Pollack, Norman. *The Populist Response to Industrial America.* Cambridge, Mass.: Harvard University Press, 1962.

Randall, John H. *The Landscape and the Looking Glass.* New York: Houghton Mifflin, 1960.

Rosowski, Susan J. "Willa Cather's *A Lost Lady*: The Paradoxes of Change." *Novel* 11 (1977): 51-62.

Schroeter, James, ed. *Willa Cather and Her Critics.* Ithaca, N.Y.: Cornell University Press, 1967.

Sergeant, Elizabeth Shepley. *Willa Cather: A Memoir.* Philadelphia: J.P. Lippincott, 1953.

Slote, Bernice. "Introduction" to Willa Cather's *Alexander's Bridge.* Lincoln: University of Nebraska Press, 1977.

————. "Willa Cather." In *Sixteen Modern American Authors*, edited by Jackson R. Bryer. New York: W. W. Norton, 1973.

————, and Faulkner, Virginia, eds. *The Art of Willa Cather.* Lincoln: University of Nebraska Press, 1974.

Smith, Anneliese H. "Finding Marian Forrester: A Restorative Reading of *A Lost Lady.*" *Colby Library Quarterly* 14 (1978): 221-25.

Stouck, David. *Willa Cather's Imagination.* Lincoln: University of Nebraska Press, 1975.

Stuckey, William J. "*My Ántonia:* A Rose for Miss Cather." *Studies in the Novel.* 4 (1972): 473-83.

Van Ghent, Dorothy. *Willa Cather.* Minneapolis: University of Minnesota Press, 1964.

Walker, Don D. "The Western Humanism of Willa Cather." *Western American Literature* 1 (1966): 75-90.

Warshow, Robert. *The Immediate Experience.* Garden City, N.Y.: Doubleday, 1962.

Woodress, James. *Willa Cather: Her Life and Art.* New York: Pegasus, 1970.

HAMLIN GARLAND

Works by Garland

Back-Trailers from the Middle Border. New York: Macmillan, 1928.

The Book of the American Indian. New York: Harper and Brothers, 1923.

The Captain of the Gray-Horse Troop. New York: Harper and Brothers, 1902.

Cavanagh, Forest Ranger: A Romance of the Mountain West. New York: Harper and Brothers, 1910.

Companions on the Trail. New York: Macmillan, 1931.

Crumbling Idols. 1894. Edited by Jane Johnson. Cambridge, Mass.: Harvard University Press, 1960.

A Daughter of the Middle Border. New York: Grosset and Dunlap, 1921.

The Eagle's Heart. New York: Harper and Brothers, 1900.

The Forester's Daughter. New York: Harper and Brothers, 1914.

Hamlin Garland's Diaries. Edited by Donald Pizer. San Marino, Calif.: Huntington Library, 1968.

Hamlin Garland's Observations on the American Indian 1895-1905. Compiled and edited by Lonnie E. Underhill and Daniel F. Littlefield, Jr. Tucson: University of Arizona Press, 1976.

Jason Edwards: An Average Man. Boston: Arena Publishing Company, 1892.

Main-Travelled Roads. 1891. New York: New American Library Signet Edition, 1962.

A Member of the Third House: A Dramatic Story. Chicago: F. J. Schulte and Company, 1892.

Rose of Dutcher's Coolly. 1895. Introduced and edited by Donald Pizer. Lincoln: University of Nebraska Press, 1969.

A Son of the Middle Border. 1917. New York: Macmillan, 1922.

A Spoil of Office: A Story of the Modern West. Boston: Arena Publishing Company, 1892.

The Tyranny of the Dark. London and New York: Harper and Brothers, 1905.

"The Work of Frank Norris." *The Critic* 42 (1903): 216-18.

Other Works

Arvidson, Lloyd A., ed. *Hamlin Garland: Centennial Tributes and a Checklist of the Hamlin Garland Papers in the University of Southern California Library.* University of Southern California Library Bulletin no. 9 (1962).

Billington, Ray Allen. "Frederick Jackson Turner and the Closing of the Frontier." In *Essays in Western History in Honor of T. A. Larson,* edited by Roger Daniels. Laramie: University of Wyoming Publications, no. 37 (1971).

Cady, Edwin. *The Light of Common Day*. Bloomington: Indiana University Press, 1971.

Carter, Joseph L. "Hamlin Garland and the Western Myth." Ph.D. dissertation, Kent State University, 1973.

Davis, Jack L. "Hamlin Garland's Indians and the Quality of Civilized Life." In *Where the West Begins*, edited by Arthur R. Huseboe and William Geyer. Augustana College, Sioux Falls, S. Dak.: Center for Western Studies Press, 1978.

Dove, John R. "The Significance of Hamlin Garland's First Visit to England." *Studies in English*, University of Texas, no. 32 (1953): 96-109.

Dreiser, Theodore. *Sister Carrie*. 1900. Boston: Houghton Mifflin Riverside Edition, 1959.

Gish, Robert. *Hamlin Garland*. Western Writers Series, no. 24. Boise, Idaho: Boise State University, 1976.

Harrison, Stanley R. "Hamlin Garland and the Double Vision of Naturalism." *Studies in Short Fiction* 6 (1969): 548-56.

Holloway, Jean. *Hamlin Garland: A Biography*. Austin: University of Texas Press, 1960.

Howells, William Dean. *Dr. Breen's Practice*. Boston: Houghton Mifflin, 1881.

––––––. "Mr. Garland's Books." *North American Review* 196 (1912): 523-28.

James, Henry. *The Bostonians*. 1886. New York: Modern Library, 1956.

Keiser, Albert. *The Indian in American Literature*. New York: Oxford University Press, 1933.

McGreivey, John C. "Art and Ideas in Garland's *The Captain of the Gray-Horse Troop*." *Markham Review* 5 (1976): 52-58.

Penick, James, Jr. *Progressive Politics and Conservation: The Ballinger-Pinchot Affair*. Chicago: University of Chicago Press, 1968.

Pizer, Donald. *Hamlin Garland's Early Work and Career*. University of California English Studies, no. 22. Berkeley: University of California Press, 1960.

––––––. *Realism and Naturalism in American Literature*. Carbondale: Southern Illinois University Press, 1966.

Ravitz, A. C. "Willa Cather Under Fire: Hamlin Garland Misreads *A Lost Lady*." *Western Humanities Review* 9 (1955): 182-84.

Roosevelt, Theodore. "The Manly Virtues and Practical Politics." *The Forum* 17 (1894): 551-57.

––––––. *The Writings of Theodore Roosevelt*. Edited by William H.

Harbaugh. New York: Bobbs-Merrill, 1967.

Savage, George Howard. " 'Synthetic Evolution' and the American West: The Influence of Herbert Spencer on the Later Novels of Hamlin Garland." Ph.D. dissertation, University of Tulsa, 1974.

Smith, Henry Nash. *Virgin Land: The American West as Symbol and Myth.* Cambridge, Mass.: Harvard University Press, 1950.

Spencer, Herbert. *Man Versus the State.* 1884. New York: D. Appleton, 1908.

SINCLAIR LEWIS

Works by Lewis

Arrowsmith. 1925. New York: New American Library Signet Edition, 1961.

Babbitt. 1922. New York: New American Library Signet Edition, 1962.

Cass Timberlane. New York: Random House, 1945.

"The Death of Arrowsmith." *Coronet* 10 (July 1941): 107-10.

Dodsworth. 1929. New York: New American Library Signet Edition, 1961.

Elmer Gantry. 1927. New York: New American Library Signet Edition, 1967.

Free Air. New York: Grosset and Dunlap, 1919.

The God-Seeker. New York: Popular Library, 1949.

"The Greatest American Novelist." *Newsweek* 11 (January 3, 1938): 29.

[Tom Graham]. *Hike and the Aeroplane.* New York: Stokes, 1912.

The Innocents. New York: Harper and Brothers, 1917.

The Job. New York: Harcourt, Brace, 1917.

Kingsblood Royal. New York: Random House, 1947.

Main Street. 1920. New York: New American Library Signet Edition, 1961.

"Main Street's Been Paved!" *The Nation* 119 (1924): 255-60.

The Man from Main Street: Selected Essays and Other Writings. Edited by Harry E. Maule and Melville H. Cane. New York: Pocket Books, 1963.

Mantrap. New York: Harcourt, Brace, 1926.

"Minnesota: the Norse State." *The Nation* 116 (1923): 624-27.

"One Man Revolution." *Newsweek* 10 (November 22, 1937): 33.
Our Mr. Wrenn. New York: Harcourt, Brace, 1914.
The Prodigal Parents. Garden City, N.Y.: Doubleday, Doran, 1938.
The Trail of the Hawk. New York: Harcourt, Brace, 1915.
Work of Art. Garden City, N.Y.: Doubleday, Doran, 1935.
World So Wide. New York: Random House, 1951.

Other Works

Aaron, Daniel. "Main Street." In *The Americal Novel*, edited by Wallace Stegner. New York: Basic Books, 1965.

Anderson, Sherwood. "Four American Impressions." *The New Republic* 32 (1922): 171-73.

Andrews. Wayne. *Architecture, Ambition and Americans.* New York: Harper's, 1955.

Carpenter, Frederick I. "Sinclair Lewis and the Fortress of Reality." In his *American Literature and the Dream.* New York: Philosophical Library, 1955.

Cowan, Michael. *City of the West: Emerson, America, and the Urban Metaphor.* New Haven, Conn.: Yale University Press, 1967.

Dooley, D. J. *The Art of Sinclair Lewis.* Lincoln: University of Nebraska Press, 1967.

Geismar, Maxwell. *The Last of the Provincials.* Boston: Houghton Mifflin, 1949.

Grebstein, Sheldon. *Sinclair Lewis.* New York: Twayne Publishers, 1962.

Howard, Ebeneezer. *Garden Cities of Tomorrow.* 1902. Cambridge, Mass.: Massachusetts Institute of Technology Press, 1965.

Kaul, A. N. *The American Vision.* New Haven, Conn.: Yale University Press, 1963.

Kramer, Maurice. "Sinclair Lewis and the Hollow Center." In *The Twenties: Poetry and Prose*, edited by Richard E. Langford and William E. Taylor. Deland, Fla.: Everett Edwards Press, 1966.

Lea, James. "Sinclair Lewis and the Implied America." *Clio* 3 (1973): 21-34.

Lewis, Claude. *Treaty Trip.* Edited by Donald Green and George Knox. Minneapolis: University of Minnesota Press, 1959.

Light, Martin. *The Quixotic Vision of Sinclair Lewis.* West Lafayette, Ind.: Purdue University Press, 1975.

Lundquist, James. *Sinclair Lewis*. New York: Frederick Ungar, 1973.

Manson, Alexander. "The Last Days of Sinclair Lewis." (As told to Helen Camp.) *Saturday Evening Post* 223 (March 31, 1951): 27, 110-12.

Miller, Perry. "The Incorruptible Sinclair Lewis." *The Atlantic* 187 (April 1951): 30-34.

Mumford, Lewis. *Sticks and Stones*. 1924. Second revised edition. New York: Dover, 1955.

Noble, David. *The Progressive Mind*. Chicago: Rand McNally, 1970.

Schorer, Mark. "Afterword" to Sinclair Lewis's *Arrowsmith*. New York: New American Library Signet Edition, 1961.

————. *Sinclair Lewis: An American Life*. New York: McGraw-Hill, 1961.

Scully, Vincent. *American Architecture and Urbanism*. New York: Praeger, 1969.

Tunnard, Christopher, and Reed, Henry Hope. *American Skyline*. Boston: Houghton Mifflin, 1955.

Ward, John William. "The Meaning of Lindbergh's Flight." *American Quarterly* 10 (1958): 3-16.

Whipple, T. K. *Spokesmen: Modern Writers and American Life*. New York: Appleton, 1928.

Wright, Frank Lloyd. *A Testament*. New York: Horizon Press, 1957.

————. *Writings and Buildings*. New York: Horizon Press, 1960.

FRANK NORRIS

Works by Norris

The Argonaut Manuscript Limited Edition of Frank Norris's Work. 10 volumes. Garden City, N.Y.: Doubleday, Doran, 1928.

Frank Norris of "the Wave." San Francisco: Westgate Press, 1931.

The Letters of Frank Norris. Edited by Franklin Walker. San Francisco: Book Club of California, 1956.

The Literary Criticism of Frank Norris. Edited by Donald Pizer. Austin: University of Texas Press, 1963.

Other Works

Crane, Stephen. "The Bride Comes to Yellow Sky." 1898. In his *Twenty Stories*. New York: Alfred A. Knopf, 1940.

————. *Maggie: A Girl of the Streets.* 1893. New York: Norton Critical Edition, 1979.

French, Warren. *Frank Norris.* New York: Twayne Publishers, 1962.

Giles, James R. "Beneficial Atavism in Frank Norris and Jack London." *Western American Literature* 4 (1969): 15-28.

Goldsmith, Arnold Louis. "The Devlopment of Frank Norris's Philosophy." In *Studies in Honor of John Wilcox.* Detroit: Wayne State University Press, 1958.

Graham, Don B. *The Fiction of Frank Norris: The Aesthetic Context.* Columbia: University of Missouri Press, 1978.

Hart, James D. "Introduction" to Frank Norris's *A Novelist in the Making.* Edited by James D. Hart. Cambridge, Mass.: Harvard University Press, 1970.

Hollander, John. *The Untuning of the Sky.* Princeton: Princeton University Press, 1961.

Howells, William Dean. "Frank Norris." *North American Review* 175 (1902): 769-78.

James, Henry. *The American.* 1877. Boston: Houghton Mifflin Riverside Edition, 1962.

Johnson, George W. "The Frontier Behind Frank Norris's *McTeague.*" *Huntington Library Quarterly* 26 (1962): 91-104.

Marchand, Ernest. *Frank Norris.* Stanford: Stanford University Press, 1942.

Markham, Edwin. *The Man with the Hoe and Other Poems,* New York: Doubleday and McClure, 1899.

Pizer, Donald. *The Novels of Frank Norris.* Bloomington: Indiana University Press, 1966.

Pomeroy, Earl. *In Search of the Golden West: The Tourist in Western America.* New York: Alfred A. Knopf, 1957.

————. *The Pacific Slope.* New York: Alfred A. Knopf, 1965.

Royce, Josiah. *California: A Study of American Character.* 1886. Santa Barbara: Peregrine, 1970.

Starr, Kevin. *Americans and the California Dream.* New York: Oxford University Press, 1973.

Taylor, Walter F. *The Economic Novel in America.* Chapel Hill: University of North Carolina Press, 1942.

Walker, Franklin. *Frank Norris.* Garden City, N.Y.: Doubleday, Doran, 1932.

Ziff, Larzer. *The American 1890s.* New York: Viking Press, 1966.

Index